AF531488

GLOBALISATION AND WOMEN EMPOWERMENT

MULTIDIMENSIONAL APPROACHES

Edited by

BIPIN KUMAR

DEEP & DEEP PUBLICATIONS PVT. LTD.
F-159, Rajouri Garden, New Delhi - 110027

GLOBALISATION AND WOMEN EMPOWERMENT
Multidimensional Approaches

ISBN 978-81-8450-211-4

Typeset by THE LASER PRINTERS, 8/15, 3rd Floor, Subhash Nagar, New Delhi-110027.

Printed in India at MAYUR ENTERPRISES
WZ Plot No. 3, Gujjar Market, Tihar Village, New Delhi - 110 018.

Published by DEEP & DEEP PUBLICATIONS PVT. LTD.,
F-159, Rajouri Garden, New Delhi-110027. Phones: 25435369, 25440916.
E-mail: ddpbooks@yahoo.co.in • ddpubs@gmail.com
Sales Showroom: 2/13, Ansari Road, Daryaganj, New Delhi-110002
Phone/Fax: 23245122

CONTENTS

Preface ix

Contributors xv

PART I

EMPOWERMENT OF WOMEN AND GLOBALISATION

1. *Bipin Kumar*
   Empowerment of Women and Globalisation 3

2. *Indradeo Sharma*
   Growth, Transformation and Unorganised Women Workers: A Case for Enhanced Public Investment in Agriculture 30

3. *Parmanand Singh*
   Globalisation, Empowerment Question and the Case of Women Workers in India: An Analysis 42

4. *Parveen Azad*
   Women's Empowerment and Globalisation 56

5. *Mahesh Chandra Prasad*
   Women Empowerment and Development During Globalisation 66

6. *Praveen Sharma*
   Globalisation and Economic Empowerment of Women (Some Issues for Discussion and Policy Intervention) 83

7. *Reyaz Ahmad*
Gandhian Philosophy and Women's Empowerment 91

PART II

EMPOWERMENT OF WOMEN AND EDUCATION

8. *Mithilesh Kumar Sinha*
Women Empowerment: A New Roadmap Required 105

9. *Anjali Prasad and Jyoti Prasad*
Women Empowerment: Stress and Mental Health 125

10. *Talat Jabeen and Murshid Alam*
Women and Education in India 143

11. *Rajesh Shukla, Ranjana Shukla and Rajesh Ranjan*
Women: Education and Health 158

12. *Sanjeev Kumar Singh and Roma Rupam*
Empowerment of Women and Education 170

13. *R.U. Singh*
Economics of Women Education: An Overview 175

PART III

GENDER DEVELOPMENT AND EMPOWERMENT

14. *Rashmi Akhaury*
Women's Empowerment Through Gender Budgeting: A Review in the Indian Context 185

15. *Birendra Kumar Jha*
Issues of Gender Equality and Empowerment of Indian Women 211

16. *Nayan Kumar, Subalal Yadav and Rana Pratap*
Gender Budgeting and Women Empowerment 233

17. *Shamim Akhtar and Shaishta Nagien*
Theory of Gendered Approach to Development in the Third World Perspective 247

18. *Shakeel Ahmad Khan*
Gender Equity and Rights of Women: An Islamic Analysis 266

PART IV

CRIME, VIOLENCE AGAINST WOMEN AND EMPOWERMENT

19. *Reeta Kumari*
Violence Against Women: An Educated Woman can Eradicate Violence 285

20. *Ravindra K. Choudhary and Manoj Kumar Mishra*
Crime Against Women and the Scope of Women Empowerment 295

Index 310

PREFACE

Globalisation has presented new challenges for the realisation of the goal of women's equality, the gender impact of which has not been systematically and fully evaluated. Benefits of the growing global economy have been unevenly distributed leading to wider economic disparities, the feminisation of poverty, increased gender inequality through deteriorating working conditions and unsafe working environment especially in the informal economy and rural areas. Countries across the world have making designed strategies to enhance the capacity of women and empower them to meet the negative social and economic impacts, which may flow from the globalisation process.

Empowerment of women involves many things—economic opportunity, property rights, political representation, social equality, personal rights and so on. The process of empowerment is taking place at so many levels that it is quite difficult to gauge the actual nature and extent of empowerment in improving status of women.

The position of women and their status in any society is an index of its civilisation. Women are to be considered as equal partners in the process of development. But exploitation and subjugation from centuries, Indian women have remained at the receiving end. In this context, in order to provide a big push, institutional support is necessary to empower Indian women in general and rural women in particular. Women empowerment demands a "life-cycle" approach where empowerment is viewed as a process and not as an event. History reveals that females in most of the developed countries like USA, Sweden, Japan were not equally empowered with their male counter-parts before industrial revolution. But presently these countries are also considered having high gender empowerment as per the indicators used by protagonists of gender. The political representation of women, ratio of female administrators and managers in organisation, women's real GDP per capita, female economic activity rate, literacy ratio, etc. are high in these countries. So, the Gender Development Index (GDI) and Gender Employment Measure (GEM) Index are also high enough. Men like almost all other societies of the world are dominating the Indian society. Males take the responsibilities outside the home and females carry on their household chores. In ancient religions, we find those women were always free as subordinate to man which were recalled by our Hindu Texts like Manu, Samhita, Vedas, etc. Women occupied a very important place in the ancient traditional society. In primitive societies, women enjoyed superior status in comparison to men. Vedic society was patriarchal where a man used to command over his wife and children. However, in spite of this, the status of women in Rig Vedic society was much higher than in later time.

The post-Vedic period is considered crucial in determining the present status of women in India. In the two great epics, the Ramayana and the Mahabharata women were treated with honour and adorned. The Bhakti movement brought a new message and hope for women and the downtrodden. In Bhagawat Gita, Lord Krishna gave due honour to the women folk. However the status of women deteriorate during Muslim rule specially due to the intrusion of polygamy in the society. The Sati Pratha, child marriage and Purdah system during that period also lowered the women status in the society. The 1931 Karachi Session of the Indian National Congress (INC) took the historic decision committing itself to political equality of women regarding of their status and qualifications. The father of the nation, Gandhiji advocated for more empowerment to women participated in the national movement in the village reconstruction programme. He was in favour of socio-economic equality to women to attain all round development in the society. Gandhi and the independence movement finally led to emancipation of Indian women to a great extent in the twentieth century.

With the acceptance of the Constitution of India, Article sixteen, equality of opportunity in public employment, The

Preambles, the Directive Principles of State Policy and the Fundamental Rights have well accorded the right to women in different dimensions. Different commissions have been set-up in independent India. Among them the prominent Durgabhai Deshmukh Commission (1956), Hansa Mehta Committee (1961), Bhakta Vatsalam Committee (1965), National Education Policy of 1986. Since the Sixth Five Year Plan of India, multi-pronged strategy have been adopted to empower women relating to employment and economic independence, education, access to health care and family planning, support services to meet gender needs.

The Ninth Five Year Plan gives special attention to the empowerment and the objective of the plan was stated as "Empowering women as the agents of social change and development". The term empowerment has the most conspicuous feature containing the world 'power' which means control over material assets, intellectual resources and ideology. Empowerment is an active, multi-dimensional process, which enables women to realize their full identity and power in all spheres of life. The most innovative strategy which is emerging today as a unique response to the challenge of equality, development and peace for empowerment of women.

Women empowerment is a most vital component for sustainable development. It is a global issue and is being discussed all over the world. Globally, gender equality and women empowerment have been recognized a vital components to achieve over all development. Empowerment is a process and awareness and capacity building, leading to greater participation, to greater decision-making power and control, and to transformative action. Empowerment of women is essential as their throughout and value system lead to the development of a good family, good society and ultimately, good nation.

This present edited volume on "Empowerment of Women and Globalisation: Multidimensional Approaches" is divided into four parts. Part-I: Empowerment of Women and Globalisation, Part-II: Empowerment of Women and Education, Part-III: Gender Development and Empowerment, and Part-IV: Crime, Violence against Women Empowerment.

Part-I concentrates on *Empowerment of Women and Globalisation*. This section consists of seven papers, covering the major issues regarding empowerment of women in context of globalisation. The main contributors in this are Dr. I.D. Sharma, Dr. Bipin Kumar, Dr. Parmanand Singh, Dr. Praveen Sharma and Dr. Reyaz Ahmad.

Part-II is concerned with *Empowerment of Women and Education*. In this section, an attempt has been made by several scholars about empowerment of women in context of education. No doubt, education is the first and foremost important weapon for empowering women. In the era of globalisation, where resources for the social sector will come out of an ever-shrinking common pool, the burden on women to 'make do' in the household will increase, and this will jeopardize their ability to generate human resources. Education is the engine of economic growth and social change. It creates motivation for progress and brings revolution in the ideas necessary for the progress of the country. Education would emancipate and endow women with ability to control her life, accomplish her dreams and enhance her status; the task is challenging yet not impossible. Education and the empowerment of women are both essential and indispensable for prosperous nation. The main contributors in this section are Dr. Mithilesh Kumar Sinha, Dr. Sanjeev Kumar Singh and Roma Rupam, and Dr. R.U. Singh.

Part-III discusses the issues regarding *Gender Development and Empowerment*. Empowerment of women is an effective strategy to cope with gender-based discrimination and attain gender equality. Pursuit of equality aims at three levels namely polity, economy and society. Over the past few years, gender equality and empowerment of women have been receiving special emphasis. The 8th March in every year has been celebrated as the 'International Women's Day'. India celebrated the year of 2001 as the 'National Women's Empowerment Year'. However, in practice, it is flattering due to various factors such as low literacy, restrictive social structure, predominance of patriarchal society, low exposure to growth opportunities, non-involvement in income generating activities as well as continuing socio-economic dependence over the years. The prominent contributors in this section are Dr. Rashmi Akhauri, Dr. Birendra Kumar Jha, Dr. Nayan Kumar, Dr. Shamim Akhtar and Dr. Shaishta Nagien and Shakeel Ahmad Khan.

Part-IV relates with *Crime, Violence Against Women and*

Empowerment. Crime against women is the most evocative, traumatism and political subject for discussion within India. Although it is not a direct issue of development yet it affects women's development; it restricts them from full participation in national development efforts and obtaining their due share in developmental efforts. Women are victims of crime like 'murder', 'robbery', 'cheating', etc. Only the crimes which are directed against women are characterized as 'crime against women'. Domestic violence has been clearly defined in the 'Domestic Violence Act, 2005'.

Violence against women is socially a very sensitive issue and more so in our country where we have a special place for 'Family Honour'. Any act which affects the family honour is not tolerated and very strongly put down. Therefore, the acts of violence are seldom talked out of the family honour is not tolerated and very strongly put down. Violence against women is widespread and viewed as one of the cruelest social mechanisms to suppress women. Unequal power relations have led to discrimination against women. Violence on women manifests even before birth and early life, married life as domestic violence, rape, murder, dowry, death, etc. It is said that violence violets human rights of life, liberty, equality, dignity, development and peace. The prominent contributors in this section are Dr. Reeta Kumari, Dr. Ravindra Kumar Choudhary and Manoj Kumar Mishra.

This book provides a comprehensive coverage to the issues arising out of the present process of globalisation and the manner in which it affects the development of women. It shows how the market-oriented economy has resulted in the feminisation of labour activity and poverty and has disturbed the existing patterns of social relationships. This work will be highly useful to development planners, researchers and all others who are interested in gender studies.

The book is a collection of papers written by 29 eminent Scholars. The present volume contains twenty papers. In completion of the book, I have received help from numerous eminent research scholars from all concerns of the country who have ably undertaken the tedious task of preparing research papers despite of their heavy engagements within the shortest time. I would like to place them on record my deep appreciation and gratitude to all contributors.

I feel highly privileged to express my profound regard and heartfelt indebtedness to Dr. I.D. Sharma, Professor and Head, Department of Economics, A.N. Sinha Institute of Social Studies, Patna and Dr. Tapan Kumar Shandilya, P.G. Department of Economics, College of Commerce, (Patna) M.U. Bodh Gaya for their constant help and encouragement in my academic pursuits. I express my sincere regards to Dr. Mithilesh Kumar, Professor and Head, Department of Economics, Nagaland University, Nagaland who encouraged me throughout the academic work. I am also thankful to my friends and one-time colleagues, Dr. Sanjeev Kumar Singh, Department of English, R.R.S. College, Mokama (Patna), Dr. M.S. Gupta, Department of Commerce, R.K.D. College, Patna. I am thankful to Mr. Prakash Kumar (Patna) and Mr. Rajesh Kumar Singh (Sintoo) of L.N. Mishra Institute of Social Development and Economic Change, Patna.

I am also thankful to all my colleagues, friends and relatives who helped me one way or other, words are insufficient to appreciate the affectionate and co-operation of my wife, Suman Rani who helped me to maintain the time schedule in completing the book. Thanks a lot to my children, Divyanshu Bhardwaj and Priyanshu Bhardwaj whose humour kept me to concentrate in this venture.

Finally, I express my gratitude for the help extended by Mr. G.S. Bhatia of Deep & Deep Publications Pvt. Ltd., Rajouri Garden, New Delhi for his endeavour to ensure the timely publication.

BIPIN KUMAR

Contributors

Bipin Kumar, Head, Department of Economics, R.R.S. College, Mokama (Patna), Magadh University.

Indradeo Sharma, Professor & Head, Department of Economics, A.N. Sinha Institute of Social Studies, Patna.

Parmanand Singh, Head, Department of Economics, B.N.M. College, Barahiya, T.M. Bhagalpur University, Bhagalpur.

Parveen Azad, Research Scholar, Department of Philosophy, Aligarh Muslim University, Aligarh.

Mahesh Chandra Prasad, Senior Lecturer in Commerce, Department of Applied Economics and Commerce, Patna University, Patna.

Praveen Sharma, Assistant Professor, Department of EAFM, University of Rajasthan, Jaipur.

Reyaz Ahmad, Research Associate, Centre for Study of Social Exclusion and Inclusive Policy, BSBRAU (A Central University), Lucknow.

Mithilesh Kumar Sinha, Head, Department of Economics, Nagaland University, Hqrs. Lumami, Mokokchung.

Anjali Prasad, Department of Economics, TPS College (Patna), Magadh University.

Jyoti Prasad, Department of Psychology, Nirmala College, Ranchi University, Ranchi, Jharkhand.

Talat Jabeen, Councillor (B.Ed.), Indira Gandhi Open University (IGNOU).

Md. Murshid Alam, Lecturer in Commerce, D.A.V.P.G. College (Siwan), J.P. University, Chhapra.

Rajesh Shukla, Department of History, S.M.D. College, Punpun (Patna).

Ranjana Shukla, Research Scholar, Department of Sociology, Magadh University.

Rajesh Ranjan, Research Scholar, Magadh University.

Sanjeev Kumar Singh, Lecturer, Department of English, R.R.S. College, Mokama (Patna), Magadh University.

Roma Rupam, (M.A.) History, Nalanda Open University, Patna.

R.U. Singh, Lecturer, P.G. Department of Commerce & Coordinator (B.B.M.), College of Commerce, Patna.

Rashmi Akhaury, Lecturer, Department of Economics, College of Commerce, Patna.

Birendra Kumar Jha, Reader and Head, Department of Economics, D.B.K.N. College, Narhan, Samastipur (Bihar).

Nayan Kumar, Centre for Operations, Research & Training (CORT), 402, Woodland Apartment, Racecourse Circle, Vadodara, Gujarat.

Subalal Yadav, Research Scholar (Magadh University), Naryad, District-Kher (Gujarat).

Rana Pratap, Research Scholar, Magadh University.

Shamim Akhtar, Lecturer in Krishna College, Bijnor (U.P.)

Shaishta Nagien, Lecturer in R.B.D. College, Bijnor (U.P.)

Shakeel Ahmad Khan, Lecturer, Department of Economics, Oriental College, Patna City.

Reeta Kumari, Department of Economics, B.S. College, Danapur (Patna).

Ravindra Kumar Choudhary, Senior Lecturer in Economics, MJK College, Bettiah, B.R.A. Bihar University, Muzaffarpur.

Manoj Kumar Mishra, Research Scholar, B.R.A. Bihar University, Muzaffarpur.

PART I

EMPOWERMENT OF WOMEN AND GLOBALISATION

Empowerment of Women and Globalisation

Bipin Kumar

INTRODUCTION

President A.P.J. Abdul Kalam remarked, "Empowering women is a prerequisite for creating a good nation, when women are empowered, society with stability is assured. Empowerment of women is essential as their throughout and their value system lead to the development of a good family, good society and ultimately a good nation."

—*President A.P.J. Abdul Kalam*

The role of women in economic development, in developing human resources, in governance, in leadership, in marketing and in evolving sacro-civic society has outstandingly been covered under three broad themes. They are general perspectives, priorities and issues, implications and action. The year 1975 was declared as "year of women" by the United Nations. Since then there is increased concern of women's sufferings and empowerment in the society. The UNDP has brought out its 'Human Development Report', 2003, which speaks about the millennium development Goals. It lists eight goals out of which the third goal to be achieved is gender equality and empowerment of women. Women empowerment is a global issue, which has gained momentum in recent decades. In India besides ratification of international conventions, there are provisions in the constitution and several legislative acts have been passed to ensure women empowerment.

In 1995, the Human Development Report quoted that out of 1.3 billion poor people living in developing countries, 70 per cent are women. Poverty among rural women is growing faster than among rural men. Over the past 20 years, for example, the number of women in absolute poverty rose by 50 per cent as against some 30 per cent for rural men. Women in India form 89 per cent of the informal and unrecognized sector. Women's work participation rate is higher in rural areas, women make up for one-third of the force of India and 90 per cent of the rural and 10 per cent of the urban women workers are unskilled.

The vast majority of the people in India live in rural areas and are engaged in agricultural earning, a substance wage. Development, which has been focused on them, seems to have just passed them by. Rural population involves women folk also to make almost half of it. However, rural women have acquired a secondary status in social life, economic activities and decision-making among their families. Their role in work productivity, employment generation and income-oriented activities are hindered by many Socio-economic constraints.

HISTORICAL PERSPECTIVE OF WOMEN EMPOWERMENT

Empowerment of women involves many things—economic opportunity, property rights, political representation, social equality, personal rights and so on. The process of empowerment is taking place at so many levels that it is quite difficult to gauge the actual nature and extent of empowerment in improving status of women. Certainly the process is entangled in struggles of civil society against the state, and under the weight of historical practice and ongoing debates over the appropriate role of ideologies.

Historically the world over, either by law or by custom, the status of women is undermined by asymmetrical power relationships in decision-making, personal and social rights, access to resources and entitlements. Women in many countries still lack rights to inherit property, own land, get educated, obtain credit, earn income or work outside home, control their fertility; they are still widely under-represented in involvement in decision-making at the household or social level. Empowerment by means of modest income-generating projects is clearly insufficient to ameliorate the prospects for a higher quality of life for women.

The position of women and their status in any society is an index of its civilisation. Women are to be considered as equal partners in the process of development. But because of centuries of exploitation and subjugation, Indian women have remained at the receiving end. In this context, in order to provide a big push institutional support is necessary to empower Indian women in general and rural women in particular. Women empowerment demands a "life-cycle" approach where empowerment is viewed as a process and not as an event. History reveals that females in most of the developed countries like USA, Sweden, Japan were not equally empowered with their male counterpart before industrial revolution. But presently these countries are also considered having high gender empowerment as per the indicators used by protagonists of gender. The political representation of women, ratio of female administrators and managers in organisation, women's real GDP per capita, female economic activity rate, literacy ratio, etc. are high in these countries. So the Gender Development Index (GID) and Gender Employment Measure (GEM) index are also high enough. Men like almost all other societies of the world are dominating the Indian society. Males take the responsibilities outside the home and females carry on their household chores. In ancient religions we find those women were always free as subordinate to man which is recalled by our Hindu Texts like Manu, Samhita, Vedas, etc. Women occupied a very important place in the ancient traditional society. In primitive societies women enjoyed superior status in comparison to men. Vedic society was patriarchal where a man used to command over his wife and children. However in spite of this, the status of women in Rig Vedic society was much higher than in later time.

The post-Vedic period is considered crucial in determining the present status of women in India. In the two great epics the Ramayana and the Mahabharata women were treated with honour and adorned. The Bhakti movement brought a new message and hope for women and the downtrodden. In Bhagawat Gita Lord Krishna gave due honour to the women folk. However the status of women deteriorate during Muslim rule specially due to the intrusion of polygamy in the society. The Satidah Pratha, child marriage and Purdah system during that period also lowered the women status in the society. The 1931 Karachi session of the Indian National Congress (INC) took the historic decision committing itself to political equality of women regarding of their status and qualifications. The father of the nation Gandhiji advocated for more empowerment to women participated in the national movement in the village reconstruction programme. He was in favour of socio-economic equality to women to attain all round development in the society. Gandhi and the independence movement finally led to emancipation of Indian women to a great extent, in the twentieth century.

With the acceptance of the Constitution of India, Article sixteen guarantees equality of opportunity in public employment, The Preambles, The Directive Principles of State Policy and The Fundamental Rights have well accorded the right to women in different dimensions. Different commissions have been set-up in independent India. Among them Durgabhai Desmukh Commission (1956), Hansa Mehta Committee (1961), Bhakta Vatsalam Committee (1965), National Education Policy of 1986. Since the Sixth Five Year Plan of India multi-pronged strategy have been adopted to empower women relating to employment and economic independence, education, access to health care and family planning, support services to meet gender needs.

STATUS OF WOMEN

Literacy and education are the most essential inputs for empowerment of women. Our constitution has given equal rights and opportunities to both men and women in the political, economic and social spheres and it also prohibits any kind of discrimination against women. A critical analysis of the five-year plans over the years starting from independence, they reflect that in the earlier phase of developmental planning, the concept of women development was mainly 'welfare' oriented. During sixties, women's education and maternal and child health received priority. During seventies, there was a shift from 'welfare' to development, which started recognizing women as participants of development. The eighties adopted a multidisciplinary approach with a special thrust on health, education and employment and a number of programmes were launched for the propose under different sectors of agriculture and its allied activities. Recognizing the role and contribution of women in development, in early nineties made a beginning in concentrating on training for employment-*cum*-income generating programmes for women with the ultimate objective of making them economically independent and self-reliant. No doubt, that because of these developmental efforts have brought lot of positive changes and achievements towards betterment of women folk.

INTERNATIONAL STATUS

It is global phenomenon that many women are not involved in the political decision-making process. There are, no doubt, exceptions to it. Some countries like Sweden and Norway have sufficient number of women representation in their parliament and women had been Prime Ministers in some countries including India. Even women are currently also Prime Ministers in some countries in the world; yet emancipation of women from the various types of discriminations are very slow. It is appreciating that India has allowed 33 per cent of women representation in the local bodies and efforts are also being made for their representation in parliament where their share of total seats amounted to only 9.3 per cent in 2005. Their representation at the ministerial level was even much lower constituting only 3.4 per cent in the same year. One of the most alarming aspects of the gender inequalities in India is the declining female population. It amounted only 48 per cent of total population in the country according to 2001 population census. It has occurred mainly due to certain patriarchal practices and social customs such as preference for male child, bride burning and female foeticide, etc.

India is ranked 127 for Human Development Index (HDI) out of 177 countries and 98 for Gender Development Index (GDI out of 140 countries in 2003 as reported in the Human Development Report, 2005). It is shown in Table 1.

TABLE 1

Country	*Human Development Index (HDI)*		*HDI Rank*		*Gender Development Index (GDI)*		*GDI Rank*	
	1997	*2003*	*1997*	*2003*	*1997*	*2003*	*1997*	*2003*
Norway	0.927	0.963	2	1	0.967	0.960	2	1
Australia	0.922	0.955	7	3	0.921	0.954	4	2
Sri Lanka	0.721	0.751	90	93	0.712	0.747	76	66
China	0.701	0.755	98	85	0.699	0.754	79	64
Indonesia	0.681	0.697	105	110	0.675	0.691	88	87
India	0.545	0.602	132	127	0.525	0.586	112	98
Pakistan	0.508	0.527	138	135	0.472	0.508	116	107
Bangladesh	0.440	0.520	150	139	0.428	0.514	123	105
Nepal	0.463	0.526	144	136	0.441	0.511	121	106
Mozambique	0.341	0.379	169	168	0.326	0.365	138	133
Niger	0.298	0.281	173	177	0.286	0.271	143	140

Source: UNDP, Human Development Report, 1999 and 2005.

As Table 1, shows India is behind many developing countries including Sri Lanka, China and India both in terms of HDI and GDI values and ranks. It signifies that HRD and/or gender equalities are not the automatic process. The translation of growth to the HRD and/or gender equalities requires appropriate strategies for targeting particular groups. The performance of Sri Lanka or even Kerala at the regional level in India is akin to the developed countries in many respects of gender equalities because of the effective governance providing better education and health facilities to all. Even Bangladesh being the poor country is paying greater attention to the education of girls and involving women in economic activities and thus improving its HDI and GDI ranks relatively at rapid rate.

According to the International Labour Organisation's (ILO) Report on Global Empowerment Trends for Women, 2004, more women work today than ever before: in 2003 out of the 2.8 billion people that had work, 1.1 billion were women. However, for women there is no real socio-economic empowerment, including an equitable distribution of household responsibilities, equal pay for work of equal value, and gender balance across all occupations. Women are more likely than men to find employment in the informal economy, outside legal and regulatory frameworks, without social security benefits. They, therefore, experience a high degree of vulnerability. This also means that the units that employ women are not likely to follow any environmental regulations and the work itself may be hazardous.

Women have a higher share than men in agricultural employment in Asia, sub-Saharan Africa, the Middle East, North Africa, in some Latin American Economics, and the Caribbean. In all developing countries, women's share in industry is lower than men's.

Of late, almost everywhere in developing countries, micro-finance has been mentioned as an important instrument to combat poverty. Especially during the past 10 years, micro-finance programmes have been introduced in these countries to help the rural poor and particularly women. Gramin Bank System of group lending established in 1976 by Muhammad Yunus, a Bangladesh banker and economist, Banco Sol Bolivia and Bank Rakyat in Indonesia, are the classic examples, in this regard. Further, to support the view that micro-finance can be an important instrument to fight poverty, the UN declared 2005 as the International year of Micro-credit. That apart, very recently, the attention for micro-finance and its role in reducing poverty have further enhanced when Muhammadyunus received the Nobel peace prize. (Neel Hermes, Robert Hensink, 2007). In India micro-finance has been provided through Self Help Groups in rural areas, primarily.

In brief, data related to global women status highlight the factual truth.

- Of the world's 1.3 billion poor, nearly 70 per cent are women.
- Between 75-80 per cent of the world's 27 million refugees are women and children.
- Only 24 women have been elected as heads of governments in the last century.
- Women hold only 10.5 per cent of the seats in world's parliament.

- Of the world's one billion illiterate, two-thirds are women.
- Two-thirds of 130 million children world-wide, who are not in school, are girls.
- In most countries, women work approximately twice the unpaid time men do.
- Rural women produce more than 55 per cent of all food grown in developing countries.
- The value of women's unpaid house work and community work is estimated at 35 per cent of GDP world-wide.
- HIV is increasingly affecting women. Today, about 42 per cent of the estimated cases are those of women.

20 million unsafe abortions are performed every year resulting in the deaths of 70,000 women.

NATIONAL STATUS

Human deprivations in India or for that matter in other developing countries are largely due to the neglect of women. Human distresses in these countries could have been minimized if adequate attention paid to the empowerment of women. It is shown in Table 3 explain the human deprivations in India in terms of human poverty, populations lacking access to safe drinking water and improved sanitation, child deprivations and women deprivations.

The Table shows that nearly one quarter of our population is still below poverty line and about one-fifth of the people are undernourished. There were 39 per cent adult illiterates in 2003. Human Poverty Index (HPI) in the country stood 31.3 per cent in the same year. There were 14 per cent of our people lacking access to improved water sources and 70 per cent to improved sanitation in 2002.

Child and women deprivations are still widespread. Infant mortality rate (IMR) in India amounted to 63 per 1,000 live births and less than 5 mortality rates per 1,000 live births amounted to 87 in 2003, which are still quite large. 16 per cent of the children joining primary schools do not complete grade 5. There are 47 per cent underweight children under age 5 indicating their poor health. According to population census 2001 there are 12.5 million children working as child labour in the age group of 5 to 14 whereas existing laws prohibit their employment. Adult female illiterates in India were 52.8 per cent in 2003, which is more than half of the female population. Maternal mortality rate per 100,000 live births is 540 in 2005 while it stood only 56 in China, 92 in Sri Lanka and 380 in Bangladesh in the same year. It means that a large number of children do not see their beloved mothers after births. Half of adult female population is out of economic activities in our country reducing their access to income.

NEED OF WOMEN EMPOWERMENT

Above discussion pinpoints the earnest need of women empowerment as women play a vital role in the all-round development of a nation and in shaping the character of the country's future generation. The reality is that the women population produce 50 per cent of the world's food supply, account for 60 per cent of working force and contribute upto 30 per cent of the official labour force, receive only ten per cent of world's economy but own less than one per cent of World's real estate (*University News* (31), August 21, 2000, p. 11). In spite of the constitutional provision and provision of different Acts on developing the status of women, even now many more miles to go for complete empowerment of women in India, with many more physical and social problems. Indian women hardly can fight for financial independence and self-reliance. The Hindu Succession Act provides equal rights to girl child to inherit her parents' property. In practice women hardly even given their due share of property and much depends on husband and son's money. However, empowerment of women is increasing in modern India as they are playing longer role in shaping the socio-economic, political and other aspects of national life.

The question that needs to be answered is that in a society where men control the destiny of women how is it possible to empower women? Before we discuss practical and associated difficulties in the process of empowerment of women let us look at what does the national policy of empowerment of women in Indian state.

The national policy of empowerment of women has set certain clear cut goals and objectives. The goal of this Policy is to bring about the advancement and empowerment of women. The Policy will be widely disseminated so as to encourage active participation of all stakeholders for achieving its goals. Specially, the objectives of this Policy include:

- Creating an environment through positive economic and social policies for full development of women to enable them to realize.
- The *de-jure* and *de-facto* enjoyment of all human rights and fundamental freedom by women on equal basis with men in all spheres—political, economic, social, cultural and civil.
- Equal access to participation and decision-making of women in social, political and economic life of the nation.
- Equal access of women to healthcare, quality education at all levels, career and vocational guidance, employment, equal remuneration, occupational health and safety, social security and public office, etc.
- Strengthening legal systems aimed at elimination of all forms of discrimination against women.
- Changing societal attitudes and community practices by active participation and involvement of both men and women.
- Mainstreaming a gender perspective in the development process.
- Elimination of discrimination and all forms of violence against women and the girl child.
- Building and strengthening partnerships with civil society, particularly women's organisation.

The social welfare policies are built on the premise that women lack power, they are denied basic rights as individuals have limited income and access to resources. It is clear that efforts to improve income and living conditions (the basis of the early social welfare approach) are insufficient in empowering women unless considerations of the basic patriarchal feature of society are brought into the equation and the responsibility of states to address its negative effects is addressed. Policy-makers must also take note of the resistance women have faced in their entry into public space, and coordinate vigorous efforts to continue legal reform and enhance women's participation in social, economic and political spheres.

Indicators of Women Empowerment

There are several indicators of empowerment. At the individual level participation in crucial decision-making process, ability to prevent violence, self-esteem, improved health and nutrition conditions and at the community level, existence of women's organisations, increased number of women leaders involvement of women in designing development tools and application of appropriate technology, etc. At national level the indicators are, for example, awareness of her social and political rights, adequate representation in legislative bodies, integration of women in particular in national development plans, etc. (Medel-Anouevo, 1995).

Improvement in economic status is a more visible indicator of women empowerment. This naturally gets reflected in improved social, political and cultural status of women. Self-confidence and self-esteem of women proceed simultaneously with their empowerment. In brief, all indicators can be classified into two broad categories namely visible and invisible indicators. Amongst visible indicators a mention could be made of women's representation in parliaments. Thirty per cent (30%) of total women parliamentarians in the world come from just seven countries. Their share in national parliaments of a few selected developed and developing countries is shown in Table 2.

It can be seen from Table 2, that both in developed and developing countries women hold less seats than the men. However, in developed countries their representation is relatively higher than developing countries. In this context it can be said that increasing the number of women in parliaments and also raising women's visibility in positions of authority and decision are quite necessary for their empowerment, particularly and economically as well.

TABLE 2

Seats in Parliaments Held by Women (as % of Total)

Sl. No.	Developing Countries	Percent Countries	Developing Countries	Percent Countries
1.	China	21.8	Sweden	45
2.	Pakistan	21.6	Denmark	38
3.	Morocco	10.8	Norway	36.4
4.	India	8.8	Finland	36.1
5.	Indonesia	8.0	Netherlands	36
6.	Nepal	5.9	Iceland	34
7.	Egypt	2.4	Austria	33
8.	Bangladesh	2	Newzealand	29

Source: Human Development Report, 2003.

Gender Discrimination

Despite concerted efforts at individual and institutional levels there exists wide scale gender discrimination, both open and concealed. Here we restrict ourselves to only two such types, one, discrimination expressed in terms of burden of work on women and the other being in concerned by women. It is shown in Table 3.

Table 3 points out burden of work explained in terms of minutes of work per day. It is clear from this table that in almost all countries, except in Canada, Women are putting in more amount of work than men. It is evident from Table 3 that the male member's burden of work is less than the females in developed and developing countries as well. For example, in USA in 1985 the work burden of females is 453 minutes per day. In India in 2000, total work time of women is 391 minutes per day. Despite this women are earning less than men as is clear from Table 4 that contains figures of estimated earned income of males and females in different countries.

It is clear from Table 4 that women earn less than men. For example, in Indonesia the estimated earned income of a female is $ 1987 whereas a male is getting $ 3893. In India it is $ 1531 and 4070 respectively. It is also eminently clear from Table 3 that not only women are earning less but also the relative difference too between the two is also very huge. In almost all cases men are earning twice higher than women. "Much of women's work never appears in the national statistics because it is seen as an extension of their earning and nurturing functions rather than as materially rewarding activity. All of it is taken as unpaid family labour; but if it is quantified the world's gross national product would increase by 20-30 per cent". (Choudhary: 2004).

TABLE 3

Total Work Time: Wage Employment Outside Agriculture (Minutes/Day)

Sl. No.	*Countries*	*Year*	*Females*	*Males*
1.	Indonesia	1992	378	366
2.	Nepal	1978	579	554
3.	Bangladesh	1990	545	496
4.	India	2000	457	391
5.	South Africa	2000	332	273
6.	Australia	1997	435	418
7.	Canada	1998	420	429
8.	France	1999	391	363
9.	Japan	1996	393	363
10.	United Kingdom	1985	413	411
11.	USA	1985	453	428

Source: Human Development Report, 2003.

TABLE 4

Estimated Earned Income (PPP US$ 2001)

Sl. No.	*Countries*	*Female*	*Male*
1.	China	3169	4825
2.	India	1531	4070
3.	Swaziland	2395	6453
4.	Bangladesh	1153	2044
5.	Nepal	867	1734
6.	Pakistan	909	2824
7.	Nigeria	505	1191
8.	South Africa	7047	15712
9.	Indonesia	1987	3893

Source: Human Development Report, 2003.

WOMEN EMPOWERMENT AND GLOBALISATION

Women empowerment is a globally important issue and international agencies now focus on women centric gender-based policy initiatives. One of the Millennium Development Goals of the UN is to promote gender equality and women's empowerment. The stated goals to eradicate poverty and hunger achieve universal primary education, reduce child mortality, fight with some fatal diseases, ensure environmental sustainability and develop and global partnership for development are directly or indirectly linked with gender-based strategy. In this global world masses are being driven away towards a new world of consumerism which results in expansion of market, less employment opportunities as there are certain restriction on them that reduces economic independence. The impact of new technologies and globalisation on women's job is very much limited. It has failed to generate adequate job opportunities to the Indian women. Internet and Information technology facilities have provided jobs to urban elite group of women. The liberalisation of trade and financial markets also fails to provide much impact on the empowerment of women, as most of the women are unskilled and untrained to work in elite industries.

ISSUES OF WOMEN IN AGRICULTURE AND ALLIED ACTIVITIES

In India, as high as 76 per cent of rural population is engaged in agricultural production and rural women comprise about 50% of agricultural force. There are more than 30 million as agricultural labourers and 10 million employed in animal husbandry, handicrafts and related activities. In hilly regions of our country female labourers out number the male labourers. In family farm labour, women play an important role in all states in all stages of crop raising, starting from land preparation to harvest and post-harvest processing. The type and extent of participation by farm women in farm operations vary from State to State, while the participation rate of women in crop production in Haryana, Punjab is only 1.45 and 4.28 per cent, respectively. It is higher in Maharashtra and Tamil Nadu, i.e., 29 and 24 per cent, respectively and the rate is still higher in North-eastern region and Andhra

Pradesh accounting for 70% and 96%, respectively (Singh and Bhattacharya, 1990).

On the threshold of the twenty-first century, we find that the condition of our women folk, particularly those of rural community is still very deplorable. In view of the tremendous contribution that women are making and can yet make, it is not a matter of little concern, rather time has come when it has been realized that for speedy and over all development of agriculture, their involvement needs to be properly assessed and known. In the production-oriented programmes for rural development, there has been very little or practically no effort to evaluate the role played by the rural women.

Today, 44 per cent of the world's food is produced by women which indicate how important their role is in farming. Rural women in general and farm women in particular are engaged in different activities. Despite their substantial contributions, women continue to be marginalized, under valued and unrecognized. There is a tendency among most administrators and policy-makers to see "men as farmers" and "women as farmers' wives" and highlight their 'supportive role' rather than their 'productivity role'. Further, recently studies reveal that 50-90 per cent of agricultural operations are carried out by women only. It can therefore, be forcefully established that their contribution to agriculture and allied activities in rural India is immense. It is shown in Table 5.

UN Secretary General Kofi Annan has rightly stated, "Gender equality is more than a goal in itself. It is a precondition for meeting the challenge of reducing poverty, promoting sustainable and building good governance."

Indian agriculture cannot improve without making the women equal partners in its development efforts. As women play key role in many facets of the composite farming system practiced by farm families, their pauperisation will increase rural poverty, because the poorest families are the most dependent upon women's economic productivity.

To improve the position of women workforce it is necessary to improve their production potential by treating them as important economic actors, not as dependent members of the family. In dealing with women as economic actors, interventions should be made on all fronts of the farming system in which each of them are involved. Institutional interventions should be made to provide them with productive resources around their vocations.

TABLE 5

Status of Women (Census, 2001)

Total Population	1025.25 million
Total Women	25.67%
Rate of participation of women in work force out of total women in the country	25..67%
Rate of participation of men in work force out of total men in the country	51.93%
Total cultivators	127.62 million
Female cultivators	41.29 million (32.35%)
Total Agricultural labourer	107.44 million
Women Agricultural labourer	47.94 million (44.62%)
1995-96	
Total land holdings	115.58 million
Land holdings belonging to Women	11.01 million

Society has institutionalized a sharp demarcation of social roles according to sex, in which one half of its members voluntarily accept a role subordinate to the other half. The fact that such a division of labour, extending into both economic and political spheres, has existed throughout history and in most areas of the world does not lessen the impact of such a secondary role on women. Men virtually monopolize the high status of positions of decision-making and formulation of goals in major economic, political and cultural institutions of society. The rationale, such as it is, for this perception stresses that women want it that way, supported by studies which show that women are relatively apolitical; women prefer the domestic sphere, of home and family, and thus choose to leave political and civic affairs to men. This raises the question whether it is traditional feminine values and sex stereotyping which causes women to lower their own separations not only with respect to social roles, but also within the full spectrum of political attitudes and participation. If interrelatedness between traditional feminine values, sex stereotyping and political awareness could be demonstrated; it might serve to explain the well-known myths of women's preconceived attitude and pattern of behaviour.

It is surprising that political scientists have excluded women, as deserving major concern and attention. Few little efforts have been made to question the widely held belief that politics is strictly a masculine affairs and that women's place is in the home. On the contrary, the profession evaded the question by relying on cultural gender role definition for the status of women in politics rather than actually investigating the nature of status. The lower status of women in politics has been perpetuated and accepted because culture contrived and supported the myth of inferiority of women and their unsuitability to take up politics. Man's role revolves around his occupation, the women's around her family.

For a very long period women have secluded themselves from politics. Public Administration and politics, by and large, are considered to be the exclusive privilege of men. In recent years women's participation in politics and in policy-making spheres has significantly increased. The importance of women's participation in politics arises from the fact that 'politics' confers authority to exercise power, i.e. the power to make policies, make decisions and to implement the policies and the decisions. It also provides an effective control over government machinery. During the freedom movement in India, a very large section of women came out of their domestic seclusion and participated in Dharnas, picketing and protests side by side with men. But after independence women's participation in politics has been disappointing. The percentage of seats held by women in parliament is very low at 11.8 per cent. Particularly in developing countries like India the share is only 7.3 per cent. In Industrial countries it is somewhat better at 15.3 per cent than in other countries. The representation of women in Indian Lok Sabha for various years is given in Table 6.

A cursory glance at Table 6 indicates that the proportion of male voters to total males was 53 per cent. Later it increased to 70.79 per cent in 1989, which again decelerated to 52.56 per cent in 1991. At the same time, the proportion of female voters to total females also soared from 37.10 per cent in 1952 to 47.42 per cent in 1991 amidst fluctuations. The number of seats won by females also rose from 23 to 54 between 1951 and 2004. In relative terms, the percentage of female M.P.s in Lok Sabha was 4.40 per cent in 1952. It surged to the highest level of 7.90 per cent in 1984 and later it plummeted to 6.60 per cent in 1991 but once again surged to 8.16 per cent in 2004. These statistics clearly indicate that the representation of women in Lok Sabha, the highest decision-making body in country is lawfully low, far lower than their legitimate share of 50 per cent. The sporadic efforts of government to bring about 1/3 reservation in Indian parliament and state legislatures has been thwarted by certain vested interests accustomed to power.

TABLE 6

Representation of Women in Indian Lok Sabha

Year of Election	*% of male voters*	*% of female voters*	*No. of seats won by females*	*% of women M.P.s in Lok Sabha*
1952	53.00	37.10	23	4.40
1957	56.00	38.77	27	5.40
1962	62.10	46.63	35	6.70
1967	66.70	55.48	31	5.90
1971	69.70	49.15	22	4.20
1977	65.62	54.96	19	3.40
1980	57.69	51.22	28	5.14
1984	63.61	68.17	59	7.90
1989	70.79	43.90	28	5.30
1991	52.56	47.42	33	6.60
1996	NA	NA	39	7.20
2004	NA	NA	44	8.16

Note: NA: Not Available.

Sources: 1. Bharat Gyan Vigyan Samiti, Panchayat Raj—Mahila Gyan Vigyan Vedika, p. 34.

2. For 1996 and 2004, Election Commission of India (Web site).

The 73rd and 74th Amendments (1993) to the Indian Constitution have served as a break-through towards ensuring equal access and increased participation in political power structure for women at grass root level. Based on these Amendments, almost all the states have enacted new Panchayati Raj Act. So it is high time to examine the problems and prospects involved in this attempt of establishing gender justice and the changes brought about in the political sphere by the 1/3 participation of women in Panchayati Raj Institutions (PRIs) and in the society at large. Political/Social experience is a favourable factor for women empowerment. Therefore, the political parties should encourage women in large numbers and various assignments should be given to them so as to acquire leadership equalities.

GENDER EQUALITY, ECONOMIC GROWTH AND GOVERNANCE

Economic Growth

All over the world, women and men spend the major portion of their lives working. Some of the work may be paid and some may be unpaid. The conditions under which women work and women's access to employment and productive resources can differ considerably from those of men. As observed in the Beijing platform for action, almost every where, women are now working more outside the home, but there has not been a parallel lightening of their responsibilities for unremunerated work in the household and community. For women in paid work, obstacles remain that hinder them from achieving their potential and women are poorly represented in economic decision-making as well as in certain occupations and sectors. Unemployment and under employment are serious problems in many countries, especially for women. Where formal employment opportunities are not accessible, women often seek livelihood for themselves and their dependents in the informal sector, some becoming self-employed or owners of small scale enterprises.

Gender discrimination remains pervasive in many dimensions of life-worldwide. This is so despite considerable advances in gender equality in recent decades. The nature and extent of the discrimination vary considerably across countries and regions. But the patterns are striking. In no region of the developing world are women equal to men in legal, social and economic rights. Gender gaps are widespread in access to and control of resources, in economic opportunities, in power and political voice. Gender inequalities impose costs on productivity, efficiency and economic progress. By hindering the accumulation of human capital in the home and the labour market and by systematically excluding women or men from access to resources, public services or productive activities gender discrimination diminishes an economy's capacity to grow and to raise living standards. Losses in output result from inefficiencies in the allocation of productive resources between men and women within households. In households in Burkina, Faso, Cameroon and Kenya more equal control of inputs and farm income by women and women could raise farm yields by as much as a fifth of current output (World Bank Research Report, Oct. 2000).

Low investment in female education also reduces a country's overall output. One study estimates that if the countries in South Asia, Sub-Saharan Africa and the Middle East and North Africa had started with the gender gaps in average years of schooling that East Asia had in 1960 and closed that gender gap at the rate achieved by East Asia from 1960-92, their income per capita could have grown by 0.5-0.9 percentage points higher per year substantial increases over actual growth rates. Another study estimates that even for middle and high income countries with higher initial education levels, an increase of 1 percentage point in the share of women with secondary education is associated with an increase in per capita income of 0.3 percentage point. Both studies control for other variables commonly found in the growth literature (World Bank Research Report, Oct. 2000).

For these reasons, gender equality is a core development issue. Gender equality means women and men have equal opportunities to realize their individual potential, to contribute to their country's economic and social development and to benefit equally from their participation in society. Gender equality strengthens countries' abilities to grow, to reduce poverty and to govern effectively. Promoting gender equality is thus an important part of a development strategy that seeks to enable all people-women and men alike—to escape poverty and improve their standard of living.

Governance

Greater women's rights and more equal participation in public life by women and men are associated with cleaner business and government and better governance. Where the influence of women in public life is greater, the level of corruption is lower. This holds even when comparing countries with the same income, civil liberties, education and legal institutions. Although still only suggestive, these findings lend additional support for having more women in the labour force and in politics—since women can be an effective force for rule of law and good government. Women in business are less likely to pay bribes to government officials, perhaps because women have higher standards of ethical behaviour or greater risk aversion. A study of 350 firms in the republic of Georgia concludes that firms owned or managed by men are 10 per cent more likely to make unofficial payments to government officials than those owned or managed by women. This result holds regardless of the characteristics of the firm, such as the sector in which it operates and firm size and the characteristics of the owner or manager, such as education. Without controlling for these factors, firms managed by men are twice as likely to pay bribes (World Bank Research Report, Oct. 2000).

Gender Equality and the Millennium Development Goals

In September 2000, Heads of State and Representatives of the Governments of 191 countries met at the United Nations and adopted the Millennium Declaration. The Declaration outlines the central concerns of the global community—peace, security, development, environmental sustainability, human rights and democracy and articulates a set of inter-connected and mutually reinforcing goals for sustainable development. These, the Millennium Development Goals (MDGs) are based on the major goals and targets agreed upon at the UN Conferences of the 1990s, which have been synthesized into a global agenda for development.

The Millennium Declaration commits the international community and member-states of the UN to the achievement of the following eight major goals.

1. Eradication of extreme poverty and hunger.
2. Achievement of universal primary education.
3. Promotion of gender equality and empowerment of women.
4. Reduction of child mortality.

5. Improvement in maternal health.
6. Combating HIV/AIDS, malaria and other diseases.
7. Ensuring environmental sustainability.
8. Developing a global partnership for development.

Quantitative targets have been defined for each goal, most of which are to be achieved by 2015. Indicators have been selected to monitor progress on each of the targets. A list of 18 targets and 48 indicators has been agreed upon to ensure comparability across countries and facilitate tracking of progress at global, regional and national levels.

POLICY COMMITMENTS FOR WOMEN CONSTITUTIONAL PROVISIONS

The commitment to gender equity is well entrenched at the highest policy-making level—the Constitution of India. A few important provisions for women are:

- Article 14—Equal Rights and Opportunities in Political, Economic and Social Spheres.
- Article 15—Prohibits discrimination on grounds of sex.
- Article 15(3)—Enables affirmative discrimination in favour of women.
- Article 39—Equal means of livelihood and equal pay for equal work.
- Article 42—Just and Human conditions of work and maternity relief.
- Article 51(A)(e)—Fundamental Duty to renounce practices, derogatory to dignity of women.

The National Policy for Empowerment of Women, 2001 envisaged introduction of a gender perspective in the budgeting process as an operational strategy.

These provisions are effected and supplemented by the legal framework. A few laws and legislations that are in place:

Women Specific Legislations

- Immoral Traffic (Prevention) Act, 1956.
- The Maternity Benefit Act, 1961.

- The Dowry Prohibition Act, 1961.
- Indecent Representation Women (Prohibition) Act, 1986.
- The Commission of Sati (Prevention) Act, 1987.
- Protection of Women from Domestic Violence Act, 2005.

Economic

Factories Act, 1948, Minimum Wages Act, 1948, Equal Remuneration Act, 1976. The Employees' State Insurance Act, 1948. The Plantation Labour Act, 1951 and The Bonded Labour System (Abolition) Act, 1976.

Protection

Relevant provisions of Code of Criminal Procedure, 1973; Special provisions under IPC, The Legal Practitioners (Women) Act, 1923, The Pre-Natal Diagnostic Technique (Regulation and Prevention of Misuse) Act, 1994.

Social

Family Courts Act, 1984, The Indian Succession Act, 1925, The Medical Termination of Pregnancy Act, 1971, The Child Marriage Restraint Act, 1929, The Hindu Marriage Act, 1955, The Hindu Succession Act, 1956 (Amended in 2005), The Indian Divorce Act, 1969.

DEVELOPMENT OF WOMEN DURING PLAN PERIOD

In recent years, empowerment of women has been recognized as a central issue in determining the status of women. Empowerment covers aspects such as women's control over material and intellectual resources. Empowerment is a process, not an event, which challenges traditional power equations and relations. Abolition of gender-based discrimination in all institutions and structures of the society and participation of women in policy and decision-making processes at domestic and public levels are few dimensions of women empowerment.

All round development of women has been one of the focal points of planning process in India. The First Five Year Plan (1951-56) envisaged a number of welfare measures for women. Establishment of the Central Social Welfare Board (CSWB), Organisation of Mahila Mandals or Women's Clubs and the

Community Development Programmes were a few steps in this direction. In the Second Five Year Plan (1956-61), the empowerment of women was closely linked with the overall approach of intensive agricultural development programmes. The Third and Fourth Five Year Plans (1961-66 and 1969-74) supported female education as a major welfare measure. Similarly, the Fourth Five Year Plan (1969-74) co: tinued the emphasis on women's education. The Fifth Five Year Plan (1974-79) emphasized training of women, who were in need of income and protection. Functional literacy programmes got priority. This plan coincided with International Women's Decade and the submission of Report of the Committee on the Status of Women in India. In 1976, Women's Welfare and Development Bureau was set-up under the Ministry of Social Welfare. It was to act as a nodal point to coordinate policies and programmes for women's development. The Sixth Five Year Plan (1980-85) saw a definite shift from welfare to development. It recognized women's lack of access to resources as a critical factor impending their growth. The Seventh Plan (1985-90) emphasized the need for gender equality and empowerment. For the first time, emphasis was placed upon qualitative aspects such as inculcation of confidence, generation of awareness with regards to rights and training in skills for better employment. The Eighth Five Year Plan (1992-97) focused on empowering women, especially at the grassroots level, through Panchayati Raj Institutions. The Ninth Five Year Plan (1995-2000) adopted a strategy of Women's Component Plan, under which not less than 30 per cent of funds/benefits were earmarked for women-specific programmes. The Tenth Plan (2002-07) approach aims at empowering women through translating the recently adopted National Policy for Empowerment of Women (2001) into action and ensuring Survival, Protection and Development of Women and Children through Right Based Approach. Eleventh Five Year Plan (2007-12) approach Paper: The theme of the draft approach paper to the Eleventh Five Year Plan titled "towards faster and more inclusive growth" is indeed very attractive. At this stage of development, India definitely needs faster and more inclusive growth. The question, however, is whether the strategy underlying the approach paper ensures a more inclusive growth or not. That is whether the underlying approach will be able to include the excluded the poor, the women, dalit and others.

Approach paper: The approach paper starts by starting that the Indian economy is in a much stronger position today than before, with the average growth rate of about 7 per cent in the Tenth Plan. The reasonably high rates of savings (28 per cent) and investment (27.5 per cent), comfortable position of foreign exchange reserves (at US $ 151.6 billion) and low rate of inflation (about 4.8%) during the Tenth Plan has put the economy in a position to grow faster, at 8.5 per cent in the coming years. The economy is now poised to grow at 9.9 per cent in industry, 9.4 per cent in services and 4 per cent in agriculture.

SUGGESTIONS AND CONCLUSIONS

Problem of gender discrimination needs to be addressed with several fronts such as economic, legal, social, educational and political. Women may be empowered by various activities such as calculating the amount of their labour and add it to be GDP proper enactment of legislation, mobilisation and purposeful action, uprooting the Dowry system, to instill and understanding of the dangers of gender discrimination among all persons in the society, stopping the politicians to follow the divide and rule policy in the society on the basis of religion, castes and creed. So compulsory female education, strengthening adult literacy programme, holding seminars and debates at the grass root level are essential to empower the women. Enactment of equal remuneration act, more research works in women empowerment, preparation of more relevant curriculum, which will make the girls self-reliant, are quite important. Empowering the communities with response through local management mechanism, organizing career campaigns in the college for the girls will certainly help in strengthening the women empowerment. Last not the least is a multifaceted approach covering the regional and local needs must be strengthened. After all a concerted effort by all the sections of the people in the society, the voluntary organisations and the government is must to empower women. Developing skills and techniques on women, setting up of micro-enterprises for women will definitely help in increasing women empowerment.

Now a conclusion can be drawn though the nation is marching towards the path of panned development, yet women's plight, plunder and perversion are on increasing in most areas. The path of development is yet to bring a perceptible change on women's empowerment. So to improve the status of women in India socio-economic aspects concerning women empowerment must be carefully addressed. Hence all efforts on the part of the government at the central, the state and the local, the NGOs and the people as a whole must work together to combat with problem of women empowerment. Let us work together to build India with equal development of both men and women.

REFERENCES

Agrawal, Rashmi and B.V.L.N. Rao (2004), "Gender Issues—A Road Map to Empowerment," Shipra, New Delhi.

Beteile, Andre (1994), "Empowerment", *Economic and Political Weekly*, Vol. 34, Nos. 10 & 11.

Batliwala, Srilatha (1994), "Women's Empowerment in South Asia", Max Mueller Bhava, New Delhi.

Choudhary, Sarmisttha (2004), "Invisible Activities of Rural Women," *Kurukshetra*, July.

Hirway, Indira (1999), "Economic Reforms and Women's Work", in Papola and Sharma (eds).

Hirway, Indira (2006), "Where is Gender in Eleventh Approach Paper"? *EPW*, August (12-18), Vol. XLI, No. 32, pp. 3464-66.

Joseph, Cherian and Prasad, K.V. Eswara (1995), "Women, Work and Inequity", (The Reality of Gender) eds. National Labour Institute.

Medel-Anouevo, Carolyn and Bettina Bochynek (1995), The International Seminar on "Women's Education and Empowerment", UNESCO, Institute for Education.

Magnifying Mal-Development, Alternative Economic Survey, India, Rainbow Publishers, Zed Books, London.

Mukhopadhyay, Swapna and Ratna M. Sundarshan (2003), "Traking Gender Equity Under Economic Reforms—Continuity and Change in South Asia (eds.), IDRC and Kali for Women, New Delhi.

Papola, T.S. and Sharma, Alakh N. (1999), "Gender and Employment in India", Vikas Publishing House, New Delhi.

Peerzade, Sayed Afzal and Parande, Prema (2005), "Economic Empowerment of Women: Theory and Practice," *Southern Economist*, March.

Rustage, Preet (2005), "Women's Work and Income Promotion: Policy Related Issues", International Conference at IHD, New Delhi.

Sharma, Kumud (1992), "Grassroots Organisations and Women's Empowerment: Some Issues in The Contemporary Debate," in Samya Shakti, Centre for Women's Development Studies, New Delhi.

Sharma, Alakh N. and Singh, Seema (1993), "Women and Works Changing Scenario in India," B.R. Publishing Corporation, Delhi.

Sundaram, Satya (2005), "Women Empowerment and Globalisation," Southern Economist, November.

World Development Report, 2003.

World Development Report, 2004.

World Development Report, 2005.

Yojana, January 2005.

Yojana, August 2005.

Yojana, October 2005.

Yojana, January 2006.

Yojana, August 2006.

Yojana, October 2006.

Growth, Transformation and Unorganised Women Workers: A Case for Enhanced Public Investment in Agriculture

Indradeo Sharma

CONTEXT

Organised workers, as the name indicates, are those who are working in the organised sector. The organised sector in India includes all establishment in the public sector (Government, Semi-Government, Government Undertakings, Local Bodies, etc.) and non-agricultural establishments employing 10 or more workers in the private sector. Within agriculture, it covers only the plantation sector. It does not cover household establishments as well as self-employed or independent workers. Within the government sector, again, it does not cover employment in Indian missions/ embassies abroad and defence forces due to administrative reasons. Organised industries include those industrial units which are covered y the Factories Act. On the other hand, the informal or unorganized sector can be said to constitute one which is defined as the absence of any formal structure of organisation and operation. These organisations do not follow the general principles of accounting, management and according wages and other benefits as laid down by the government from time to time. In these organisations, the rules of functioning are largely laid down by individual owners/families. And, all those working in the unorganized/informal sector are known as unorganized workers. The significance of the organized sector lies in that it constitutes the most productive sector in the Indian economy. It employs only around 8 per cent of all main workers in India but is generating over 40 per cent of its net domestic product. The sector is extremely paying to workers as well. It accounts for around 64 per cent of the total wage bill in the Indian economy. And, it is for jobs in this Sector that most of the educated youth in the country are aspiring. On the other hand, the unorganized sector is extremely low in productivity as well as payments per workers.

DEVELOPMENT STRATEGY AND EMPLOYMENT

Based on the development experience of western industrialized countries, economic development in the third (developing) world, too, has been perceived to require a rapid structural transformation of the economy from one largely based on agriculture to a more complex modern industrial and service society (Todaro, 1981, p. 252). The role of agriculture in this development process is thought to be largely passive and supportive to provide sufficient low priced food and cheap man-power to the expanding industrial sector which is considered the dynamic: 'leading sector' in the over all strategy of economic development.

The first and the best known model of the development process for labour surplus third world nations developed by the 1979 Nobel Laureate W.A. Lewis provides the most outstanding example of the theory of development that places heavy emphasis on rapid industrial growth with agriculture fuelling process of industrial expansion with its cheap food and surplus labour (Lewis, 1954). In the growth model of Lewis, the economy consists of two sectors: the traditional rural subsistence sector characterized by zero or very low productivity surplus labour and high productivity modern urban industrial sector into which surplus labour and a high productivity modern urban industrial sector into which surplus labour from the subsistence sector is gradually transferred. The primary focus of the model is both on the process of labour transfer and growth of employment in the modern sector which are brought about by rapid expansion of output in the modern sector which takes place faster with the development process on account of its high income elasticity of demand as compared to the output of the traditional sector which does not grow so fast on account of its low income elasticity of demand. In India, the government has played an active role in the development process. Besides providing basic social and economic infrastructure, it has also promoted large (basic industries in its own sector. All these have led to rise in employment in the organized (public) sector.

PLANNING AND ORGANIZED SECTOR EMPLOYMENT

Data showing the growth of employment in the organized sector are contained in Table 1. As shown in the table, there has been significant expansion of employment in the organized sector over the plan period till 191, i.e. from 120.90 lakh in 1991 (at the rate of 2.68 per cent per annum). As a percentage to all main workers, it has risen from 6.41 to 9.51 over the same period, reflecting the fact that the rate of rise in the organized sector employment has been higher. After 1991 however, there has been a marked reversal in this trend, especially since 1997. The number of persons employed in this sector has gone down from 282.45 lakh in 1997 to 264.43 lakh in 2004, i.e. at the rate of 2.57 lakh per annum. The percentage share of the organized sector employment in total has gone down from 10.12 in 1981 to 8.18 in 2004. The expansion of women employment in this sector, however, has been steady and much faster over the period 1961-2001. Hence, the percentage share of women in total organized sector employment has gone up from 10.90 in 1961 to 18.66 in 2004. As percentage to all women workers, it has improved from 2.22 in 1961 to 6.49 in 2004. Some of the reasons cited for preference for women employment in this sector are that women workers are docile, less demanding, more disciplined and punctual in work. Moreover, they are expected to leave their jobs soon after their manage, making no claims for retirement benefits. Despite these, however,

TABLE 1

Dynamics of Organised Sector Employment (1961-2004)

As on End March	*Organized Sector Employment in '000*				*% share of women in organized employment*	
	India		*Bihar*			
	Persons	*Women*	*Persons*	*Women*	*India*	*Bihar*
1961	12090 (6.41)	1318 (2.22)	NA	NA	10.90	NA
1971	17473 (9.68)	1922 (6.13)	NA	NA	11.00	NA
1981	22879 (10.12)	2791 (6.13)	NA	NA	12.20	NA
1991	26733 (9.51)	3769 (5.96)	NA	NA	14.10	NA
1997	28245 (9.42)	4637 (6.74)	NA	NA	16.42	NA
2001	27789 (8.88)	4949 (6.79)	577.3 (2.74)	38.0 (1.07)	17.81	6.58
2004	26443 (8.18)	4934 (6.49)	527.1 (2.42)	31.5 (0.82)	18.66	5.98

Figures in brackets indicate organized sector workers as percentage to all main workers (organized + unorganized).

Sources: 1. Directorate General of Employment and Training, Ministry of Labour, GOI, New Delhi, Employment Review of relevant years.
2. Census of India of relevant years.

the hard fact remains that the share of the organized sector in employment is extremely low, including that of women, and this share is declining fast. The situation is extremely poor is this regard in the case of Bihar where the organized sector covers only 2.42 per cent of all main workers. This coverage is not even one per cent in the case of women workers in the state. And, the organized sector employment figures both for men and women in the state declining fast even in absolute terms.

REGIONAL AND SECTORAL SPREAD—HIGH DEPENDENCE ON AGRICULTURE

The organized sector employment also depicts large disparities across states in India, especially in the case of women employment. The percentage share of organized sector workers in all main workers in the case of women in 2001 comes to 28.12 in Assam followed by that in Kerala (27.35), Delhi (23.24), Goa (22.72), Karnataka (10.40), Tamil Nadu (9.79), Punjab (9.50), the all India average being 6.79. On the other hand this share is the lowest at 1.07 in Bihar followed by that in Chhattishgarh (1.79), M.P. (2.98), Rajasthan (3.76), U.P. (4.17), Uttaranchal (4.85), Andhra Pradesh (4.37), etc. The coverage under organized sector employment is better in states where the over all employment structure is more diversified and the level of women education is relatively better. In both these respects, the position of Bihar is extremely poor. The state depicts extremely high dependence of the labour force (main worker) on agriculture (over 76%) and extremely low level of literacy, especially of women (33.57) per cent against 54.16 per cent for India. These factor primarily go to explain why the state depicts extremely high dependence of its workers, especially of women workers, on the unorganized sector. At the same time, the dependence of workers including those of women (both in India and Bihar) has been growing on the unorganized sector over recent years in which both productivity and hence wages per worker are extremely low. Data depicting the distribution of workers both in the organized and unorganized sectors across different (broad) sectors in the economy are contained in Table 3. Within the unorganized sector, women workers depict very high dependence on the agricultural sector in the country as well as in Bihar. The percentage of the women (Main) workers engaged in agriculture comes to as high as 86.22 in Bihar and 75.01 in India. However, the value of output per worker in agriculture is extremely low in relation to other sectors in the Indian economy. In India, agriculture and allied activities employ around 58 per cent of all main workers but produce less than 25 per cent of its net domestic product. However, for decades to come, this large dependence of unorganized workers on agriculture is going to remain. Hence, the major solution of their wages and employment lies in accelerated agriculture development which in turn will lead to substantial rise in productivity. This is turn is crucially dependent on the level of investment in agriculture, especially public investment. The actual developments during the period of reforms, however, have not been on right lines.

TABLE 2

State-wise spread of Organised Sector Employment—As in March 2001

State	*Organised Workers (in '000)*			*As % to Main Workers*		
	Persons	*Males*	*Females*	*Persons*	*Males*	*Females*
Punjab	847.7	713.3	133.9	10.81	11.10	9.45
Haryana	652.7	562.5	90.2	10.46	11.40	6.89
Himachal Pradesh	304.5	257.4	47.1	15.51	19.30	7.47
Jammu and Kashmir	210.1	187.5	22.6	8.05	8.42	5.92
Delhi	841.1	719.5	121.6	19.48	18.96	23.24
Rajasthan	1248.3	1075.7	172.6	7.16	8.38	3.76
Uttaranchal	270.4	237.3	33.1	11.64	14.48	4.85
Uttar Pradesh	2223.8	2015.5	208.3	5.65	5.87	4.17
Madhya Pradesh	1179.1	1028.7	150.4	6.17	7.32	2.98
Chhattisgarh	348.1	306.7	41.4	4.93	6.47	1.79
Bihar	577.3	539.3	38.0	2.74	3.08	1.07
Jharkhand	953.4	880.5	72.9	14.79	17.15	5.55
Orissa	828.8	730.1	98.7	8.64	9.12	6.23
West Bengal	2324.7	2071.2	253.5	10.10	10.62	7.18
Assam	1116.4	760.7	355.7	15.69	13.01	28.12
Other N.E. States	407.5	318.8	88.7	12.00	13.81	8.16
Maharashtra	3694.6	3129.9	564.7	10.63	12.81	5.47
Gujarat	1696.0	1490.3	205.7	9.96	11.06	5.80
Goa, Daman and Diu	125.2	100.9	24.3	25.40	26.15	22.72
Andhra Pradesh	2075.3	1656.2	419.1	7.15	8.51	4.37
Karnataka	1879.7	1310.9	568.8	9.71	9.43	10.40
Kerala	1241.7	755.8	485.9	15.07	11.70	27.35
Tamil Nadu	2505.8	1776.3	729.5	10.55	10.90	9.79
India	27789.2	22839.9	4949.3	8.88	9.51	6.79

Source: Directorate General of Employment and Training, Ministry of Labour, GOI, New Delhi, and Census of India, 2001.

PLAN EROSION AND CRISIS IN AGRICULTURE

In a developing economy like India, the government has to play an active role in the process of economic growth by providing social and economic overhead capital, i.e. those basic services without which primary, secondary and tertiary economic activities can not function properly. These include all public services from law and order through education and public health to

TABLE 3

Sector-wise Distribution of Organized and Unorganized Workers, 2001

(in '000)

Sectors	*India*				*Bihar*			
	Organised		*Unorganised*		*Organised*		*Unorganised*	
	Persons	*Women*	*Persons*	*Women*	*Persons*	*Women*	*Persons*	*Women*
Agriculture	1434.5 (5.16)	512.8 (10.36)	175544 (61.55)	50850 (75.01)	4.90 (0.93)	0.02 (0.06)	16110 (78.36)	3034 (86.22)
Industry	9520.6 (34.26)	1207.3 (24.39)	47364 (16.61)	9214 (13.59)	73.35 (13.91)	0.50 (1.59)	1932 (9.40)	313 (8.89)
Services	16833.9 (60:58)	3229.2 (65.25)	62274 (21.84)	7731 (11.40)	448.91 (85.16)	30.98 (98.35)	2516 (12.24)	172 (4.89)
All Sectors	27789.2 (100.00)	4949.3 (100.00)	285183 (100.00)	67795 (100.00)	527.15 (100.00)	31.50 (100.00)	20558 (100.00)	3519 (100.00)

Figures for Organized Workers for Bihar are of the year 2004.
(Figures in brackets indicate as percentage to total).

transportation, communications, power and water supply, as well as such agricultural overhead capital as irrigation, flood control and drainage systems (Hirschman, 1960). These are of vital significance for economic growth without which investments in different sectors can not be fully productive. They promote different areas (sectors) by generating large external economies to them. However, the economies they generate to other sectors are not reflected in their own rate of return. Hence, they seldom attract much of private investments. Therefore, in general, these services are provided by public agencies either free of charge or at nominal rates. They have been subjected to public control, regulation and support even when provided through private agencies. In India, the government has played a key role in providing these services in agriculture such as those of irrigation, flood control and drainage as well as those in agricultural research, etc. Under the new economic policy, in the name of privatisation and fiscal consolidation, however, there has been a perceptible decline in the role of the government as an investor. First, there has been a decline in the level of public expenditure which has gone down from around 40 per cent of the net domestic during 1985-90 to around 36 per cent of the domestic product during 1990-05. The decline has been much more in plan expenditure. The plan expenditure as percentage to public expenditure has gone down from 39.25 during 1980-90 to 30.45 during 1990-05. Thus, the size of plan expenditure, as a percentage to the net domestic product in the country, has gone down from 14.31 during 1980-90 to 10.98 during 1990-05. The decline has been much more in that on agriculture and irrigation, including flood control and command area development. Their combined share in total plan expenditure over the same period has gone down from 16.11 to 12.62 per cent.

TABLE 4

Plan Expenditure on Agriculture and Irrigation in India (1951-2005)

(in Rs. crores at 1981-82 Prices)

Period	*Plan Expenditure*				*Plan Expenditure as % to*	
1951-61	4814 (12.59)	—	5128 (13.41)	38233 (100.00)	41.93	5.64
1961-69	8316 (14.18)	—	4452 (7.59)	58630 (100.00)	37.80	7.94
1969-80	15983 (13.69)	—	11068 (9.48)	116724 (100.00)	35.46	9.07
1980-90	18810 (7.47)	16952 (6.73)	21767 (8.64)	251939 (100.00	39.25	14.31
1990-05	35353 (5.64)	48285 (7.71)	43697 (6.98)	626019 (100.00)	30.45	10.98

Figures in Brackets indicate percentage share in total plan expenditure.
CAD = Command Area Development.
Source: Computed by Authors from Data contained in Economic Survey, Government of India, of relevant years and from other sources.

ADVERSE TERMS OF TRADE

One major factor promoting better growth in Indian agriculture was the favourable terms of trade that this sector enjoyed during 1980s, i.e. agricultural prices rose higher that those of other commodities, especially in relation to key agricultural inputs like fertilizers, fuel, etc. Thus, with 1981-82 as the base (100) the whole sale price index of foodgrains rose to 179 in 1990-91, the same for fertilizer and diesel stood at 99 and 156. Data depicting movements in whole sale price index of some commodities are contained in Table 5. It is clear from the table that price movements have not been favourable for agricultural commodities, during the period of reforms especially for foodgrains after 1999-2000. Thus, between 1999-2000 and 2005-06 (till December) while the price index for foodgrains rose by only 12 points, those of fertilizer, diesel, and electricity in agriculture rose by 59,345 and 221 points respectively. These price movements have adversely impacted the real terms of trade of agricultural produce, especially of foodgrains. The terms of trade (with 1990-91=1) of foodgrains during 2005-06 stood at 0.46, 0.57 and 0.84 in relation to diesel, electricity for irrigation, and fertilizer respectively. The abnormal rise in the price of fuels (especially diesel and electricity) has really broken the backbone of Indian agriculture, as energy has become an important input in agriculture. It is needed for operating irrigation pump sets and other agricultural implements. Thus, the terms of trade have become very adverse for agriculture during reforms which have very adversely impacted its growth process. It has raised the cost of irrigation through ground water to abnormal heights and made agriculture unremunerative.

TABLE 5

Wholesale Price Index (1990-91 = 100)

Year	*Food Articles*	*Foodgrains*	*Fertilizer*	*Diesel*	*Electricity for Irrigation*
1994-95	160	167	212	152	186
1999-00	235	257	262	246	251
2000-01	242	253	290	319	317
2001-02	250	251	296	352	371
2002-03	254	254	308	381	409
2003-04	257	257	310	419	430
2004-05	264	258	313	503	433
2005-06*	277	269	321	591	472

*Till December, 2005.

Source: RBI, Handbook of Monetary Statistics of India, 2006.

CRISIS IN FOODGRAINS PRODUCTION

The decline in the level of public investment in agriculture has been followed by a perceptible decline in the growth of irrigation which has been the basis of agricultural breakthrough during the second half of the twentieth century. The annual rate of irrigation expansion in India has come down from 2.37 per cent during 1978-81 and 1988-91 to 1.60 per cent during 1988-91 and 2000-03. In fact, there has been an absolute decline in the net irrigated area in the country by about 2 million hectares since the closing years of the last century, mainly due to the decline in the area irrigated through government canal. This has been followed by a marked decline in the net sown area from 142.41 million hectares in 1988-91 to 138.42 million hectares in 2000-03. Again, there have been marked deceleration and declines in the use of chemical fertilizers and electricity in agriculture, mainly due to rise in this prices caused by reduction in subsidies on them. The annual consumption of fertilizer has declined from 17.2 million tonnes during 1998-01 to 16.75 million tonnes during 2002-04. Over the same period, the average annual use of electricity in agriculture has gone down from 91 to 85 billion kwh. This is extremely disturbing in view of the fact that cheap electric supply to agriculture has played a crucial role in promoting ground water irrigation which has been the most dynamic element in irrigation—the basis of green revolution since the mid-1960s. Ground water has accounted for over 90 per cent of the net addition to the irrigated area in the country over the period 1962-65 to 2000-03. As a result of all these, there has been a sharp deceleration in the rate of growth of agriculture in the country. Thus, the annual compound growth rate of agricultural gross domestic product has gone down from 3.70 per cent during 1978-81 and 1988-91 to 2.37 per cent during 1988-91 and 2002-05. The deceleration has been much more in the production of food grains which grew at the rate of only 0.97 per cent annum during 1988-91 and 2002-05 against 3.38 per cent per annum during 1978-81 and 1988-91. As a result, the per capita annual production of foodgrains in the country, instead of going up, has gone down from 208 kg during 1988-91 to 181 kg during 2002-05, which is much below the level needed for self-sufficiency (194 kg. per person per year). These trends are extremely disturbing from the

TABLE 6

Some Key Inputs in Agriculture

Period	*Area in Million hectares*			*Cropping Intensity*	*Fertilizer Use (Million Tonnes)*	*Electricity Use in Agri-culture (Billion kwh)*
1948-51	19.99	21.52	110.59	1.13	0.05	0.15
1962-65	26.05	29.96	136.98	1.15	0.59	1.22
1978-81	38.43	49.10	140.63	1.23	5.30	13.32
1988-91	46.96	62.06	142.41	1.29	11.78	44.42
1998-01	56.22	76.08	141.59	1.34	17.19	90.95
2001-04	54.61@	75.61@	138.42@	1.33@	16.75	85.44

@ relate to the period 2000-03.

Source: Central Statistical Organisation, New Delhi, Statistical Abstract of India (Various Volumes) and Ministry of Agriculture, Government of India, Land Use Statistics of Relevant years.

TABLE 7

Sector-wise Growth in GDP at 1993-94 Prices (Compound Annual Growth Rate)

	Pre-reform Decade (1978-81 to 1988-91)	*Reform Period (1988-91 to 2002-05)*
Agriculture and Allied Activities	3.45	2.43
Agriculture	3.70	2.37
Mining and Industry	6.45	5.85
Services	6.45	7.60
All Sectors	5.35	5.72
Agriculture and Industry	4.67	4.14

Source: Computed by the author.

point of view of food security which need to be corrected on a priority basis by making a quantum jump in the level of public investment in agriculture including those in irrigation, rural electrification, flood control and drainage. This needs to be supplemented by other suitable measures relating to pricing, marketing and subsidies needed for agricultural development. Otherwise, the way things are moving under the new economic policy, the country is limping towards food insecurity even in the limited sense of the term, i.e. self-sufficiency in foodgrains. In fact, the government has already decided to import foodgrains to the tune of 5-7 million tonnes during 2006-07.

CONCLUSION

The fate of most unorganized workers in the country and the state, including women workers, is directly linked to that of agriculture which is their main source of livelihood. However, the developments during the period of reforms in the country have been such that its agricultural sector is in deep crisis, characterized by marked deceleration in the growth rates, especially of foodgrains and other food items such as oilseeds, sugar, potato, etc. The self-sufficiency in foodgrains which the country assiduously attained over the first four decades of planning has been lost as a result of plan erosion during the period of so-called reforms. And, in so far as growth in agriculture provides a natural solution to the problem of poverty and low wages (as has happened in Punjab), it can be safely said that the growth process during reforms is not promoting equity, i.e. growth with social justice. The country has really fallen into a deep crisis on its food front which needs to be remedied on a very urgent basis by undertaking suitable policy measures, especially by strengthening the planning process and having a congenial price regime. Some other solutions lie in occupational diversification and skill generation by providing education, especially technical and professional education. In this respect also, public investment in technical education has to play a key role.

REFERENCES

Hirschman, A.O. (1960), *The Strategy of Economic Development*, New Haven, Yale University Press, pp. 83-84.

Lewis, W.A. (1954), *Economic Development with Unlimited Supplies of Labour*, Manchester, Manchester School.

Todaro, M.P. (1981), *Economic Development in the Third World*, Orient Longman, New York, London.

Globalisation, Empowerment Question and the Case of Women Workers in India: An Analysis

Parmanand Singh

INTRODUCTION

Globalisation has initiated a process of change in the realm of economics and politics in which freedom of economic forces that is market forces and liberty of masses matters more. This has let loosen the restrictions which regard to conditions of work and wages. This new wave has reduced the position of labour forces be it male or female and increased the role of capital as a class. Thus the capital or capital owning class is getting a favour. They are aided and awaited by the state. This situation produced by globalisation reflects the underlying conflicting objectives of these two classes. The labour class requires increasing access to opportunity of employment and the capitalist class desires profit maximisation with innovative use of technology with the least possible capital investment in the merging new scenario. Faced with this situation empowerment question requires adequate skill and expertise to cape with and increasing capability domain for upward movement of the labouring class on the skill formation ladder be it male or female.

Thus, empowerment question in the context of globalisation requires increasing space for capability building and skill formation awareness and human capital investment, thus become the core issue.

In India, capital with a lot of help from India states has positioned itself for maximizing growth and efficiency in the economy, i.e. for increasing accumulation. The labour as a class has to strive for maximizing equity and development in the economy. The weakness of labour as class is that it has not positioned itself for the task, as a vast majority of its brotheren are weak, unskilled and unorganized while capital as a class is well organized with a lot of help from the state. It is, thus better placed for gain. The pity for the labour is that there is wide devide in them between those who are organized and unorganized. The organized labour class is well equipped with legal conditions and protection of work and better terms for wages. But their number is very few roughtly 7% of the work force. There members are on a decreasing trend these days.

The unorganized sector labour with least protection in working conditions and poorly paid wages are on increase, their problems are not well addressed. They are not taken seriously, they an left redundant and thus it is weakening the labouring community as a class in new emerging scenario. The empowerment debate of any kind like this should address these phenomena arising out of globalisation process in the Indian economy via creation of vast non-farm informal sector in urban areas, and vast exodus of rural proletarians to thiborea. This take of women labour force in such a situation is even worsening.

Labour in India finds itself in a much stronger position during the first two decades after independence. Labour in present during the new regime is facing adverse working situation with widening divide between organized and unorganized and this has weakened the empowerment process in the make of globalizing Indian economy these increasing the space for informality in various sectors thus the worst suffers are the women labour force in this new emerging situation.

II
THE THEORETICAL PERSPECTIVES AND THE GLOBALISATION

There are have been various theoretical perspectives evolved to explain the globalisation process. The most popular theoretical framework has been propounded by the neo classical thinkers. The new classical thinker suggests that organized class workers with their organisation activities creates rigidity in labour markets via wages and working conditions and is thus incompatible with objectives of growth and efficiency. As a result we have decreasing space for unionism. And as a result of it, we have shrinking domain of organized working class with stable employment opportunity in the new liberal regime of the globalizing world. This is called the distortionist view of labour market provided by a number of economists, by Freeman, 1992, Fallen and Lucas, 1989, Lucas, 1988 and World Bank, 1995. In the neoclassical framework, self interest is the glue that binds all in economic and other matters.

We have another broader looking Marxian lenses on the other, which rests on the interpretation of class and class interests. It, thus changes the basis of organisational interest from self to community. This calls for shift in the basis of organisation from pecuniary logic to associational logic that will be solidaristic in nature and helps to broad base the organisational being. Some bargaining will take place with capital as a class and therefore the economy is wideved. This will also mean that bargaining act of broad-based organisations will pressurise the state to ensure the minimum requirements for consumption (though minimum wages as well as antipoverty programmes) will be addressed along with basic needs and capabilities as housing, health and education. Thus, Marxian view in this new phase of globalisation, does not emphasis on redistribution of resources in pure and simple sense but the Marxian perspective be looked as a part of strategy of development through increasing labour productivity by not merely via competition and efficiency but via capacity building-based participation. It thus makes the process of growth democratic, decentralized and intensively inclusive which in turn will become a strategy to address simultaneously the question of egalitarianism and efficiency in a poor economy of ours.

We have Gandhian perspectives of looking things and interpreting the present situation. Gandhian perspective is based on enlightened self which rests on individual wisdom of leaving as many choices as possible to an individual. So the broader project of globalisation has less to do with right or left views. It is ultimately about choices exercised at global level: economic, political, life style and identity (particularly in relation to terrorism). So globalisation in Gandhian sense, in the transforming world of today is nothing more than recent movement of people, ideas and technologies, taking advantage of new era (politically and economically) of relatively easy travel, easy communication and open opportunities for education, self-betterment and self-aggrandizement. Gandhi says keep windows and door of the house be opened, let fresh air come in, but be ware that your feet could not be unrooted.

This requires that in order to benefit from the new wave of fresh breeze of globalisation one must have the wisdom of learning as many choices as possible. So anti globalisation radicalism is nothing but lack of faith in human being. Gandhian roots in the ground via faith in individual's integrity and faith in the dignity of labour and wisdom in decision-making. These traits help individual workers to prosper, via evolving entrepreneurial pursuits in the new global scenario.

Any debate on empowerment of the weak and vulnerable labouring class specially women must bear in mind these above theoretical perspectives, otherwise the debate will lead us to an inconclusive domain. It is in these perspective, we have to look in to the question of empowerment of women working class in India.

III
THE CASE OF WOMEN WORKERS IN INDIA

According to census of population 2001, there are 402.24 million workers in the country there 3.13.005 million are main workers and 89.23 million are marginal workers. Men predominance as main workers, while female predominates as marginal workers.

TABLE 1

	Main Workers	Marginal Workers	Total Workers
Workers	313.05 (M)	89.23 (M)	402.24 (M)
Male	76%	40%	77%
Female	24%	60%	23%

Source: Census 2001.

Organised sector constitutes a small share 7.07% of the total work force in the country and what is important that this share is shrinking overtime in the new liberal regime over the years.

TABLE 2

Year	Organised Sector	Unorganised Sector	Total	% of Organized Sector to Total Workers
1983	24.01	280.53	304.54	92.12%
1991	26.73	315.17	341.90	92.18%
2000	28.15	369.73	397.88	92.93%

Source: NSSO Rounds.

The growth rate of organized sector employment has been much less the same of unorganized sector between 1983 and 2000. Annual growth rate of organized sector employment was 0.52 against 1.09% of unorganized sector employment. The growing vistas of unorganized sector employment indicates the mode of production in the lower economic terrain and with their non-capitalist stamp, they are characterised as informal sector on warder academic plane since 1970's with writings of Hart, who first coined informal sector term and used it with regard to urban fresh settles in 1973. The erosion of welfare state in western world and its halting development in the third world, where it had only just began to come into sight. It can be seen as a confirmation of a trend, in which the slowly advancing emancipation of labour in recent decades, appears as if it is being reversed into its opposite subordination and growing insecurity. Globalisation insists that unfair competition could be avoided by abolishing security of employment, minimum wages and maximum working hours and labour rights which were used to apply in the formal sector. The critical researchers have observed that formal sector remained inaccessible for reasons other than inferior quality of new urbanitie's labour and their defects and rejects such an optimistic view. The failure of the new comers' effort to find stable and reasonably paid work is in this alternative perception due mainly to a development strategy that in the face of excess supply, it seeks to keep the price of labour as low as possible, allows no room for collective action to reduce these peoples' vulnerability and refuses to provide to this foot loose work force with official support. Globalisation thus under the present scenario is acting as a mechanism forecasting informal sector growth in order to make it a catchments reservoir for job seekers, who had been forced out of their rural agricultural existence. So it is because of the push factor working there due to active role of the marginalisation process revolving these. In this explanation, the emphasis is on stamina, the flexibility, the will to adopt, the ingenuity and the attempts made for upward mobility of foot loose work force, flooding into entire third world cities. The more integrated they become in their new milieu of work and life and the more skill they acequire, the better qualified they would be for the formal sector of the economy. In making this leap forward, they would form trade unions to strengthen their bargaining power *vis-a-vis* both employers and government. Researchers of pro-globalisation stream, thus support informality via disorganized sector growing employment and they frequently associate it with self-employment. This was also how Hart initially described it (Hart, 1973). In much a growing informability to which world bank's positive assessment have pointed to the accelerated shift in livelihood patterns away from agriculture and villages to cities and focus in the third world since mid twentieth century. But on practical plain it has created increasing slum space and miserable life conditions for working labour force in cities. Their connection with organized sector neighbours to some extent help but is making, the empowerment question of working class complex. Though vote bank politics has helped them achieve a reasonable basic amenities, thus their livelihood base is constant regular compare to their rural segments. Women workforce in with large part are engaged in marginal work (60%) in the unorganized sector suffer more and their empowerment becomes misnomer in the present working scenario in India.

Women workers in India is subject to be a lower partner is economic activities because of patriarchal social structure and mindsets that result in non-recognition of their work, invisibility, under valuation, lower payment being assigned to their contribution and the gender-based discrimination meted out to women. Who participates in paid spheres of economic activities. Irene Tinker, 1990, A.N. Sharma and T.S. Popular in 1999 have well highlighted these issues. We have in India and elsewhere in the third world, women folk facing persistent inequalities and gender-based discrimination in employment. Table three explains their vulnerability dimension and volatility of their employment condition. These tables explain, in fact the dimension of women work. The number of women in labour force, structure of the work force, unemployment rates, proportion of women engaged in household duties and the keenness to undertake additional income generation activities are discussed here. The nature of women's work involvement, highlighting factors that weaker women's position *vis-a-vis* labour market, which are interspersed between structural gender inequalitities and women's entitlements and capabilities in order to strategies for effecting policy planning, are some of the issues that deserve attention, while examining empowerment of women in the context of globalisation.

Labour force participation rates among men and women, both in rural and urban areas have registered a decline over the years 1993-94 to 1999-2000 in Table 3.

TABLE 3

Labour Force Participation Rates—India

MSS Rounds	*Rural*		*Urban*	
	Male	*Female*	*Male*	*Female*
1987-88 (43rd)	54.9	33.1	53.4	16.2
1993-94 (50th)	56.1	33.0	54.3	16.5
1990-00 (55th)	54.1	30.2	54.2	14.7

Source: MSSO, different years.

A part of the delay in age, at entry into the labour market it is also relate to the educational pursuits among women as well as men. Educational level of labour force by sex reflect the high proportions of illiterate workers both in rural and urban areas. This continues to be the scenario in spite of improvements noted over the years. The gap among male and female graduates, and above categories in Urban areas is gradually shirking. This positive outcome is reflected in the direct and beneficial increases in women's organized sector jobs even displacing men in these sectors. Except for this, minuscule inversion not other change, seems to be visible (Srivastava, 1999; Divakearan, 1996).

The Table 4 represents that the proportion of illiterate labourers by sex reflects high magnitude of gender disparity. In the labour force 17 per cent of rural males and 43 per cent of urban males are educated above secondary levels while the corresponding female proportions are 5 per cent and 32 per cent respectively (NSSO, 1999-2000).

TABLE 4

Percentage Distribution of Labour Force by Educational Statues

Rural	*1987-88*		*1993-94*		*1999-2000*	
	Male	*Female*	*Male*	*Female*	*Male*	*Female*
Illiterate	48.3	82.3	43.2	78.0	39.6	73.9
Literate upto Primary	29.6	12.0	28.2	14.2	27.4	15.7
Literate upto Middle	11.6	3.2	13.9	4.4	16.0	5.8
Literate upto Secondary	8.4	2.0	11.3	2.8	13.5	3.6
Literate upto Graduate and above	2.1	0.4	2.8	0.6	3.4	1.0
Total	100	100	100	100	100	100
Illiterate	19.6	51.8	17.8	45.9	15.9	41.2
Literate upto Primary	30.5	19.0	25.3	19.0	21.9	17.0
Literate upto Middle	16.0	7.3	17.6	8.9	18.8	9.7
Literate upto Secondary	21.8	12.3	24.7	14.0	26.4	15.7
Literate upto Graduate and above	11.7	9.6	14.5	12.2	16.9	16.4
Total	100	100	100	100	100	100

Note: Figures relate to usual status of individuals and population aged 15 years and above.

Source: NSSO, Different years.

Besides these I am depicting Tables 5, 6 and 7 to analyse the fact that how women working folk are denied secondary tertiary sector employment with their heavy dependence on their primary sector where per capita income generating potential is comparatively lower due to heavy dependence of population per unit of land and productivity volatility due to vagaries of nature.

TABLE 5

Per 1000 Distribution of Usually Working by Broad Industry (PS+SS) Groups—All India

MSS Rounds	*Primary*		*Secondary*		*Tertiary*	
	Male	*Female*	*Male*	*Female*	*Male*	*Female*
Rural						
1987-88	745	847	121	100	134	53
1993-94	741	862	112	83	147	56
1999-00	714	854	126	89	160	57
Urban						
1987-88	91	294	340	317	569	389
1993-94	90	247	330	291	479	463
1999-00	66	177	328	293	606	526

Source: NSSO, 2000.

TABLE 6

Per 1000 Distribution of Usually Employed by Category of Employment—All India

(PS+SS) NSS Rounds	*Self-Employment*		*Regular Employees*		*Casual Labour*	
	Male	*Female*	*Male*	*Female*	*Male*	*Female*
Rural						
1987-88	586	608	100	37	314	355
1993-94	579	585	83	28	338	387
1999-00	550	573	88	31	362	396
Urban						
1987-88	417	471	437	275	146	254
1993-94	417	454	421	286	162	162
1999-00	415	453	417	333	168	214

Source: NSSO, 2000.

The Table makes it clear that self-employment activities both among men and women is a prime characteristic of Indian labour markets (Table 6). The opportunities of regular work for rural women are extremely low. Bulk of women's labour (main marginal) in India are involved in agricultural activities Table 6 nearly 72 per cent as per census 2001. The share of A.L. constitutes 39 per cent among total female workers while another 33% are enumerated as cultivators. The women employment in primary sector is due to poverty induced compulsion, peaking of labour demand and sudden spurts in wages. Indian labour market is demand driven. Given, the surplus supplies of labour for majority of tasks the wage rate become secondary in as much as they are not crucial factor drawing labour supplies to the market. In widely and rampant unemployment situation *vis-a-vis* excessive supply of labour force and low rate of employment generation creates a situation in the Indian economy, in which women are not actually reflected in the magnitude of the unemployed, as scarce employment avenues push women out of the labour force. The decline in participation rate both LFPR and WPRs (work force as well as labour force) beyond twenty-five years age groups which are not off set by increases in educational participation, reflect lowering employment avenues obviously, besides it also hit at more non-recognized and vulnerable participation, that is not amenable to being netted (Hirway, 2002).

The fact is that women work force vulnerability emanates from their participation in extended SNA kind of activities. Among SNA activities the share of women's time spent on unpaid work is far higher than men's. Tables 7 and 8 explains this situation clearly.

There is no denying the fact, that women's roles are defined to include domestic work and responsibilities, their labour market participation in sheer physical sense of number of hours available to them to hire out labour supplies for paid work are limited by household work runtime. This is one dimension that contests with the understanding of their need for income promotion and the creation of employment avenues for them. Half of the women engaged in domestic chores express their inability to participate in the labour markets, since there is no other persons in their households. Who can take up these activities. Nearly 36% rural and 15 per cent urban women in 1999-2000 were engaged in household duties. The burden of these responsibilities reflect an increase over 1990's on wards for the 30 to 60 years age group of urban females. Table 9 makes it clear that the number of women engaged in household duties per 1000 thousand females usual principal status.

TABLE 7

Age Specific Unemployment Rates by Sex in India

Age group (in years)	*Rural*				*Urban*			
	1993-94		*1999-00*		*Male*		*Female*	
Rural	*Male*	*Female*	*Male*	*Female*	*Male*	*Female*	*Male*	*Female*
5-14	1.6	0.8	2.2	1.2	4.5	2.6	5.7	3.3
15-29	4.9	3.2	5.1	3.7	10.8	19.6	11.5	16.6
30-44	0.4	0.4	0.6	0.4	1.1	2.8	1.4	2.8
45-59	0.1	0.2	0.1	0.2	0.4	0.4	0.4	0.5
60 and above	NA	NA	0.2	0.4	0.3	NA	0.0	0.0
Total	2.0	1.4	2.1	1.7	4.5	8.2	4.8	7.1

Source: NSSO, 2000.

TABLE 8

Weekly Average Time (in hours) Spent on SNA Extended SNA and Nox. SNA Activities by Sex and Sector

	SNA	*Extended SNA*	*Nox. SNA*	*Total*
Rural	32.72	18.40	116.89	168.01
Female	22.53	33.95	111.50	167.98
Male	42.31	3.74	121.98	168.03
Urban	25.77	19.26	123.03	168.06
Female	9.16	36.44	122.44	168.04
Male	41.06	3.44	123.47	167.97
Combined	30.75	18.69	118.62	168.08
Female	18.72	34.63	114.58	167.92
Male	41.96	3.65	122.42	168.03

Source: CSO, 2001.

TABLE 9

Number of Women Engaged in Household Duties per 1000 Females (Usual Principal Status)

Age Group	*Rural*		*Urban*	
	1999-00	*1993-94*	*1999-00*	*1993-94*
0-14	66	99	38	51
15-29	565	592	589	601
30-44	547	565	761	755
45-59	550	562	716	711
60 above	399	430	440	460
All	358	382	453	449

Source: NSS 55th Round (1999-2000).

CONCLUSION

In the light above worsening employment and work situation facing Indian women folk and working women in particular empowerment the question of women in the new global situation is a difficult and complex task. With growing informality of the sectors and scauty principal job situation, working women are hard pressed with growing domestic duties, with in age group of 30 to 60 years produces a denting situation with regard to empowerment of women in era of globalisation and for this empowerment question of women demand some ways of compensation for undertaking household responsibilities. Karchadi questioned, the strength of globalisation to take the working women out of this morassing situation in his writings and we must be aware of that, before embarking on a practical solution on the issue of empowerment of women.

REFERENCES

Agrausal Rashmi and B.V.L.N. Rao (2004), Gender Issues—A Road Map to Employment, Shipra, New Delhi.

Agraval, Usina (1994), A Field of One's Own—Gender and Land Rights in South Asia, Cambridge University Press, Cambridge.

Antony, Piush (2001), Towards Employment: Experiences of Organized Women Workers, ILO, New Delhi.

Banerjee, Narayan (2004), "Nari Bikash Sangha: Towards Empowerment, *Indian Journal of Gender Studies*, Vol. 11, No. 2.

Bhattacharya, B.B. and S. Sakhival (2003), "Economic Reforms and Jobless Growth in India in 1990's, *Indian Journal of Labour Economics*, Vol. 46 Nov.

Bose, A.J.C. (1996), "Subcontracting, Industrialisation and Labouring Conditions in India: An appraisal, *The Indian Journal of Labour Economics*, Vol. 39, No. 1, pp. 145-62.

Breman, Jan (1995) of Peasants, Migrants and Panpees: Rural Labour Circulation and Capitalist Production in West India, Oxford University Press, Delhi.

Breman, Jan (2005), "Information of Employment," Interactive Conference on Employment and Income Rigidity in India, April 6-8, 2005.

Breman, Jan (1995), 'Labour Get Lost: A lote-capitalist manifesto, *EPW*, Vol. XXX, No. 37, Sept. 16, 1995.

Census of India, 2001.

Chandra, Navin (1997), "The Organizing Question and the Unorganised Labour" in Datta ed.

Dev, S. Mahendra (2002), Pro-Poor Growth in India: What do we know about Employment Effects of Growth 1950-5000? Working Paper No. 161 Overseas Development Institute, London.

Freeman (1992), "Labour Market Institutions and Policies: Help on Hindrances to Economic Development?" In Proceedings of World Bank Annual Conference on Development Economies.

Ghosh, Jayati (2003), Changes in World of Work, *Indian Journal of Labour Economics*, Vol. 46, No. 4.

Jhab, Vola R., R. Sudarshan and Jeemal University (eds.) (2003), Informal Economy Centre State—News Trustures of Employment Safe, New Delhi.

Kaluki, Michel (1976), Essays on Developing Economies.

Kannan, K.P. (1999), Changing Economic Structure and Labour Institutions in India: Some Reflections and Emerging Perspectives on Organizing the Unorganized, *IILE*, Vol. 42, Nov. 4, 1999.

Karet, Prakash (1984), "Action Groups Voluntary Agencies—A Factor in Imperialist Strategy," *The Markist*, April-June.

Kikeri, Sunita (1997), Privatisation and Labour—What Happens to Markets Where Government Divert," World Bank Technical Paper, World Bank, Washington DC.

NSSO various rounds.

Pattern, Chris, The World is Bumpy, *Hindustan Times*, Patna, 7th Nov. Lectare Delivered on M. Rao, Sindhiya Memorial, 1 Nov. 2007.

Thabroala Renena (2003), "Bringing Informal Workers Contrasting" in Jhabvola *et al.*

University, Jeemol and Uma Rani (2003), B. Regional Overview of Social Protection of Informal Workers in Asia: Insecurities, Instruments and Institutional Arrangements—Gender and Developments, Discussion Paper Series No. 14, United Nations Economics and Social Commisston for Asia and the Politics (UNESCAP), Bangkok.

Women's Empowerment and Globalisation

Parveen Azad

I. WOMEN'S EMPOWERMENT

Men and women have been perennially searching for justice. They have been putting up a historically long drawn-out struggle for the establishment of an egalitarian social, political and economic order across the globe. However, owing to paucity of resources and more importantly greedy and exploitative behaviour displayed by man across various historical and cultural shifts of human civilisation, the establishment of an egalitarian order has remained an unattainable goal. In modern times, the quest for justice has been further intensified owing to numerous historical factors and intellectual developments. The foremost impetus to the struggle for justice has been given by Socialist Movement in nineteenth and twentieth centuries. Directly as well as indirectly inspired by socialist thinkers and practitioners, women's rights activists have launched a world-wide movement for the betterment of women's condition. At the theoretical level, feminist thinkers are committed to the demolition of patriarchical world-view and value-system. On the plane of practice, women's rights activists are committed to achieving fully-fledged equality with the male of the species.

Presently, the question of women's empowerment is globally acknowledged. Women's political and economic rights debate is presently at the heart of various international campaigns. The Women's Movement has inspired and negotiated several crucial critiques and powerful debates throughout the world and it is through these intellectual and critical engagements that the concept of women's empowerment has originated and in course of time came to dominate the feminist agenda as well as discourse.[1]

The Women's Empowerment means greater control over finance, knowledge, information, technology, skills, training, political power, economic resources, etc. It is to challenge the ideology of patriarchy and participate in leadership and decision-making processes. It is to improve the quality of women's education with a view to making women active participants in the process of change and more importantly inculcating in them sufficient critical and questioning spirit to question the institutions and values leading to injustice and inequality.[2]

The feminity and masculinity are not naturally ordained or causally dictated concepts. They are culturally directed and ideologically sustained and reinforced categories. A fully-fledged ideology of gender has been historically crafted and culturally formulated with a view to stabilizing gender distinctions and polarities. The gender dissymmetry can be observed in almost all societies across the globe. Legal systems, customary practices, religious traditions and moral values have been so designed as to perennially sustain gender-discrimination. In all cultures across the globe the gender system is structured on cultural conceptions of male and female both being simultaneously complementary and mutually exclusive categories. A sex-gender system is also always intimately interlinked with political and economic factors in each society. The cultural construction of sex-gender system cross-culturally characterizes all societies as well.[3]

The inequality and vulnerability of women is conspicuous in all spheres of life; social, political, economic, cultural, educational, legal, etc. In view of the same, the development and empowerment of women entail an all-round or multi-sectoral intervention in formulating of policy initiatives and initiating and implementing of programmes with a view to ameliorating the social, political, economic, cultural, educational and legal status of women. To begin with, the existing system of structures unfavourably militating against the very interests of women need to be demolished and deconstructed to their very foundations. For discrimination against women is systematically and systematically anchored on ideological and cultural foundations.[4]

The women constituting half of the world's population are estimated to be working two-thirds of the total hours of work put in by both the sexes. However, they get only one-tenth of the world's total assets and properties. All the policy formulations and development plans have been systematically ignoring these gender-inequities. Rather the development plans are so designed as to reinforce these patterns of gross injustice.

II. GLOBALISATION

The globalisation is a long drawn-out historical process. We cannot trace its' origin to an exact point of time. However, the ongoing primarily economic and commercial globalisation is conveniently traced to 1970s. It was during this decade that the spatial reorganisation of production and movement of industries across borders was formally inaugurated. The spread of financial markets also resulted in flexible production methods during the same decade. The global production chains were also organized and introduced in this very decade.

Firstly, the most powerful symbol of globalisation has been the phenomenal and globally ubiquitous and conspicuous rise of multinatonal corporations. These corporations are increasingly appropriating capital and technology. They are ceaselessly in search of new markets, raw-material and cheap labour that can boost their profits. Secondly, the globalisation process is being powerfully supported by another ongoing Information Technology Revolution with its' phenomenal impact in the realm of knowledge and communication. Thirdly, technologies, products, consumption patterns and even lifestyles and moral values are being rapidly diffused across the globe resulting in great economic and societal transformation in many regions of the globe.[5]

Presently, globalisation has emerged as an unprecedented process of integration of world economy and thereby of world society and world polity. Highly complex patterns of socio-economic change are worked out by the ongoing process of globalisation in so for as it is integrating markets and product systems across national boundaries. Many deem it to be leading us to transformation of the world into a new global village. It presages the dawn of a new era in so far as it signifies the end of both history and geography. As a matter of fact, the world is getting increasingly connected through forces unleashed by the process of globalisation. The instantaneous communication is powerfully impacting the local milieu everywhere by events occurring thousands of miles away.

The ongoing process of globalisation is also powerfully impacting our attitudes, perceptions, values and norms. In fact, it is changing the very mindset we have inherited through countless cultural and ideological interactions in the past. However, globalisation is generating new political, social, economic and cultural interactions leading to tremendous transformations both at local and global levels of operation. In the process, it is impacting the social relations and discursive powers of women and men as well. This unprecedented transformation process is renegotiating the gender relations at local levels and articulating new identities.

The vital transformative impact gobalistion is making at macro-level across the globe cannot be denied or wished away. However, a few studies have tried to provide empirical evidence on how processes that are initiated at one place are responded to by people at the receiving end. Anthropological studies of globalisation are presently trying to work out its' impact on the daily lives of people and their local responses and strategies within this global process of change.[6]

III. THE ADVERSE IMPACT

It was in the very 1970s that the third world women workers entered both the formal and informal labour force of the global economy. The phenomenon came to be known as the 'feminisation of labour'. The phenomenon was conspicuously ubiquitous in Asia and Latin America, although it emerged with a big bang in other countries as well. To begin with, women were preferred for certain jobs in the global economy especially in manufacturing companies. However, the process of globalisation has not changed the gender division of labour. The least skilled levels of work with lowest remunerations continue to be assigned to women following the universal gender division of labour and patterns of work oragnisation.

More than enough statistical data can be cited to substantiate that India along with other developing countries did not pay enough heed towards formulating and executing policies leading to the establishment of a just and egalitarian society wherein marginalized sections of the people such as women could feed a sense of belonging.[7] On the other hand, forces opposed to the establishment of a just human society gradually consolidated themselves in India and other developing countries. They established themselves in politics, economy, bureaucracy, media, culture, academics, etc., and oriented public opinion towards the espousal of neoliberal ideology. The gradual espousal of neoliberal values and norms steadily paved the way for large-scale appropriation and celebration of a world-view and value-system underlying the current or ongoing process of globalisation.

The advocates of globalisation claim that it promotes economic efficiency and brings better standards of living for people across the globe. They are driven by the gospels of free trade and competitive markets. However, the powerful rhetoric of globalisation-proponents notwithstanding, its' repercussions are being increasingly felt among the vast majority of mankind. For example, it has been pointed out in Annual Human Development Reports of United Nations that while collapse of space, time and borders is creating a global village, it is promoting the interests of an elite minority. Billions of underprivileged people are finding the borders as high as ever. The more the globalisation process expands the opportunities for the privileged few, the more it shrinks them for the overwhelming majority of the underprivileged people.[9] It may be integrating economy, government and culture but it is disrupting and fragmenting the societies across the globe.

For the women of high education, sophistication and exceptional skills and training, the process of globalisation has opened up vast opportunities of professional advancement.

However, for poor women, the existing inequalities and insecurities have been further intensified by the ongoing process of globalisation. Many unskilled women have lost their livelihoods. For some women workers, it has meant loss of basic rights and social security benefits.

The overwhelming majority of Indian women workers are employed in the Informal or Unorganised Sector. Thus, despite their massive contribution to national economy, their role remains unacknowledged till date and they continue to be exploited by middlemen, contractors and extortionists throughout the length and breadth of the country. Presently women are massively employed in Farming or Agricultural Sector as men are continuously moving up to higher paying jobs. Mostly, these women workers in Agriculture Sector are amongst the most underpaid workers. To add salt to their injuries, they are exploited, demoralized and even dehumanized by landlords and rural warlords in view of their vulnerable position in the Unorganised Sector they are engaged in.

The collective socio-economic and political impact of the ongoing process of globalisation is getting increasingly adverse on women. Those who are adversely getting affected by globalisation, include disproportionately large segments of women. The women belonging to weaker sections of society in less developed regions of the world are all the more adversely affected by the overall societal, political and economic forces unleashed by globalisation. Therefore, the gender implications and gender concerns of globalisation need to be brought out with a view to understanding its' impact on the empowerment of women. The lack of sufficient data in this regard does constitute a grave methodological problem. However, the emerging socio-economic trends intimate enough signals to work out an informed analysis of the adverse impact of globalisation on the empowerment of women especially in third world countries.

The foremost impact of globalisation on weaker sections and marginalized people in the third world must be measured in terms of the accelerated impetus it is giving to the elitist and consumerist culture already entrenched in the developed countries. Especially the hyperconsumerist culture being exceedingly reinforced by the tidal waves of all pervading globalisation is creating an atmosphere of violence, anger, greed and aggression in which the dignity and security of women is seriously compromised. For in such an atmosphere it becomes all the more easier to exploit the vulnerabilities of women.

With the onset of globalisation, there has been a steady decline in employment for women. Especially, in rural India, there has been a stagnation in the number of women workers while there has been no corresponding increase in the girl student population ratio. For women workers, there has been no clear movement away from the agricultural to non-agricultural sectors as warranted by a modernizing economy under the benign supervision of globalisation. The primary livelihood for a very high proportion of female workers continues to be agricultural labour, known to be one of the most insecure and poverty-prone forms of employment.

The process of globalisation is not having a beneficient impact on the employment situation or employability of women. The ongoing globalisation has been constantly and rapidly introducing modern methods of production. Consequently, new products go on entering the market giving rise to new consumer preferences. In response to this feature of globalisation, traditional products lose their appeal. This leads to large-scale displacement of women workers from traditional modes of earning livelihood. These women who are displaced from their traditional modes of employment do not have the requisite training, skills, resources and contacts which can fetch them compensatory employment in the newly emerging areas in modern industrial and technological economy.[10]

What is known as feminisation of production under globalisation actually amounts to massive employment of women in labour intensive units of production. However, as these units of production introduce highly sophisticated technological modes of mass production, women are elbowed out and greater number of men are employed in the technology driven sectors of economy. This trend has been noticed in studies conducted in various developed and developing countries across the globe. The women driven out as technologically advanced processes are introduced in labour intensive industries, find themselves joining the Unorganized Sector where working conditions are notoriously adverse, wages are lowest and areas of exploitation are large.

The process of globalisation is leading to increasing

casualisation and flexiblisation of labour. In the ongoing phase of globalisation, the giant multinational corporations constantly compete for markets and profits. They increasingly resort to cost-cutting through the strategy of flexible employment. The strategy is to replace full-time labourers entitled to various rights and benefits by casual workers. These workers are not entitled to social security provisions. The casual women workers are not entitled to maternity and childcare benefits as well. In this newly emerging Casual Sector, more and more women find themselves employed as casual workers. These women become easy prey to exploiters and extortionists.

The impact of liberalisation and privatisation, concomitantly operating with the process of globalisation, has also been adverse on the economic well-being of women. The processes of liberalisation and privatisation have led to declining public expenditure in critical areas such as healthcare, education, housing, rural development, etc. in different parts of the world. The process of transformation and transition should have entailed devising and enlarging policy networks with a view to ameliorating condition of women. Instead, post-liberalisation budgetary allocations specifically curb the programmes benefiting women. There is a globally discernible trend to reduce allocations to schemes directly or indirectly benefiting women in different parts of the world. The trend can be discerned in Indian Central Government's budgetary policies and proposals as well. Needless to say, the State Governments are faithfully following the budgetary additions and alterations stipulated by Central Government in keeping with the imperatives entailed by the merciless onslaught of globalisation.

The increasing virtual withdrawal of state from Social Sector can spell great hardships for women in years to come. It will increasingly entail additional demands for women's labour. The total burden on women would aggravate in view of the greater upcoming compulsions for meeting out the survival requirements and sustenance needs in the families. In such an emerging scenario, the girl child will be further neglected as meager family resources are spent on the education and health of boys whom tradition defines as the torch-bearers of the family's future. Thus, in view of the shift in policies and programmes inspired by the considerations of profit and loss of Multinational Corporations—

the chief engines of globalisation—gender disparities will persist for decades to come.

There is no doubt that benefits of growing global economy are being unevenly distributed gender-wise. This is leading to increased gender inequality. Women are increasingly facing deteriorating working conditions, especially in the Unorganised Sector and rural areas. What is needed is the designing of strategies enhancing the capacities of women and empowering them to meet the challenges posed by the process of globalisation.

As Women's Movement moves increasingly to higher levels of empowerment, it is bound to negotiate entrenched resistance from male-dominated society, polity and economy as excusive male privileges are threatened. The capitalists, landlords, tradesmen, contractors, bureaucrats, police officials, legal and judicial authorities and other state structures are bound to raise roadblocks in the onward march of Women's Empowerment Movement. These patriarchically designed as well as evolved establishmentarian vested interests are by temperament and upbringing incapable of recognizing women as individuals and equally endowed persons.

The Women's Empowerment Movement should not address itself to the improvement of social, political and economic conditions of women. It should not be aiming at the amelioration of women's situation by recourse to inauguration of certain welfare measures here and there. The Movement should rather be aiming at equal participation of women in the decision-making process and equal control over resources. The Movement should also be aiming at appropriate legal, constitutional and statutory initiatives and safeguards with a view to stabilizing the social, political and economic gains thereof. The purpose of Women's Movement should be attainment of complete socio-political and economic equality and equality of opportunities. It should be a transition from welfare measures to complete equal control.

The question of the empowerment of women cannot be taken up in isolation from other cognate areas of contemporary human endeavour. There are other equally significant problems on which depend the survival of human civilisation. Women's Empowerment must be linked to the quest for the empowerment of all the marginalized people. There are several ongoing movements such as Peace Movement, Environment Movement,

Working Class Movement, Human Rights Movement, etc. Those who struggle for the empowerment of women must put up a collective front with such movements. They must also work in tandem with the movement for greater decentralisation and democratisation. Women's struggle is ethically and spiritually in tune with the rise and fall of these ongoing struggles. They must swim or sink together.

Lastly, it must be readily admitted that Indian women's participation in the emerging IT Sector has been phenomenal. Even globally women have a strong presence in the IT sector. This is a positive trend from the point of view of women's employment in non-traditional sectors. However, here again the highly skilled women belonging to advanced or upcoming sections of society can hope to be registering their presence in years to come.[11] However, we will have to take an overall or holistic view of the women's problems and prospects and devise strategies or initiate policy formulations and implementations with a view to ameliorating women's condition to begin with and subsequently empowering them. Only a concerted and dedicated policy implementations programme backed up by continuous data-based research can lead to the empowerment of women and the establishment of a really egalitarian society. Women of the world unite. You need to do two things; firstly, educate yourselves and then agitate for your rights. You will lose nothing but your disempowerment.

Notes and References

1. Sahay Sushma, "*Women and Empowerment,*" Discovery Publishing House, New Delhi, 1998, p. 201.
2. *Ibid.*, 215.
3. Moghadam, 1990: 1.
4. Sahay, *op. cit.*, p. 10.
5. Mukherjee, Mukul, *Indian Journal of Gender Studies*, 11:3 (2004), p. 276.
6. *Ibid.*, p. 286.
7. Saradamoni, K., *Women's Watch*, April-June 2004, p. 19.
8. *Ibid.*, p. 20.
9. Mukherjee, Mukul, *op. cit.*, pp. 276-77.
10. *Ibid.*, p. 279.
11. Parkash Moirangthem, *Women's Link*, October-December, 2006, p. 22.

WOMEN EMPOWERMENT AND DEVELOPMENT DURING GLOBALISATION

MAHESH CHANDRA PRASAD

I. INTRODUCTION

Empowerment of women has emerged as an important issue in our society in recent times. The economic empowerment of women is being regarded these days as a *sine-qua-non* of progress for a country, hence the issue of economic empowerment of women is of paramount importance to political thinkers, social scientists and reformers, women activists, politicians, academicians and administrators. Gender inequality is now receiving greater attention. Women, better known as half of the humanity, have long been neglected in their role as beneficiaries in the process of development. Though they contribute two-third of the World's work hours, they earn only one-third of the World's resources. The Governments are keen to ensure that women are empowered both economically and socially and they become equal partners in national development along with men.

Nehru has said rightly that in order to awaken the people, it is the woman who has to be awakened. "Once she is on the move, the household moves, the village moves and the country moves and through the woman her children are brought into the picture and given the opportunity of higher life and better training. Thus, we give the opportunity of women of today we build the India of tomorrow." Now-a-days women are becoming more conscious of their rights, society as a whole has begun to respond. More and more women are adopting careers and finding fulfilment as individual while contributing to the building of participation in rural economy of India. But this is a fact that, whether in traditional or modern situations, they have to work harder than men and to bear more burden and more participation in the development of rural economy of India.

Long before 'Empowerment' word became popular, women were speaking about gaining control over their lives and participating in the decisions that affect them in home, community, in government and international development policies. The word 'Empowerment', captures this sense of gaining control over their lives, participating and decision-making. Recently the world has entered the vocabulary of development particularly in the case of women development. Empowerment is a comprehensive process, and is not, therefore, something that can be given to people. The process of empowerment is both individual and collective, since it is through involvement in groups that people most often begin to develop the awareness and the ability to organize to take action and bring about change.

The present position and status of women in general and rural women in particular is not satisfactory rather their position in society is in no way better than second class citizen. Theoretically women are considered important and equal partners in the process of development, but in practice they are generally ignored. Inspite of so many statutory protections, women still remain under privileged, under-valued and exploited and various kinds of discriminations continue to persist against them. The contribution of Indian women to the country's development process since Independence and during the freedom struggle has been creditable. It has been a source of unique strength for reaching national goals. As housewives women have kept the home fires burning so that their menfolk can go out to work and their children attend school and college. The unpaid job of bringing up the family, a labour of love, has never been evaluated in terms of money. A wholly dedicated lot, working silently most of them have been too busy to think of their own rights.

With rising prices and the spread of education, the pattern of life has changed in some measure in towns and cities where both husbands and wives go out to work. The concept of shared housework is catching on. In rural areas where 70 per cent of the population lives, women have always shared their part of farming activities. Agriculture is the one field where women participate in decision-making. This they do with regard to seed management, bio-mass-utilisation, marketing and other post-harvest processes besides livestock management.

In the world as a whole women are under represented in all wings of the government legislative, executive and judiciary. In the political area, women have made the least headway in contemporary world and politics appears to be last male stronghold. Notwithstanding the fact that females make up approximately 50 per cent of the World's population, rather throughout the world, their representation in public life is remarkably small.

II. WOMEN'S CONTRIBUTION TO NATIONAL ECONOMY

Gainful employment of women is identified as a major entry point in promoting their economic conditions. Realizing this fact, some young women entered the fields of industry, public service as well as business, and are successful in these fields. The vital role of women in the Indian labour force and their contributions to the national economy have been established beyond doubt. Women are engaged in a wide variety of occupations especially in the unorganized sector. In the rural unorganized sector, women care for cattle, sowing, transplanting, harvesting, weaving, working in the handlooms, and producing handicrafts mostly as low paid wage earners or unpaid family workers. In the urban informal sector, women are working as petty traders. They are also engaged in producing and selling a variety of goods such as vegetables, fruits, flowers, cooked food, groceries, etc. or work as domestic workers. In both rural and urban areas, they are also engaged as construction workers. In addition to this, women spend, on an average, seven to ten hours a day in domestic chores.

According to 2001 census, out of the total population of 1,027,015,247, the female population was 495,732,169 accounting for 48.2 per cent of the total population. But, their participation in economically productive activities is often underestimated. For last two decades, women's work participation rate increased from 22.73 per cent in 1991 to 28.6 per cent during 2001.

Women workforce in the service sector is very meagre compared to the total employable population of women. Hence, it is necessary to encourage and guide women to organize business and services to enable them to join business and services in large numbers.

III. WOMEN EMPOWERMENT AND PLANNING PROCESS

All round development of women has been one of the focal points of planning process in India. The First Five-Year Plan (1951-56) envisaged a number of welfare measures for women. Establishment of the Central Social Welfare Board (CSWB), organisation of Mahila Mandals or Women's Clubs and the Community Development Programmes were a few steps in this direction. In the Second Five-Year Plan (1956-61), the empowerment of women was closely linked with the overall approach of intensive agricultural development programmes.

The Third and Fourth Five-Year Plans (1961-66 and 1969-74) supported female education as a major welfare measure. Similarly, the Fourth Five-Year Plan (1969-74) continued the emphasis on women's education. The Fifth Five-Year Plan (1974-79) emphasized training of women, who were in need of income and protection. Functional literacy programmes got priority. This plan coincided with International Women's Decade and the submission of Report of the Committee on the Status of Women in India. In 1976, Women's Welfare and Development Bureau was set-up under the Ministry of Social Welfare. It was to act as a nodal point to coordinate policies and programmes for women's development.

The Sixth Five-Year Plan (1980-85) saw a definite shift from welfare to development. It recognized women's lack of access to resources as a critical factor impending their growth. The Seventh Plan (1985-90) emphasized the need for gender equality and empowerment. For the first time, emphasis was placed upon qualitative aspects such as inculcation of confidence, generation of awareness with regards to rights and training in skills for better employment.

The Eighth Five-Year Plan (1992-97) focused on empowering women, especially at the grassroots level, through Panchayati Raj Institutions. The Ninth Five-Year Plan (1995-2000) adopted a strategy of Women's Component Plan, under which not less than 30 per cent of funds/benefits were earmarked for women-specific programmes. The Tenth Plan (2002-07) approach aims at empowering women through translating the recently adopted National Policy for Empowerment of Women (2001) into action and ensuring Survival, Protection and Development of Women and Children through Rights Based Approach.

IV. APPROACHES FOR EMPOWERMENT

The approaches for empowerment of rural women can be divided into four broad heads:

- Educational Empowerment.
- Social Empowerment
- Economic Empowerment
- Technological Empowerment

Educational Empowerment

Education is the key which opens the door to life, develops humanity and promotes national development. Education can be an effective tool for women's empowerment. It enables rural women to acquire new knowledge and technology required for improving and developing their tasks in all fields. Therefore, at least one Functional Literacy Centre should be opened in each Gram Panchayat area with a view to make all and rural farm women functionally literate and adult education necessary.

Social Empowerment

Empowering women contribute to social development. Economic progress in any country whether developed or underdeveloped could be achieved through social development. Hence, women's empowerment cannot be ignored, while devising various policies for rural and socio-economic development.

(i) Status of Women

Even country has made progress in developing women's

capabilities, but inequalities continue to exist between women and men. The low status of women is the outcome of a variety of causes in which patriarchal values reinforced by tradition, media and other socio-political institution play a major role. Thus, the institutional bases of women's oppression have to be sensitized to accept the gender equality and moreover, women's perception of themselves would also need to be changed.

(ii) Gender Bias

Cultural traditions and economic necessity have always mean a significant role for women in agriculture. In India it is not uncommon that women do not have control over the land. Even, where women constitute a larger share of an agricultural producers but, there are cultural constraints to easy communication between men and women, because almost all extension workers are men.

(iii) Health and Nutrition

Health and nutrition are two very important basic needs for empowerment of rural women. To achieve real and quicker development in health sector, an extensive as well as intensive "Health Education and Awareness Campaign" (HEAC) needs to be given topmost priority and it should mainly stress on nutritional education, benefits of immunisation, family planning, etc.

Economic Empowerment

Empowering women with economically productive work will enhance their contribution to agricultural development.

(i) Access to Resources

The farm women need to have control over limited resources like land and livestock, so that they could take away decisions and implement them in any way that is required. Ownership and control over productive assets will create a sense of belonging and owning. It will thus help to take responsibility in family and local group activities. Other impact of control is to enhance their decision-making ability to meet some physiological needs like self-esteem and confidence.

(ii) Micro-Credit Programmes

Micro-credit programmes extend small loans to poor people for self-employment projects that generate income allowing them to care for themselves and their families. In most cases, micro-credit programmes offer a combination of services and resources to their clients in addition to credit for self-employment. Access to productive resources is critical for enhancing women's economic choices. Since, formal credit institutions rarely lend the poor, special institutional arrangements may become necessary to extend credit to those who have no collateral to officer their enterprises. In order to have access to credit, setting up self-help group, local banking system by women, Non-Governmental Organisations and provision of facilities by Government need to be established. The policy challenge is to support effective grass-roots credit schemes and intermediaries and ensure that low-income have assured credit from the formal financial system.

(iii) Access to Cooperatives and Local Women's Organisations

Collectivisation has been recognized as a tenet of women's empowerment. It has been defined as a process of bringing a group of women together at a base to become an integral part of an economic activity. Organisational efforts should be made for integrating farm women into development. Organisation of Mahila Mandals, Cooperatives Societies and Discussion Groups will serve this purpose. The control of these organisations should be in the hands of womenfolk themselves. Also, the present beneficiary approach to women's development should be replaced by participatory approach.

Technological Empowerment

Though women are involved in almost all agricultural operations, in rural areas yet, they have inadequate technical competency due to their limited exposure to outside world. This has compelled them to follow the age old practices which in turn result in poor work efficiency and drudgery and needed computer, internet latest informations.

(i) Capacity Building

Capacity building and empowerment are important for

which there should be decentralized capacity building among the rural women particularly farm women. Empowerment projects should go beyond the provision of basic social services for all. They should include components vital for enabling the poor to participate in economic activities. It is important to develop the skills among farm women in order to increase their productivity and to keep them abreast of modernisation and technological changes for being competitive in the market.

(ii) Exposure to Mass Media

The transfer of technology approach, which mainly includes mass media are also not paying due attention towards dissemination, of adequate and timely agricultural and marketing information to the farm rural women. Therefore, there is outmost need to provide adequate coverage to the programmes related to women and they must get exposure to mass media for improving their communication and meditation skills to strengthen their capacity to contact and mediate with external world.

(iii) Appropriate Training Programme

Training is an important component of HRD which enhances knowledge, skill and attitude. For building technical competency among farm women, need-based skill-oriented training programmes to reinforce their role in farm activities need special attention. The training programmes should initially be organized on their field-needs and then be switched over to unfelt but essential needs. To achieve this sacred task, infrastructural facilities in terms of more numbers of KVKs, FTCs and BRLP should be established in the district on priority basis.

(iv) Appropriate Technology for Women

In order to cater the technological needs of farm rural women, women specific technologies should be developed. While evolving agricultural technologies, indigenous practices used by women should be paid due attention for blending with the frontier ones for greater adoption. Also there is need to strengthen linkage between various research and extension organisations engaged in transfer of technology.

Rural Women and New Millennium

Empowerment of Women and Rural Development go together. Rural Development Schemes which are implemented over the years are target-oriented. The benefits are not proportionately reached to women. The ensuing rural population in India according to 2001 census 741,660,293 (55.33 per cent) out of which female population is 360,519,109 (44.36 per cent). Though the proportion of rural population was high, i.e. 72.22 per cent and the percentage of female population is also high, i.e. 51.17 per cent. The total outlays of rural development programmes meant for women are remaining at the low level. The programme meant for women in Rural Development Schemes is only DWCRA which is now carried on under SGSY.

India is an agricultural country and thus agriculture is the basis of our national economy on which the future of over seven million families directly or indirectly rests. In India, women play a significant and crucial role in agricultural development and allied fields including the main crop production, livestock productions, horticulture, post-harvest operations, agro-social forestry, fisheries, etc. Unless the rural economy of India is developed, no progress in industrial economy of the country is possible.

The status and role of rural women and issues related to it have attracted the attention of the academicians, political thinkers and social scientists both in developing as well as the developed countries, partly due to the observance of the International Decade of Women and partly because of the widely accepted truth that a society built on the inequality of men and women involves wastage of human resources which no country can afford. In Indian villages, women work from the initial stage of agriculture to the harvesting of the crop. They also contribute in transporting of the crops to the markets, running up of village industries, discharging household duties and all allied activities. Without the active participation of rural women, industries cannot be developed. As a matter of fact, role of the rural women is obviously handicapped on most fronts. There is the biggest casualty of the participation in rural economy. The alarming low rate of female literacy prevents women from imbibing new ideas and programmes related to their welfare. This handicap has come in the way of creating women consciousness and in getting full benefit of opportunities created by developing process. It acts as a barrier to any kind of modernisation and helps in perpetuation of living patterns in the family and outside which are discriminatory to them.

One of the economic fronts the situation is also still worse. There is definite sex-based discrimination in respect of job opportunities, employment conditions and wage rates. There is a clear-cut dichotomy in the labour market where only residual unskilled jobs are reserved for women. Exploitation, oppression, lack of safety, long working hours, absence of crèches and other recreational facilities have made their lot still harder. On the top of it, the women are mostly considered the non-working class because of the narrow definition of work. In regard of rural women Gandhi rightly said, "If villages perished India will perish too. India will be no more India. Her own mission in the world will be lost." In India agriculture accounts for 32 per cent of the Net National Product (NNP). About 70 per cent of the total working population and 84 per cent of all economically active women are involved in agriculture. Women make up 48.4 per cent of the total agriculture workforce. It is rightly pointed out that the developing countries like India and most of the Asian and African countries largely depend on the labour of its women population. However, the women as a component of human resources has not been fully utilized in the national development.

The nature and extent of women's involvement in agriculture, no doubt, varies greatly from region to region. Even within a region, their involvement varies widely among different ecological sub-zones, farming systems, castes, classes and stages in the family cycle. But regardless of these variations there is hardly any activity in agricultural production except plaguing in which women are not actively involved. In some of the farm activities like processing and storage, women predominate and, therefore, male workers are numerically insignificant. According to 2001 census, the male cultivators have increased in the country by 11.67 per cent from 7.67 crore in 1981 to 8.56 crore in 1991. The female cultivators, however increased at a much faster rate of 45.23 per cent from 1.48 crore in 1981 to 2.15 crore in 2001. The number of male agricultural labourers increased by 31.48 per cent, but that of female by 36.45 per cent. 74 per cent of the entire female working force is engaged in agricultural operations. 28 per cent as cultivators and 46 per cent as agricultural labour. About 60 per cent of agricultural operations like sowing of seeds, transplantation of sampling winnowing, storage of grain, etc. are handled almost exclusively by women; while in other jobs they share the work with men. Apart from participation in actual cultivation, women participate in various forms of processing and marketing of agricultural produce.

As the households in the rural India depend mainly on agriculture and allied occupations, the prosperity of the household depends on the prosperity of agriculture and allied occupations in any particular point of time *vis-a-vis* the role of women in innumerable activities connected with farming, dairying, sericulture, etc. But the women hands are invisible even to this day, so it seems looking at the agricultural extension activity which is mainly a male-oriented pursuit.

V. ACTIVITIES OF RURAL WOMEN AND EMPOWERMENT

Agriculture: Sowing, transplanting, thinning, weeding, irrigation, fertilizer application, plant production, harvesting, winnowing, storing, etc.

Domestic: Cooking, child rearing, water collection, fuel wood gathering, household maintenance, etc.

Allied activities: Cattle management, fodder collection, milking, selling, cottage industry.

Mainly rural women are engaged in agricultural operations in three ways depending on the socio-economic status of their family and regional factors. They work as:

> (i) Paid labourers, (ii) Cultivators doing labour on their own land, and (iii) Managers of certain aspects of agricultural production by way of labour supervision and participation in post-harvest operations.

The participation of rural women in agriculture is increasing in spite of scientific and technological developments. The average time spent by a farm women varies from village to village according to social customs. The share of farm women in agricultural operations has been shown in the following Table 1.

TABLE 1

Share of Farm Women in Agricultural Operations

Activities	*Involvement Percentage*
Land preparations	32
Seed cleaning sowing	80
Inter-cultivation activities	86
Harvesting—reaping, winnowing, drying, cleaning and storage	84

Women perform agriculture operations with the use of traditional tools and implements. In present time women are engaged in livestock, forestry, fishing, plantation, orchard and allied activities. Time and energy expenditure for domestic activities of women has been shown in Table 2.

TABLE 2

Time and Energy Expenditure for Domestic Activities

Activities	*Duration minutes*	*Heart beat minutes*	*Energy rate Kcal/Min*	*Energy Kcal*
Cooking	150	96	1.816	272
Washing clothes	98	99	1.912	187
Water collection	75	112	2.390	179
Household maintenance	75	110	1.984	149
Firewood collection	30	120	2.868	86
Child care	25	80	1.195	30
Total				903

Table 3 given below shows that the average time spent by farm women in household and agricultural activities on ordinary days was five to seven hours per day. In the peak season an active farm women spent five to nine hours per day on the farm. Maximum time was utilized for domestic activities by the women. Agricultural and allied activities took almost equal time and energy at par with household chores.

Problems encountered by farm women varied from region to region, cultural attitudes and status of women. Main problems are non-availability of water, lack of assistance, inadequate income and lack of time saving equipments, etc. The multifarious activities resulted in poor health and low nutritional status of women.

TABLE 3

Time and Energy Distribution by a Rural Women

Activities	*Duration Hours/Minutes*	*Energy Kcal*	*Percentage*
Domestic activities	7.55	903	40.58
Agricultural and allied activities	7.00	283	39.69
Sleep	6.50	284	12.76
Rest and recreation	2.15	155	6.97
Total	23.20	2225	100.00

It may be stated that social change in rural India would be impossible unless the roles of women are properly integrated into the main stream of development efforts. Besides, the women's role in agriculture and other subsidiary occupation is of paramount importance, but she is not given due credit because of lack of proper identification of her role in productive activities of the rural households.

In order to achieve the objective of empowerment of women the government intends to gradually introduce gender budgeting in India. This means that the budget data will in due course be presented in a manner that the gender sensitivities of the budgetary allocation are clearly highlighted. The expert group on classification system of Government transactions had already outlined the broad issues and concerns involved in gender budgeting.

TABLE 4

Fund Allocation for Women Empowerment

(Rs in Ten crore)

	2001-02		*2002-03*		*2003-04*		*2004-05*
	BE	*RE*	*BE*	*RE*	*BE*	*RE*	*BE*
Women Specific Schemes	325.98	303.48	335.82	285.26	367.53	289.68	355.54
Pro-women Allocation in Pro-Women Schemes	1059.63	1120.44	1303.60	1370.04	1329.74	1495.60	1500.12

Source: *Yojana*, October 2006.

Though gender budgeting has been integrated to the planning process, it is too early to evaluate its impact on redressing the gender imbalance. However, the objective of gender budgeting will be fulfilled only when it crosses the domain of departments and ministries of both state and central government to reach the needy and deprived women in very part of India.

This is also a fact that increasing attention has been paid to help the rural women in India since independence through various social legislations and socio-economic development schemes which are expected to bring in progressive social change. Largely the Government itself is striving to help the weaker sections of the society, particularly the women. The programmes, schemes/legislations have been formulated so that it covers the women of all sections of society irrespective of class or cast consideration. The rural development schemes on employment for women are:

1. TIWF—A special scheme to provide technical training to women farmers in agriculture and allied areas and entrepreneurial skills.
2. DWCRA—Development of women and children in Rural areas to provide credit and employment opportunities to women.
3. NREP—National Rural Employment Programme.
4. RLEGP—Rural Employment Guarantee Programme.
5. JRY—Jawahar Rozgar Yojana under wage employment programmes with 30 per cent benefits earmarked for women.
6. IRDP and TRYSEM—(Integrated Rural Development Programme) and Training Rural Youth for Self-Employment. Under Poverty Programmes with 40 per cent benefits reserved for women.

Most of the developing countries have undertaken multiple programmes for rural development, but the unwilling effect of these appears to distribute the benefits unevenly and often increase inequality between different sectors of the population and between men and women. Programmes of women have been marginal in economic development activities initiated in agriculture, animal husbandry, handicrafts, small scale industries and fisheries. Social welfare services (Home economics, nutrition, child care and family planning) appear to be offered to rural women as some sort of compensation for the lack of attention given to them to increase their productivity and income earning capacity.

VI. POLICIES FOR WOMEN EMPOWERMENT

Empowerment of women in the prime objective of all development programmes and policies. These programmes could be planned properly and implemented effectively in order to attain self sufficiency and self-reliance. U.N. Commission on status of women says, women constitute half of the world's population, accomplish about two-thirds of its work hours, receive one-tenth of the world's income. The following measures can strengthen women in new world.

A few suggestions for the effective empowerment of women are:

1. At the outset the educational programme for rural women need to be a Development Education Programme through the establishment of village Literacy Home with active community support.
2. The vocational education, i.e. (i) Preparation of toys, pickles, jam, jelly and other materials with locally available materials, (ii) preparation of paper bags, knitting, tailoring, candle making, papad making, masala making, kitchen gardening and other handicraft activities with the locally available materials are a few major content areas. The women need to be taught how to effectively utilize their time to raise their family income and quality of life. This process of "Learning by doing and earning" would empower women not only with education but also, with socially and economically useful productive work.
3. The Human Resource Development of Women political functionaries is very essential to enable them function effectively at the grass roots. Appropriate training on various developmental activities and programmes would improve their knowledge, attitude and skill to

perform their job efficiently and effectively. These functionaries are required to be given training in the following areas:

(i) rudiments of government system, i.e. legislative, executive and judiciary at the center, state, district and block level;

(ii) different forms of education existing at the village level, i.e. formal education, non-formal education, adult education and education through ICDS and also vocational education for income generating activities;

(iii) different developmental programme i.e. IRDP, Jawahar Rozgar Yojana, Indira Awas Jojana, DWACRA, etc. and other national society security schemes launched from time-to-time for the benefit of people;

(iv) financial management of funds allotted for different developmental activities; and

(v) other state specific responsibilities assigned to Panchayat.

VII. CONCLUSION

Women are very important segment in development at local to global levels. Economic independence and education of women will go a long way in attaining self-reliance for women. Experience, awareness, education and competence, willingness, confidence, self-motivation, encouragement from family and society contribute to empowerment of rural women.

The structural features of political life also tend to exclude women from positions of power. Although the representation of women in Parliament, in the Assemblies and the Union and State cabinets of India is larger than it is in many other countries of the world, it is not proportionate to their number in the total population and does not even approximate to the figure that political parties consider to be a fair allocation.

REFERENCES

B.S. Rao and Y.I. Kumari (2005), *Empowerment of Women and Rural Development*, Serials Publications, New Delhi.

Bhola Nath Ghosh (1996), *Scope and Constraints of Rural Women Leadership*, with special reference to experimentation in self-government bodies.

Census, 2001.

Economic & Political Weekly, October 30th to Nov. 15th, 1999.

Employment News, 4-10th Nov. 2000.

Gopal Singh (2003), *Economic Empowerment of Rural Women in India*, RBSA Publishers, Jaipur.

International Conference on Women & Development, 13th Feb. to 16th Feb. 1985.

K.R. Murugan (1999), *Self-Employment for Rural Women*, Third Concept, 13(151).

Kurukshetra (2005), November.

Kurukshetra (2007), March.

R. Ram and H.L. Swarup (1994), *Women and Globalisation*, Ashish Publishing House, New Delhi.

Role of Rural Women in Development, *International Seminar*, 5th Jan. to 10th Jan. 1977.

Rural India (2001), January.

Social Welfare (1999), Vol. 46, No. 6, September.

Social Welfare (2000), Vol. 47, No. 2, May.

Sushila Kaushik (1993), *Women & Panchayati Raj*, New Delhi.

Yojana (2005), October.

Globalisation and Economic Empowerment of Women (Some Issues for Discussion and Policy Intervention)

Praveen Sharma

I begin my introduction by stating the premise for discussion. This is that I consider economic self-reliance and autonomy as an important ingredient for empowerment. The UN has asserted that women's autonomy should be considered as a basic human right and essential to human dignity (UNDP, HDR, 1995). I have deliberately used two terms, viz., Self-reliance and autonomy as integral for empowerment, I believe that the subservient status of women inside the family as well as outside originates from lack of economic independence and the denial of economic right to women. This denial is with respect to:

- Ownership of property,
- Recognition Women's work as economically productive,
- Providing education and market skills to girls,
- Social obligations and restrictions put on them with

respect to what work they will be permitted to do outside the home boundaries,

- Equality in the matter of wages, salaries and opportunities for advancement at the work place, and
- Providing facilitating environment to enable women independent to work and become independent economically. These aspects have been extensively discussed in various forums—academic as well as policy planning.

I discuss the general issue concerning women's work and women empowerment to highlight the point that even though women's work is important there are several other aspects of work and the social environment of work that need to be considered. I then discuss some of the impacts of globalisation that influence women's work. The priorities for action are summarized in the concluding paragraph.

WOMEN'S WORK AND WOMEN'S EMPOWERMENT

According to Census 2001. there were 27 million women in a population of 56.5 million in Rajasthan. The total number of women workers was 9 million. This implies a participation rate of 33.5% compared to 25.7% at the all-India level. The participation rate for rural women was 41% and for urban women it was only 9%. The rate for rural women was higher than the all-India average but was lower for urban women. The second source of data is NSSO. NSSO estimates of participation rates are somewhat higher. Most of the women workers (83% of total) were working as cultivators or as agricultural labourers. The remaining were employed in household industry and in a diverse range of service occupations from teachers, doctors and administrators laundry women and cleaning (safai karamcharies) workers. Changes that have occurred are that the number of women workers or participation rate shows an increase but the structure of employment remains broadly unchanged at the macro-level.

Women's workforce participation is a central component of the Gender Empowerment Measure of the UNDP Human Development reports. The first question is, does the increase in the number of women workers indicate greater empowerment of women? The answer will depend upon whether the increase in number is the result of economic need (poverty) or the result of more women working in capacities that they were earlier not doing. This would be the case if more women workers had higher levels of education and skill. In that case we may be right to conclude an improvement in women's empowerment status. However, this does not appear to be the case today. In fact, macro-data as well as some micro-level observations indicate that participation rates go down as the level of education increases. In fact illiterate women continue to be the predominant part of the women workforce. When larger number or women with no or with low education, low skills low productivity and getting low wages are working, it is a so associated with low prestige and status. In short it does not enhance the autonomy, self-reliance of empowerment of women. This is not happening, as the structure of the work force is not changing. Women are employed either in agriculture or in household non-agricultural activities and in the service occupations both in rural and in urban areas without significant change in the status of their autonomy. Autonomy in this context may be understood as the capacity influence and control one's personal environment and or the degree of access to and control over material and social resources within the family, in the community, and in society. We need to focus attention not only on the aggregate number of women workers (or the aggregate amount of work that they do) but also on the type of work and the conditions of work. Family workers not only work outside the protection of labour laws but are also denied the social interactions that workers in organized industry or work places have. Such conditions lower women's awareness of their bargaining position and therefore lower their autonomy. The self-employed in small household-based enterprises suffer from similar disabilities. On the other hand women employers who manage a larger number of employees have greater self-reliance, self-confidence and autonomy. For example, beedi workers may be working on contract. Such women have more mobility and greater social interaction than home-based beedi workers and therefore display more confidence and self-reliance. This is only an example to show that when we talk of the status of a woman worker. It is not only urban women that we are talking about. The focus is equally on women workers in rural areas who are engaged in diverse activities but only as unpaid household workers.

Work can be differentiated by remuneration (cash kind or unpaid) or by location or by status. In Rajasthan most of the women workers classified as cultivators are unpaid family workers. For them autonomy and empowerment is not in more work but in more productive agriculture. Even if work is differentiated according to type of work, the relationship between work and autonomy would be difficult to capture. The attempt should however be made in more studies that would not only differentiate between type or work but also define indicators of autonomy carefully. This would enable rural development workers to focus of factors that are likely to enhance women's autonomy. In urban areas there appear to be more visible changes in that more women are now seen in work places such as offices, banks, retail sale, media, schools, colleges and health professions. This is especially so in bigger urban centres. However, these changes have so far, not increased the participation rates of urban women. Finding work has become more difficult even though more and more women are seeking work. As a result, the recorded urban unemployment rates are going up. The issues in the urban sector are concerned largely with the impact of the new economic policies (globalisation) on employment.

GLOBALISATION

Without getting into a debate on the meaning of globalisation. I would like to highlight only some aspects that could be of relevance to a state like Rajasthan. These are: liberalisation of trade and industrial policies replacing market-based pricing policies for subsidy supported production and supply of goods and services policy change necessitated by the need for fiscal balance and privatisation or withdrawal of the state from activities traditionally supported by it. All of these are interrelated aspects. I shall discuss only a few in the paras below.

The fact that the new policies are not generation adequate employment opportunities is widely recognized. Nevertheless, it should be recognized that the structural changes that have become necessary in the state sector would result in lower employment. One of the problems of the public sector in India has been inflated salary bills because of an unjustified increase in the number of workers. Therefore, one of the thing that became necessary was downsizing, i.e reduction in the numbers employed. This is being achieved through VRS schemes and through a drastic reduction in new recruitment. The increase in employment is expected through higher rates of investment in several sectors. Unfortunately, Rajasthan is suffering because the flow of investment has been inadequate. This has a negative impact on growth of employment. At the same time, several sectors such as road building and construction have become more capital-intensive and more mechanized. This has further restricted the growth of employment. At the same time employment has also become more skill intensive. Road building sector used to employ a large number of women. This is no longer the case. You may witness any site on the national highways in the state.

Rajasthan is not an industrially advanced state although it has some large industries that contribute a significant share of industrial output of India. Agriculture continues to be the predominate production and employment sector in the economy. The impact of the new policies on this sector has, so far, been marginal. The main large-scale industries in the state are cement, synthetic fabrics, textiles, fertilizers and non-ferrous metals (zinc and copper). None of these industries employ women worker in large numbers. In fact it would not be an exaggeration to say that industrial employment in the state as predominantly male employment. And it so happens none of the industries mentioned above are negatively impacted by trade liberalisation. Copper is probably the only exception.

Industrial policy liberalisations has meant the withdrawal of concessions to small-scale industry. Even during the eighties the small-scale industrial sector in the state was not healthy. A large number of units were closed. This trend has accelerated further. This has a negative impact on the growth of employment of the sector. At the same time, some sectors like tourism and export of handicrafts are positively affected by liberal trade policies. Both these sectors employ relatively large number of women. Growth in demand of several handicrafts from the state has certainly given a push to growth of the handicraft sector. Readymade garments and printing of textiles has emerged as an important employment creating sectors. All the export sectors employ women in fairly large numbers but each of them is undergoing technical upgrading. This leaves women workers at a disadvantage. Garment making from cutting to saving buttons to ironing and packing are increasingly handled by new machines. Women often are left out or displaced in these activities as they lack the required skills or training. Educated workers familiar with the use of cell phones and computers can handle marketing of crafts better. These are only examples of technical up-grading that is now required even in the traditional sectors.

The new sectors related to information technology—radio, TV, journalism, computers software development and related activities are relatively more women friendly. The same can be said about new service sectors that are growing viz. financial services, education and health. In Short, except for small industries, most other sectors are not negatively impacted from the point of view of employment of women workers. But there are some aspects that are of concern. The environment in which these activities are operating has become highly competitive and employers have become cost conscious. This has been accompanied by privatisation. As a result many of these sectors are now characterized by long hours of work without any union pressures and also without any state support for meeting minimum wage or social security protection to the workers. One of the major concerns of state policy now has to be with provision of social security systems for workers in the private sector particularly workers in the non-formal activities sector.

For women in these sectors there is an additional concern. This is of physical security while going work or returning from it and in the process of job search. In urban areas, commuting to work has become one of the main problems. Low paid women workers in the service sectors are being relocated in order to create better urban environment through clearing slums or removing illegal occupation on public land. Both these are laudable objectives but the needs of the workers have not been given importance private bus service that is costly is provided but regulation of the number of passengers in a bus is at best, ineffective. In most cases it is non-existent. People including women are packed in the bus almost like sardines during the morning and evening hours. How women are physically abused can only be guessed. There is no organized resistance or regulation of these conditions. Special buses for women have been withdrawn even where the existed ion the past for reasons of economy. Similarly, recruitment in may new sectors is through private placement agencies. This method provides another opportunity for exploitation particularly of women workers, in short, women are working and earning but their conditions of recruitment and of work or conditions of travel to work should be matters of concern.

Another characteristic is the substitution of contract work for salaried employment. This is euphemistically called flexi-work. Flexi-workers combine a disparate group of non-regular workers. All of them lack entitlement to statutory protection. Some are in the high remuneration categories but many are not earning high remuneration. Consultancy and contract employment has become a common mode of employment in may urban service occupations including state services.

The replacement of the welfare state with market friendly state has created a crisis of social protection that seems to be intensifying along with crisis from a scenario of jobless growth. From the policy perspective, one of the prime concerns of political-economic policy as to shift to creating employment with growth, without employment the other objectives of equity, poverty eradication and empowerment of women would became unachievable.

My Priorities for state action would be:

1. Adopt economic strategies to create more jobs work for men and for women.
2. Create social protection mechanisms.
3. Consider the impact on women more carefully in sectors like education in which withdrawal of the state from quality education or reduction of state support for education will have a greater negative impact on women.

4. Put greater emphasis on skill enhancement of women workers to cater to the needs of more sophisticated markets both in rural and in urban areas.
5. Consider the impact on women due to privatisation of the health sector as well.
6. Cost recovery in drinking water needs to be pursued more gradually because of the impact of higher cost on household budget. Use of special purpose cess for collecting revenue would probably be a better option than pricing water to achieve full cost recovery

GANDHIAN PHILOSOPHY AND WOMEN'S EMPOWERMENT

REYAZ AHMAD

Mahatma Gandhi's vision of Swaraj in all its facets and from different perspectives has permeated the discourse on India's contemporary history. As the most towering figure in India's freedom struggle Gandhi's role will remain unchallenged. All over the world the imprint of his moral philosophy as a workable political ideology has been particularly indelible. Yet Mahatma Gandhi's positions on social, political and economic matters are transparently evolutionary, a continuing examination of reality, the human condition and truth. Gandhi's attitudes towards women were as much shaped by his innate sense of comparison and justice as they were by the patriarchal albeit benevolent conservatism that was the sheet anchor of his cultural and social discourse. The contradiction between his liberal feminist pronouncements, his egalitarian, loving and respectful concern for women, his belief in their role in politics and in society are sometimes difficult to reconcile. Yet Gandhi, more than anyone else, struggled with these paradoxes in the existing social milieu. Comparing his vision of women with the current status of women and the ongoing struggle for women's empowerment will provide a measure of what has been achieved.

In a letter written to Rajkumari Amrit Kaur from Wardha on 21 October, 1936 Gandhi writes, "If you women would only realize your dignity and privilege, and make full use of it for mankind, you will make it much better than it is. But man has delighted in enslaving you and you have proved willing slaves till the slaves and the slave-holders have become one in the crime of degrading humanity. My special function from childhood, you might say, has been to make women realize her dignity. I was once a slave-holder myself but proved an unwilling slave and thus opened my eyes to my mission. Her task was finished. Now I am in search of a woman who would realize her mission. Are you that woman, will you be one?"

Gandhi was able to devote himself to such a mission and formulated views on all aspects of a woman's life, political, social, domestic and even the very personal or intimate. He was able to do this by liberating himself from the sexual desires that identify the difference between man and woman and thereby positioned himself well above the feminist, becoming instead a reformer of humanity. "True affection does not demand identity of outlook . . . my passion for brahmacharya has that meaning. I must be wholly pure, if I have true love for womankind" (July 1938). While this gave him the right to demand far-reaching changes in the attitudes of society towards women and the attitudes of women about themselves, he rooted his views on distinctly Indian soil. It was also for the non-Intellectual among Indian woman. "I began work among women when I was not even thirty years old. There is not a woman in South Africa who does not know me. But my work was among the poorest. The intellectuals I could not draw . . . you can't blame me for not having organised the intellectuals among women. I have not the gift . . . but just as I never fear coldness on the part of the poor when I approach them, I never fear it when I approach poor women. There is an invisible bond between them and me." (8 July, 1938). This mass of poor women were those whose dignified upliftment Gandhi craved. Poor women understood what he was saying because he spoke in the idiom of Hindu religion and culture. He wanted them to drop the figurative veil while continuing to wear the real one. He referred to ideal women in the religious pantheon and referred to the facts of caste and gender. Sometimes highly progressive, other times conservative, he created an empathy with his audience through this cultural fine tuning.

This is particularly clear in his response to a question asked of him in an issue of the *Harijan* in 1934, in which described the ideal within which he placed as the real "What would determine a woman's Varna? Perhaps you will answer that before marriage a woman would take her Varna from her father; after marriage from her husband. Should one understand that you support Manu's notorious dictum that there can be no independence for woman at any stage of her life . . .?" In his reply Gandhi analysed the prevailing social situation and went on to state an ideal objective and finally reiterated the reality embedded within the question. He says: . . . owing to the confusion of Varnas today, the Varna principle has ceased to operate. The present state of Hindu society may described as that of anarchy; the four Varnas exist today in name only. If we must talk in terms of Varna there is only Varna today for all, whether men or women; we are all *shudras*. In the resuscitated Varna Dharma, as I conceive it, a girl after her marriage, would naturally adopt her husband's Varna and relinquish that of her parents. Nor need . . . any such change . . . imply a slur since . . . the age of resuscitation would imply absolute social equality of all four varnas." (*Harijan*, October 1934). Not only does Gandhi automatically accept the secondary status of the woman *vis-a-vis* the social identity of her husband or father but he goes on to say, "I do not envisage the wife, as a rule, following an avocation independently of her husband."

Again, in a letter to Rajkumari Amrit Kaur in answer to a question about the religion of children in mixed marriages, Gandhi reveals his patriarchal bias. "I am quite of opinion the children of mixed marriages should be taught in the mal parent's religion. This seems to me to be self-obvious for common happiness and interest. That the instruction should be liberal goes without saying. I am considering merely the question of choice of religion. The children cannot profess two religions. They must respect the female parent's religion. If the female parent has not that much discretion and regard for her husband's religion, the marriage becomes superficial." On sees Gandhi grappling with what is just and moral at one end with the necessity to assert the paternity rights of the father at the other. In reality, even if there was no respect, and the marriage was not a true meeting of minds, the father's religion still prevails, seems to be the unsaid part of the answer.

While adopting a high moral and often conservative position he could the next moment seemingly abandon if for a more fruitful and dynamic postulation that brings him to the forefront of extreme liberalism. Typically, Gandhi was able to step out of his traditional attitudes through the medium of education. When asked to write a primer for school children by Kakasaheb Kalelkar, Gandhi did it in the form of a mother teaching her child in which she explains to her son that housework was good for both mind and body and helped in character building. "Men and women need to be educated equally in housework because the home belongs to both", he wrote. This was part of his efforts to build a wholly new society, without which he believed it was not possible to make an appreciable difference to improve the lot of mankind with the cultural discourse of society as it was, and he never shied from providing direct and practical methodologies to achieve his goals. From feminist ideas in a text book to spinning the charkha for Swaraj he always came up with a constructive proposal to bring women out of their traditional mental fetters and into a better more dignified life.

In describing the woman's role as householder and housekeeper, he goes even further in stressing the need for man and woman to "do the duty for which nature has destined us" by finding it "degrading, both for man and woman, (if) the woman should be prevailed upon or induced to forsake the hearth and shoulder the rifle for the protection of that hearth. It is a reversion to barbarity and the beginning of the end. In trying to ride the horse that man rides, she brings herself and him down. The sin will be on man's head for tempting or compelling his companion to desert her special calling. There is as much bravery in keeping one's home in good order and condition, as there is defending it against attack from without." The contemporary argument for wages to be calculated for women's work at home and the need for economic independence for them to be truly able to act in their own interest overtakes by far Gandhi's traditional perceptions. Today's liberated woman would find his position almost totally unacceptable. They would argue that while women's special calling may be child nurturing, peace loving and preservationist they are capable of performing all tasks hitherto left to men.

But Gandhi revealed a deep understanding of the pulse of society, and reflected its rhythm. He offered spinning and the salt agitation as non-violent ways for women to join the political movement for swaraj. He saw it as right as well as possible for women at that time in history. By 1940, he had provided modifications to his earlier more generalized approach to women's contribution to public life. In an issue of the *Harijan* of that year there are questions about the rising participation of women in activities outside the home:

> *Q.* The awakening of civil and political consciousness among Indian women has created a conflict between their traditional domestic duties and their duty towards society. If a woman engages in public work, she may have to neglect her children or her household. How is this dilemma to be solved?
>
> *A.* More often than not a woman's time is taken up, not by the performance of essential domestic duties, but in catering for the egoistic pleasure of her lord and master and for her own vanities. To me this domestic slavery of the kitchen is a remnant of barbarism mainly. It is high time that our women kind was freed from this incubus. Domestic work ought not to take the whole of a woman's time.

Despite a change in attitude he seems to have the middle class woman rather than the poor one in mind, and adheres to the position that a woman should be able to order her household duties in such a manner as to complete them and yet have enough time for public work were she to abjure vanities. The onus is still on the woman. However, Gandhi was always willing to modify his own stated positions. He simply resolved his contradictions by responding instinctively and practically to a situation as he saw it. For instance, in the second set of questions and answers he tackles the male offenders thus:

> *Q.* At the elections, your Congressmen expect all manner of help from us, but when we ask them to send out their

wives and daughters to join us in public work, they bring forth all sorts of excuses, and want to keep them close prisoners within the four domestic walls.

A. Send the names of all such anti-diluvian fossils to me for publication in the *Harijan*.

Liberation of woman as Gandhi saw it, was linked to a deep-seated malaise. Dr. S. Muthulakshmi Reddy wrote a long letter to Mahatma Gandhi as far back as 1929, in which she raised some fundamental issues concerning social reform. She also questioned him as to why the Congress, which was fighting for the freedom of every nation and the individual should not first liberate their women from the evil customs and conventions that restricted their healthy all-round growth. She considered it a specific instance of social tyranny. Indian women, with a few exceptions, have lost the spirit of strength and courage, the power of independent thinking and initiative which actuated the women of ancient India, such as Maitreyi, Gargi, Savitri and even today activate a large number of our own women belonging to the liberal creeds like the Brahmo Samaj, Arya Samaj, Theosophy, which is only Hinduism freed of all its meaningless customs, rites and rituals? Although Gandhi agreed with her in a rather perfunctory way, he was not prepared to tackle the issues of social and religious customs so directly at that point of time and centred his response thus, "Men are undoubtedly to blame for their neglect, nay their ill use of women, and they have to do adequate penance, but those women who have shed superstition and have become conscious of the wrong have to do the constructive work of reform. The question of liberation of women, liberation of India, removal of untouchability, amelioration of the economic condition of the masses and the like, resolve themselves by penetration into the villages, reconstruction or rather reformation of the village life." To achieve one's goal of liberation from the various shackles of society he believed that had to work for total change starting in the villages.

The late Kamaladevi Chattopadhyay, a well known freedom fighter, political and social activist, an effective constructive worker, and motivator of India's cultural renaissance asserted that while the progressive status of women in the freedom movement was amply propelled by male social reformers and Gandhi, it was actually the advocacy of women which influenced many male leaders including Gandhi.

In 1983 the women's movement in India in its currently known phase, was just beginning to mobilize itself. Kamaladevi was witness to and part of valiant efforts by women to "not only push forward their own progress but act as levers to help other oppressed sections, while facing fierce hostility . . . there were no grants to feed such activities; no awards, titles, national recognition, no press publicity instead a lot of abuse." She defines women's actions of that time to be for equal rights which could not be described as feminist. "Women's problems were never sought to be treated on a sex basis but as social maladies of a common society, men and alike. What is indeed significant is the danger signals she saw at this time. "Habit, complacency and consequent lack of vigilance which fast undermined women and eventually deprived them of whatever gain they have been able to secure over the years. There are numerous subtle ways of ignoring women and abridging their rights. She lamented that woman had docilely accepted the situation of "helper" and that their work in political parties was only to mobilise support for the party and not to assert their personalities or strength as political entities. Kamaladevi's concerns for the gains achieved during the freedom movement were well founded if we view the almost regressive situation in rural and urban society with increasing violence against women, and the decreasing number of women in the population ratio. Modern technology, consumerism and lack of effective instruments have allowed, women no real progress even while allowing greater mobility and visibility to women from the middle and elite classes. Visibility alone is not empowerment in the real sense.

Mahatma Gandhi believed that satyagraha was the most powerful weapon in a non-violent struggle. Satyagraha involves defiance. It involves the wilful, peaceful, breaking of laws that are unjust. It means picketing, protesting, squatting, obstructing, challenging and publicly resisting wrongs. Since women were the most non-violent and ardent lovers of peace, it could be sharpened and extended as a weapon in women's struggles for justice and equality. To him the ultimate ahimsa and satyagraha was when women, in vast numbers, rose up to put an end to the destructive aspects of male dominance in society. Had the momentum of freedom struggle not been slowed down, such mobilisation could have attracted many more women into public life. Political activity geared towards the transformation of society into the holistic, integrated entity as Gandhi had visualized has not yet crystallized. Satyagraha is now just a word, a mere symbol, that serves no purpose for the academic or the elite, or even the middle class feminist whose dialectic emerges from a theoretical background far removed from Gandhi's poor women who act because they have no use for words to explain themselves. Among those women who today have made satyagraha a mode of struggle for a better world are the meira peibi of Manipur who stand in clusters on the roadside outside their village with flaming torches to protest against men who indulge in drugs and alcohol which are jointly ruining the youth of north-eastern India. These women also raise their voices against the excesses the security forces and form a protective shield around their villages against them. They do not quote Gandhi nor term their struggle as satyagraha but their steadfast, powerful and peaceful picketing has all the elements of struggle in the manner, Gandhi himself would have wished.

The anti-liquor movement of Andhra Pradesh built up gradually in the minds of poor and illiterate women who for long years suffered the ill effects of alcohol consumption by their men folk. For families steeped in poverty, for women who were subject to domestic violence related to alcohol, for wives who had nothing material to lose by rebelling because they had nothing to loose, they fulfilled Gandhi's wish of deciding no longer to be slaves of the situation. "No one can exploited without his or her willing participation" said Gandhi. Gandhi said that women "strengthen my belief in swadeshi and satyagraha . . . if I could inspire in men devotion as pure as I find in the women, within a year, India would be raised to a height impossible to imagine. As for swaraj it was the easiest thing in the world." Gandhi expected them to do battle from their homes, while still fulfilling their traditional roles. "If we send them to the factories, who will look after our domestic and social affairs? If women go out to work, our social life will be ruined and moral standards will decline." The superior qualities of women and the intrinsic difference between man and woman was something Gandhi kept highlighting. Since he believed that women could bring about swaraj better: women were the very embodiment non-violence, for him they were greater soldiers and beneficiaries of his swaraj campaigns. The three famed spearheads of these campaigns were the manufacture of salt, boycott of foreign cloth and shunning of liquor which he said "were specially meant for the villages and the women would benefit especially." In 1930, Mithiben Petit reported to Gandhi that habitual drunkards were enthusiastically breaking earthen jars containing toddy and that thousands of persons in Surat who were given to drinking had started having resolutions passed by their castes prohibiting drinking.

Somewhere along the way, however, the issues close to Gandhi's heart have been largely left by the wayside by women who became part of the power structure as well as by the emancipated women's groups. Organisations involved in trade union work, social reform and development issues have in part or in whole addressed the issue of prohibition, but neither have women as a group in parliament nor through institutional structures raised this demand loudly and effectively. Prohibition is not accepted when it is presented as a moral issue alone and therefore the argument has to include developmental priorities, revenue collection, and budgetary allocations to social welfare, health and other sectors which rural women are unable to do.

The salt satyagraha and boycott of foreign cloth emphasises the indigenous, but the feminist movement has not associated itself with the swadeshi movement except for the Gandhian elements within the various groupings. The wearing of khadi and handloom among the younger activists is more as the badge of a progressive liberal rather than as a commitment to the foods of indigenous manufacture. These are no longer taken up as issues of struggle although many women are part of the wider movement against the neo colonial pressures of the new world trade regime which destroy both sovereignty and national resources.

Many institutions and organisations representing women's rights have a high visibility in the cosmopolitan arena and have effectively expressed their concerns. Not only that, their members have decisively moved far ahead of Gandhi's vision of fearless women. Alert, active and bold, they engage in constant discussion and introspection for genuine equality.

While all women's agendas prescribe peace and non-violence, the feminisation of the military and police and, the expanding membership of women in militant groups that do not abjure the use of arms are all a sad cry away from what Gandhi viewed to be a woman's special role.

While middle class women were visibly active side by side with Mahatma Gandhi, wearing khadi, going to jail, organising resistance on the British in some creative and selfless way, the socially conscious middle class woman of today has largely shunned direct political activity, preferring to seek more secure ground in funded social work through voluntary organisations. A growing number of emancipated, educated, young women are being diverted by market-oriented consumerism in the name of modernity and liberation. They become packaged products for the marriage, beauty or fashion markets, a professionalised catering to "the vanities" that Gandhi spoke of. This depoliticizes them to such an extent that the cream of young women students are unavailable to articulate the needs of their under privileged sisters. This results in a wider cultural and social divide emerging between the rural and urban woman. It also demonstrates that emancipation does not mean empowerment in the Gandhian sense if women move away from involvement with the more deep seated problems facing India.

Compared to the momentous work of stalwarts like Sarojini Naidu, Rajkumari Amrit Kaur, Dr Muthulakshi Reddy, Lakshmi N. Menon and Annie Besant and organisations like the All India Women's conference, the Arya Samaj and many others during Mahatma Gandhi's time, the collective or individual work of women in the political arena in the post-independence era has been unremarkable. This clearly does not take into account the phenomenon of an Indira Gandhi or the many successful efforts of various women's organisations in bringing about legislation to improve the status of women. Self-Employed Women's Association of Ahmedabad is a fine example of Gandhi's ideas put into practice but it lacks of political power to influence change in the society around it. The fact that women have never held more than 10 percent of the seats in parliament or jobs in the decision-making levels of the administration shows that there is a long way to go before gender parity is achieved.

While in some spheres women have accepted Gandhi's words about shedding their role as slaves and facing patriarchal challenges, women have largely slipped away from the paths of political action that Gandhi had opened out for them during the freedom movement. For instance, outside the home and far from the hearth individual women from the middle classes have achieved remarkable prominence in fields such as aviation, science and space technology, administration, education, literature and the arts. Unfortunately, the women of the rural classes are subjected to the same oppression as before, not only by the men within their caste but by upper caste communities who carryout reprisals on communities from the under castes. The recent political empowerment of the backward castes has found a corresponding rise in the suppression of their own women, reflecting the existing ethos of rural society. Neither has an effective political leadership risen from amongst them to give courage to other nor are emancipated urban women able to provide the kind of sustained leadership rural women need largely because of class and caste differences.

On paper, India is far ahead in policies and legislation favouring women. It adopted universal franchise before many other nations. Yet men in the political structure refuse to acknowledge the relationships between social justice and gender justice while women outside the political system are unable to effectively implement and integrate these two most powerful national and international agendas. The increasing criminalisation of politics and the use of vast sums of unaccounted money and ugly muscle power by caste and criminal gangs present an entire hostile environment for women who wish to pursue a political vocation. With both caste and gender groups perpetuating traditional and modern divisions and indigenous human resources being replaced by western technologies the mission of Gandhi and the dreams of women are yet to be fulfilled.

REFERENCES

Gandhi's Social Philosophy: Perspective & Relevance, B.N. Ganguli, National Gandhi Museum, Radha Publication, New Delhi, 2006.

Women in Gandhi's Mass Movements, Bharti Thakur, Deep & Deep Publication Pvt. Ltd., New Delhi, 2006.

Satyagraha—Savita Singh, New Delhi, Publication Division, 2005.

Mahatma Gandhi: His Thought, Life & Ideas, A.K.S. Parihar, New Delhi, Swastika Publication, 2007.

Gandhian Way of Peace, Non-Voilence and Empowerment, Edited by Anand Sharma, Academic Foundation, 2007.

PART II

EMPOWERMENT OF WOMEN AND EDUCATION

WOMEN EMPOWERMENT: A NEW ROADMAP REQUIRED

MITHILESH KUMAR SINHA

PROLOGUE

During the past two decades the notion of 'empowerment' of women has significantly impacted the paradigms of development. In 2001 the United Nations Population Fund (UNEPA) had promised gender equality and empowerment of women by 2005 as one of the eight Millennium Development Goals (MDGs). World Bank, World Health Organisation, UNFPA accepts women as disadvantaged gender globally, more so in developing nations. The lack of education and economic independence are the biggest factors that affect women's health. Economic background of the family does not speak about women's equality and empowerment. Lowering child sex ratio (girls per thousand boys) from 1991 to 2001 in wealthy states like Haryana, Punjab, Himachal Pradesh, Delhi, Gujarat, depicts the worst scenario. Better child sex ratio is seen among backward class, rural people who could not afford sex determination. Similar picture is seen in China, Korea and Eastern Europe, where there is strong preference for sons. The ban on sex determination was not effective. Demographic divide is wider with education and economic opportunity. The UNFPA has indicated the need of investment in women education and healthcare in order to empower them and drastically reduce the gender violence. A strategic intervention is required if MDGs are to be met.

Women empowerment enables autonomy and control over their lives. The empowered women become agents of their own development, able to exercise choices to set their own agenda and be strong enough to challenge and change their subordinate position in the society. In order to achieve this, emphasis should be on formulation of appropriate organisation for women to facilitate communication, learning and organized action. Empowerment is individual's self-esteem and collective mobilisation for challenging basis power relations like social injustice and mobilisation of resources. Empowerment is self-governance, self-sufficiency and self-maintenance. Empowerment in the Indian context means the development of women capacity to make informed choices and expansion of their capacity to manage their domestic and economic environment efficiently. It is needless to say that India's economic development is also closely intertwined with the process of women's oppression. Unless it is removed, it is not possible to achieve expected target.

I
INTERNATIONAL PERSPECTIVE

Many targets set for 2005 under the Millennium Development Goals (MDGs), to correct gender imbalances have been missed. The Millennium Development Goals (MDGs), to which 198 nations are signatories, set concrete objectives for eradicating extreme poverty and hunger, achieving universal primary education, promoting gender equality, reducing child mortality, and improving maternal health as well as combating HIV/AIDS. Specifically, the targets set for 2005 to correct gender imbalances in primary education have not been achieved. For instance, worldwide, six million girls will still not be enrolled in school by 2015, even though gender gaps in schooling are narrowing in certain parts of the world. The situation is worst in

Sub-Saharan Africa followed by some countries in South Asia. The failure to meet the 2005 school enrolment targets is evidence by the fact that even though schooling levels are rising, only about half of the countries have achieve gender parity in primary education and about 30 per cent in secondary education. Even more disconcerting is that studies suggest some of parity at the primary school level in developing countries is because boys' enrolment has dropped.

School education is also not the only indicator specified by the MDGs road map for gender equality. Other criteria are labour market opportunities for women, literacy rates, and their participation in the political process. Progress in these areas too has been insufficient. In South Asia, countries such as Sri Lanka and Bangladesh have made creditable progress. For instance, in Bangladeshi schools, the elimination of school fees for girls, as well as the provision of toilets and safe drinking water, has dramatically increased enrolment and attendance (Sinha: 2006).

The survey, published by the Geneva-based World Economic Forum—better known for its annual business bash in Davos shows that full economic and political empowerment remains a distant dream for millions of women in much of the western world, let alone developing countries. Of the 58 countries covered by the survey, only a handful of European nations—mostly the Nordic states—seem to have made real progress in lowering the glass ceiling, though it still exists even in these countries.

The report says that "no country has yet managed to eliminate the gender gap" but the Nordic states—Sweden, Norway, Iceland, Denmark and Finland—have "succeeded best" in narrowing it. They are seen to provide a "workable model" for the rest of the world to follow. Other "female-friendly" countries include Britain, Germany, New Zealand, Australia and significantly, several East European countries where women still from the support system built during the Communist era.

America, with its restrictive maternity rights regime and poor state child welfare system, does not even figure in the top 10 women-friendly countries. Even Britain, which makes it to the top 10, fares badly in a range of areas, lagging behind even India in terms of economic opportunity.

The most glaring gender inequality in Britain relates to wages where women still earn far less than men for the same work—

and this despite an Equal Pay Act passed 30 years ago. This is confirmed by official figures which show that the average income of women in Britain is almost half that of men.

Child Sex Ratio

Data on declining child sex ratio (CSRs) in the developed world have been published in the "World Population Prospects: The 2002 Revision, Volume II, Sex and Age Distribution of Population, United Nations, New York, 2003 (U.N. Secretariat, Department of Economics Social Affairs, Population Division)". The period under study covers the 50 years from 1950 to 2000.

As per the report, the average CSR (0-4 age group) in the developed regions comprising Europe, North America, Australia, New Zealand and Japan showed a steady decline in the 50-year period—from 957 female children (per 1,000 male children) in 1950 to 949 in 2000. In contrast, the CSR for this age group in the least developed countries (949 in all, 934 in Africa, 909 in Asia, 901 in Latin America and the Caribbean and 905 in Oceania) stood at 998 in 1950, much higher than that in the developed bloc, and in 2000 it was 976.

Similarly, the CSR for the 5-9 age groups was 1,002 girl children in 1950 and 977 in 2000. Though the decline is sharp, the figure remains much higher than the corresponding figure for this age grouping the more developed regions. Even in the South-East Asia, where in 1950 the CSR stood at 1,003, the figure came down to 963 in 2000, and the reasons for the decline were not entirely cultural. If they were so, then in the absence of sex-selection technology, female children would still have been eliminated by mass foeticide. As in Africa, the CSR decline in Islamic countries between 1950 and 2000 was not prominent. In fact, Afghanistan showed a marginal improvement and Iraq, reeling under the weight of U.N. sanctions, showed a dramatic improvement in the survival of the girl child in the 0-4 age group. In 2000, its CSR stood at 964, higher than the world average of 948 (Table 1).

II
PROGRESS ON THE GENDER PARITY IN EDUCATION (ASIA AND THE PACIFIC)

Several countries in Southeast Asia, including Malaysia,

TABLE 1

Global Child Sex Ratio

	0-4 Age Group		*5-9 Age Group*	
	1950	*2000*	*1950*	*2000*
North America	977	951	957	952
Latin America & Caribbean	977	962	982	964
Northern Europe	953	949	960	952
Iraq	945	964	954	965
Saudi Arabia	968	955	968	955
Iran	986	951	980	949
Afghanistan	948	947	933	939
Pakistan	968	944	999	939
Asia	944	936	956	932
China	992	898	903	897
Nepal	992	943	979	934
Bangladesh	1014	954	1003	950
Sri Lanka	758	966	868	970
India	976	941	982	934
South-East Asia	1003	963	1013	967

Source: World Population Prospects: The 2002 Revision, Vol II, Sex and Age Distribution of Population, United Nations.

Philippines, and Thailand, as well Sri Lanka and some Pacific countries, have achieved gender parity in education at relatively high levels of enrolment, but this has not translated into equal participation in economic and political affairs. Cambodia has one of the highest levels of women's economic participation in the region, but women's education and literacy remain low with gender gaps at all levels. Central Asian countries, such as Azerbaijan, Kazakhstan, and Kyrgyz Republic, have struggled to maintain education services since the fall of the Soviet Union, and girls' enrolment levels have remained high although gender gaps are widening at the secondary level. At the same time, women's wage employment and representation in national parliaments have fallen sharply (Singh: 2006).

Based on available 2001 data, the UNESCA/UNDP/ADB joint regional MDG report estimates that the vast majority of countries in the Asia and Pacific region will reach gender parity in primary enrolments by 2005 (Table 2). The countries that are farthest from the Goal 3 of MDGs target (Eliminating gender disparity in primary and secondary by 2005) are in South Asia (Afghanistan, Pakistan, India and Nepal), the GMS (Cambodia and Lao PDR) and the Pacific (Papua New Guinea). However, the country's MDG progress report confirms that gender disparities persist, although there has been substantial progress in increasing both boy's and girls' enrolment.

TABLE 2

Selected Data on Gender Parity in Primary Education

Country	*Ratio of Girls' to Boys' Enrolment 2001*	*Target data for Gender Parity (Actual or Estimated)*	*Girls' Net Enrolment 2001 (%)*	*Girls' completion 2001 (%)*	*Boys' Net Enrolment 2001 (%)*	*Boys' completion 2001 (%)*
Afghanistan	0.08	—	—	—	—	—
Pakistan	0.74	—	50	—	68	—
India	0.85	2012	76	72	89	87
Lao PDR	0.86	2013	79	69	86	77
Nepal	0.87	2003	66	67	85	80
Cambodia	0.89	2008	83	56	89	66
PNG	0.90	—	69	52	77	57
Iran, Islamic	0.96	2001	78	89	80	93
Republic THA	0.96	2001	85	83	88	86
Kyrgyz Repub.	0.97	2001	88	95	92	98
Armenia	0.98	2001	84	90	85	90
Azerbaijan	0.98	2001	79	90	81	91
Kazakhstan	0.99	2001	89	92	90	92
Uzbekistan	1.99	2001	78 (1990)	101	79 (1990)	101
Myanmar	1.00	2001	82	72	82	72
Bangladesh	1.02	2001	88	75	86	71
Nauru	1.04	—	82	102	79	82

Note: PNG—Papua New Guinea, THA—Thailand.

Source: Pursuing Gender Equality through the Millennium Development Goals in Asia and Pacific. www. adb.org/document/books/persuing gender equality/ default. Asp.

III
PERSPECTIVE OF SEX RATIO IN INDIA

Consumerist Culture-oriented economic development, commercialisation of medical profession and sexist biases in our society, combined together have created a sad scenario of 'missing girls'. Global comparisons of sex ratios shows that sex ratios in Europe, North America, Caribbean, Central Asia, the poorest regions of Sub-Saharan Africa are favourable to women as these countries neither kill/neglect girls nor do they use NRTs for production of sons. The lowest sex ratio is found in some parts of India. Deficit of women in India since 1901—violence against women over Life Cycle, from womb to tomb—female infanticide, neglect of girl child in terms of health and nutrition, child marriage and repeated pregnancy taking heavy toll of girls' lives—Selective Elimination of Female Foetuses and selection of male at a preconception stage—Legacy of continuing declining sex ratio in India in the history of census of India has taken new turn with widespread use of new reproductive technologies (NRTs) in India. NRTs are based on principle of selection of the desirable and rejection of the unwanted. In India, the desirable in the baby boy and the unwanted is the baby girl. The result is obvious. The census results of 2001 have revealed that with sex ratio of 927 girls for 100 boys. India had deficit of 60 lakh girls in age group of 0.6 years.

Just three of top ten cities in India by population—Chennai, Coimbatore and Hyderabad—have a sex ratio (numer of females per 1000 males) higher than the national average of 932. And none of the big metros figure in the top ten cities on sex ratio. The credit for that goes to smaller cities such as Kannur, Kochi & Vellore (Table 3).

TABLE 3

Big Cities Sex Ratio and Top 10 Cities in India on Sex Ratio

Cities	*Sex Ratio*	*Cities*	*Sex Ratio*
Chennai	957	Kannur	1112
Coimbatore	957	Thrissur	1079
Hyderabad	933	Kozhikode	1055
Pune	899	Thiruvanthapuram	1042
Bangalore	876	Kochi	1024
Kolkata	829	Thanjavur	1022
Delhi	821	Imphal East & West	1017
Mumbai	810	Kanniyakumari	1016
Surat	766	Mangalore	1005
		Vellore	1003

Source: City Skyline of India, 2006, Indicus Analytics.

PERSPECTIVE OF WOMEN EDUCATION

Literacy Trends

According to the census of 1951, the average general literacy rate was 18.33 with male 27.16 and female 8.86% (Table 4). The gap between male and female is 18.30. As per census 2001 report, general literacy rate is 65.38, with male 75.85 and female 54.16. This achievement in terms of general literacy growth is quite impressive, but when we compare the gap between male and female, it is contrary to the progress made in general literacy. It has increased from 18.30 to 21.70, which in ideal situation should have been reduced. Even though national average is relatively better, when we compare the States in India, there is a large variation. In progressive states like Kerala, male and female literacy rates are 94.20 and 87.86 respectively with a gap of only 6.34 per cent (Table 5).

TABLE 4

General Literacy Rate since Independence with Gender Gap

Census year	*Persons (%)*	*Males (%)*	*Females (%)*	*Male-Female gap in literacy rate (%)*
1951	18.33	27.16	8.86	18.30
1961	28.30	40.40	15.35	25.05
1971	34.45	45.96	21.97	23.98
1981	43.57	56.38	29.76	26.62
1991	52.21	64.13	39.29	24.84
2001	65.38	75.85	54.16	21.70

Source: Census of India, 2001.

TABLE 5

State-wise Variation

Literacy Rate (States)	*Males (%)*	*Females (%)*	*Gap (%)*
Kerala	94.20	87.86	6.34
Mizoram	90.69	86.13	4.56
Lakshadweep	93.15	81.56	11.59
Bihar	60.32	33.57	26.75
Jharkhand	67.94	39.38	28.56

Source: Census of India, 2001: Provisional.

Similar situation exists in Mizoram and Lakshadweep. Compared to this, Bihar has male literacy of 60.32, female literacy of 33.57 with the gap of 26.75. State of Jharkhand has also similar situation. This variation depicts gap in social and overall human development among the states. If the country as a whole is to be considered, then these gaps are to be reduced.

The census study of 1951 shows (Table 6) rural male literacy of 19.02, female 4.87 with persons literacy of 12.10, male/female gap of 14.15%, whereas the urban literacy of male is 45.06, female 22.33, persons' literacy 34.59 with male/female gap of 22.73. The urban-rural male literacy gap is 26.4; urban-rural female literacy gap is 17% with the average persons gap of 22.49%. The 2001

TABLE 6

Rural-Urban Literacy Rates

Census year		*Males*	*Females*	*Persons*	*Male/Female Gap*
1951	Rural	19.02	4.87	12.10	14.15
	Urban	45.06	22.33	34.59	22.73
	Total	24.95	7.93	16.67	17.02
Rural/Urban Gap	26.04	17.46	22.49		
1961	Rural	29.10	8.55	19.10	
	Urban	57.49	34.51	46.97	
	Total	34.44	12.95	24.02	
1971	Rural	33.76	13.17	23.24	
	Urban	61.27	42.14	52.44	
	Total	39.45	18.69	29.45	
1981	Rural	49.69	21.77	36.09	
	Urban	76.83	56.37	67.34	
	Total	56.50	29.85	43.67	
1991	Rural	57.87	30.62	44.69	
	Urban	81.09	64.05	73.08	
	Total	64.13	39.29	52.21	
2001	Rural	71.18	46.58	59.21	24.60
	Urban	86.42	72.99	80.06	13.43
	Total	75.85	54.16	65.38	21.69
Rural/Urban Gap	15.24	26.41	20.85		

Source: Census of India, 2001.

census shows rural male literacy 71.81, female 46.58 and rural persons 59.21; male/female gap of 24.60. The urban male literacy is 86.42; urban female 72.99 with urban persons 85.06. The urban male-female gap is 13.43; rural-urban gap of male literacy is 15.24, female gap is 26.41% and person's gap is 20.85%. Comparative situation of 1951 and census 2001 census shows overall good progress in literacy rate of persons 8.67 to 65.38, the gap of male literates is reduced from 26% to 15%, which is a welcome sign, but in case of female, it has increased from 17.46 to 26.41 which obviously is not a good sign. In comparison to 1951 rural literacy, male-female gap has increased from 14.15 to 24% whereas the urban male/female gap, which was 22.73 in 1951, has reduced to 13.43 in 2001. On the whole, the urban-rural analysis shows that there is persistent gap between urban-rural and rural male-female, and it needs special attention to reduce this gap.

2001 census shows persons literacy rate at national level 65.38% (Table 7) whereas the general female literacy rate is 53.67, compared to SC 41.90 and ST 34.76, which show a gap of 12% and 19% respectively.

The above data analysis shows that over all female literacy rates are poor with further low rates in rural women, of Scheduled Caste and Scheduled Tribe.

HIGHER EDUCATION

There has been a phenomenal growth in the number of women students enrolled in higher education, since independence. Women enrollment was less than 10 per cent of the total enrollment on the eve of Independence and it rose to 40.05 per cent in 2002-03. The pace of growth has been particularly faster in the last two decades. It shows that the number of women enrolled per hundred men registered almost five-fold increase during the period 1950-51 to 2002-03 (Table 7).

Though the table shows a rising tendency favouring girls, of the total population of university entrants only about one-third are women. In a country with more than a billion people only about 36,96,000 women are able to go for higher education. This means that a university course is beyond the grasp of many women. So universities have to cross over their boundary lines to reach the unreached women who never enter their portals (Janaki: 2005).

TABLE 7

Enrollment of Women in Higher Education in India

Year	*No. of Women Enrolled*	*Women Students per Hundred Men Students*	*Women %*
1950-51	43,126	14	10.9
1960-61	1,70,455	—	16.2
1970-71	6,55,822	—	21.9
1993-94	16,64,000	50	33.2
1996-97	21,91,138	—	34.1
1997-98	25,14,511	—	36.7
2002-03	36,96,000	67	40.0

Source: University Grants Commission, Annual Report, 2002-03.

Distribution of Women Enrollment by State, Stage and Faculty

(a) State-wise Distribution of Women Enrollment

Distribution of women enrollment by state-wise shows that the percentage increases has been static in the enrollment of women as compared to the total enrollment in all the states during 2002-03 over the preceding year. Among the states, Kerala with 60% topped in terms of women enrollment as a percentage of total enrollment as a percentage of total enrollment during 2002-03, followed by Goa (58.5%), Punjab (52.7%) etc. There were 17 states which had higher enrollment of women than the national percentage of 39.84%. In the rest of the states, the percentage of women enrolled was less than the national level, with Bihar recording the lowest women enrollment of 23.8% only.

(b) Stage-wise Distribution of Women Enrollment

During 2003-03, the enrollment of women as a percentage of total enrollment has consistently been going up at all stages of Higher education—Graduate, Post-graduate, Research and Diploma/Certificate (Table 8).

TABLE 8

Stage-wise Distribution of Women Enrollment

Stage	*Total Enrollment*	*Women Enrollment*	*Percentage of Women*
Graduate	82,27,417	32,85,544	39.93
Post-graduate	8,46,556	3,55,893	42.04
Research	62,213	30,918	33.74
Diploma/Certificate	92,27,833	36,95,964	40.05
	92,27,833	36,95,964	40.05

Source: UGC Annual Report, 2002-03.

But the gender gap increases as we go from the rich to the poorest: among the very poor, a man is 10 times more likely than a woman to have a higher educational degree: however, among the rich, a man is only 1.7 times more likely than a woman to have a similar degree. Gender also matters within each caste-community, with the exception of the Christians among whom women do marginally better than men. Here again the gender gap is wider at the lower end of social hierarchy: SC, ST, OBC and Muslim women are more disadvantaged *vis-a-vis* the men of their communities than upper caste Hindu women are *vis-a-vis* the men of their community (Table 9).

TABLE 9

Per Cent of Postgraduates and Professional Degree Holders by Caste/Community, Class and Gender

		All Classes	*Rich*	*Middle*	*Lower Middle*	*Poor*	*Very Poor*	*N*
1	*2*	*3*	*4*	*5*	*6*	*7*	*8*	*9*
All Caste Communities	All	2.5	8.1	6.8	1.6	0.8	0.6	26829
	Men	3.4	9.8	9.1	2.2	1.2	1.0	14345
	Women	1.4	5.8	3.9	0.8	0.4	0.1	12484
Hindu dwija upper caste	All	5.6	13.6	8.8	2.7	1.7	0.5	4148
	Men	7.4	17.8	10.3	3.9	2.7	1.0	2230
	Women	3.5	8.3	7.3	1.4	0.3	0.0	1918

TABLE 9 (*Contd.*)

1	2	3	4	5	6	7	8	9
Hindu and Sikh*	All	2.8	6.2	4.6	0.7	1.2	0.8	2521
	Men	3.5	7.3	5.8	1.2	0.9	1.7	1361
	Women	2.0	4.8	3.4	0.0	2.2	0.0	1160
OBC (Hindu & Sikh)	All	1.8	5.8	6.6	1.1	0.7	0.7	9505
	Men	2.7	6.2	10.1	1.6	1.3	1.3	5020
	Women	0.8	5.2	1.9	0.4	0.1	0.1	4485
SC (any religion)	All	1.4	4.2	8.0	1.6	0.5	0.4	4278
	Men	2.1	2.3	11.7	2.8	0.7	0.8	2287
	Women	0.6	5.0	2.6	0.2	0.2	0.1	1991
ST (any religion)	All	0.9	1.9	6.1	1.4	0.6	0.4	2181
	Men	1.3	3.3	10.0	1.6	0.3	0.7	1185
	Women	0.5	0.0	1.8	1.1	0.5	0.2	996
Muslims	All	1.8	7.1	4.0	1.5	0.3	0.0	2963
	Men	2.5	10.1	6.0	1.2	0.5	0.0	1638
	Women	0.9	1.7	1.6	2.0	0.0	0.0	1327
Christian	All	3.3	13.2	7.8	1.8	0.8	0.0	630
	Men	3.0	(11.1)	5.7	3.3	1.5	0.0	302
	Women	3.7	15.0	9.5	0.0	0.0	0.0	328

Note: All figures are for per cent of respondents belonging to a category who report having a post-graduate or professional degree. Figures based on less than 50 cases have been put within parentheses. Class categories are based on a combination of self-reported data on income and observed data on possession of assets.

* Intermediary caste (non-dwija, non-OBC).

Source: National Election Study, 2004, CSDS Data Unit. Data is weighted by state population.

(c) Distribution of Women Enrollment by Faculty

The faculty-wise distribution of women enrollment during 2002-03 is as given in Table 10.

It shows that women enrollment in the faculty of Arts has been 51.13 per cent of total women enrollment, followed by the faculty of Science (19.94), the faculty of Commerce (16.48) etc., there was no much change in the percentage of women enrolled in any faculty in 2002-03 as compared to 2001-02 except the faculty of Engg./Technology where the percentage of enrollment is increased by 0.42%.

TABLE 10

Women Enrollment by Faculty, 2002-03

S. No.	Faculty	Women Enrollment	Percentage of total women enrollment
1.	Arts	18,89,799	51.13
2.	Science	7,36,890	19.94
3.	Commerce/Management	6,08,949	16.48
4.	Education	67,096	1.81
5.	Engineering/Technology	1,54,041	4.17
6.	Medicine	1,34,364	3.63
7.	Agriculture	9,332	0.25
8.	Veterinary Science	2,982	0,08
9.	Law	61,947	1.68
10.	Others	30,564	0.83
	Total	26,95,964	100.00

Source: As on Table 9.

Women Employment Scenario

Indian women have outshone men at work a employment among women has increased 3.35% between 1998 and 2004 against a fall of about 8% in the case of men. (Assocham, an industry body: 2007). Keeping pace with the growth in GDP, the number of women employed in public and private sector has increased to 49.34 lakh in 2004 from 47.74 lakh in 1998, while the number of men employed has fallen to 215.09 lakh from 233.92 lakh during the same period, reveal the findings.

According to Assocham, the public sector has been hiring women much more aggressively than the private sector. The number of women employed in public sector has risen 4.6% to 28.9 lakh in 2004 from 27.63 lakh in 1998 while women staff in the private sector has grown 1.64% to 20.44 lakh.

IV
WOMEN IN THE ELEVENTH PLAN

The National Family Health Survey in its third round estimates the number of women in the age group 15 to 49 with no formal education at 41% as against 18% of men. The Eleventh Plan Approach says it is about to change all that. The document reads: "An important divide which compels immediate attention relates to gender. Special, focused efforts will be made to purge society of this malaise by creating an enabling environment for women to become economically, politically and socially empowered." (para. 1.7.3)

These words are very welcome. However, past Plans have all expressed similar concern with respect to gender divide. Now that the Indian Economy is on a different growth trajectory altogether, it might be useful to recall that at these growth rates, the economy will run into a crippling skill shortage very soon. This surfaced last year at the time of the OBC reservation issue.

The various working groups formed to examine the 54% seat expansion in all publicly funded educational institutions for different sectors of education found that the biggest difficulty of all would be to find qualified teachers. The seat expansion required can only be achieved if the teaching environment is radically restructured. Some of the IITs are planning virtual campuses, where classroom instruction will be beamed through television monitors. But it is not just high-level teaching skills that are in short supply.

The services-sector led growth in the Indian economy calls for a very wide range of skills, all of which will soon be in critically short supply unless there is a massive increase in effective literacy among girls, and hitherto excluded castes. The children inducted into schools will not be able to use their education or indeed absorb it unless their health status and that of their mothers improves.

The National Rural Health Mission has been formed to address this, but that mission in turn will face a critical shortage of paramedical and nursing personnel. No matter where one turns, there is a shortage of literacy-based skills that will obstruct the ambitious growth targets of the Plan, unless an attempt is made to think through why past efforts to mainstream women and other marginalized groups have failed. The high drop-out rate in primary schools does get a mention in the Approach paper. The national average reported for 2003-04 is 31%. The Sarva Shiksha Abhiyan targets universal elementary education for all children up to class 8 by 2010. A 2% education cess has been levied on all taxes and earmarked to fund this programme. An additional 1% cess has been added on in the Union Budget of 2007 to fund secondary and higher education. These funding provisions will get us nowhere unless we understand why children entering the school system leave it before completion.

The Approach paper speculates on why drop-out rates are high. The mid-day meal scheme as a twin attack on low attendance and nutrition has been a major initiative. The paper rightly calls for the meal scheme to be merged with Sarva Shiksha Abhiyan. The problem of absentee teachers, the pressures on girl children to perform domestic duties, all find a mention. But consciousness of these problems and the solutions, tried has not led to anything close to universal retention in primary education. The Approach paper quotes a NIEPA study on the poor physical infrastructure in primary schools. Only 28% of schools had electricity in classrooms, and only half had more than two teachers or two classrooms. But better infrastructure will not be sufficient to pull the girl child into school and keep her there unless the family sees some benefit (Rajaraman: 2007).

Girl children, and mothers of girl children, will want to persist with the school process for eight years, only if they see some benefit to themselves at the end of it all. The mother of the average girl in a rural school fears that schooling might turn her daughter's mind against rural life, without actually equipping her for anything else. To such mothers, the availability of a school for girls becomes a threat rather than an opportunity. For girls in rural schools within reachable distance of an urban centre, where respectable employment avenues for girls might be visible, school makes economic sense. For others, it does not.

There is an urgent need for centres of vocational training, especially those imparting women-specific skills like nursing, to link up with rural schools. This in turn will be possible only if all such centres are placed on GIS platform, Geographical Information System, GIS, is software that has been around for more than twenty years. It enables spatial planning by essentially digitizing maps. The Census of India is now available on GIS platform.

Using GIS, a vocational-primary school link can be set up for vocations not requiring a secondary schooling, and a vocational-secondary school link for vocations that do. Each vocational centre needs to be assigned responsibility for motivating and monitoring rural schools within a defined radius, showing a career path beyond the social process. The second prong of attack has to be on reducing the unproductive female work-load of fetching water from long distances. Once again, watersheds in the country need to be contoured on GIS platform. Using space technology for mapping of aquifers, a five-year plan needs to be drawn up for creating sustainable water sources within reasonable reach of rural habitations.

Survey Report

A survey to measure the NQ or the entrepreneurial quotient was conducted (1,200 middle class urban women excluding the top 20% of households and the bottom 30% in terms of social class) by India Consultancy Groups in six diverse cities—Ahmedabad, Mumbai, Coimbtore, Chandigrah, Hyderabad and Indore. This survey reveals:

1. 77% of urban housewives and 60% of rural do not work outside the home.
2. The heartening answer was that about one in every four women wanted to have a business of her own. Half of these potential entrepreneurs already are running some money-making activity from home and are ready to convert it to a formal business. The other half has so far been solely home-makers, but has given a fair degree of thought to visioning their business. Of these women, 40% had less than nine years of education, another 40% were standard tenth pass, and only 20% had an education beyond that.
3. The reasons for not studying further were forced on them in 75% of the cases, "family said enough," "financial constraints", and "got married off."
4. The touching statistic was that women with high NQ also had more educated mothers—relatively speaking, of course. Of them, 95% were married, almost all had children, and 67% had nuclear families.

What Stops Them?

Just about everything—lack of know-how, lack of space, lack of family support, lack of finances. (Interestingly that was not the first and last item on the list. It isn't just about money. It is about support in many more ways, because they have fewer role models to learn from.) Part 2 of the survey was to know more about what motivates and frustrates existing women entrepreneurs, and how they can be taken to the next level.

Four segments of women entrepreneurs exist:

Self-help groups: Those who are well served and mentored by microfinance institutions.

Grassroots entrepreneurs: Those who are driven by a need to augment the family's finances especially to secure their children's future-tailors, flower sellers, STD booth owners, paan shops. With turnover aspiration of five lakh a year, they are very work focused, as they can see any increase in their earnings as directly impacting their childrens' lives. They are hungry for formal skills and training and can clearly articulate what they want to learn that will help them earn more. Domestic family support, financial support and better infrastructure and mechanisation is what they ask for.

Mid-rung entrepreneurs: They are driven by a need to build reputation, become known, and improve quality and satisfy creative instincts. Mostly graduate+, they typically have garments shops, poultry farms, export businesses etc., with turnover aspirations from Rs. 50 lakh to Rs. 1 crore. Fairly well supported by the family, their biggest need is for know-how to take the 'quality of their businesses' to the next level. However, they do not want to scale too much, because to them, there is an optimal level beyond which, they believe their children will get neglected.

Upper Crust: Drawn from the top-most social class, very well educated, with business like export houses, travel agencies, traders in pharmaceuticals, often adjuncts to their husband's businesses, they aspire to turnovers of more than Rs. 5 crore.

V

From above perspectives of women empowerment one can question "Is now a better time to be a working woman than 50 years ago? In many ways the answer has to be yes. By and large, women everywhere have got the same legal rights as men. They also have equal access to education. The qualitative argument for having more women—with requisite skills and qualifications—in the workplace is widely accepted. They are seemingly protected by equal pay and equal opportunity. Only worrisome fact is declining child-sex ratio and male-female sex ratio. Still women today are perhaps the most under-privileged section of society. Worse, over the years their position has deteriorated in many respects as seen most glaringly in the sex ratio where female foeticide has resulted in the ratio declining from 945 in 1991 to 927 in 2001. Maternal mortality rates are at 407 per 10,000 live births as compared to just 92 in Sri Lanka and 56 in China. Wage differentials for men and women show a marked deterioration between 2000 and 2004.

What Should be New Roadmap for Women Empowerment?

A lot of work needs to be done to close the gender divide:

1. Women should proactively identify and solve problems and jettison the habit of remaining silent through meetings.
2. They should put issues, which others have been avoiding, boldly on the table.
3. Organisations must create conditions for women's long-run career development, exposing them to a variety of experiences.
4. Recognising one's distinct roles helps one to exercise leadership at home or work.
5. Gender budgeting should be emphasized
6. We should create enabling environment through various affirmative developmental policies and programmes for development of women.
7. Provision of training, employment and income generation activities should be available to women.
8. Women should be allowed to enjoy rights and fundamentals freedom on par with men in all spheres.

CONCLUSION

If suggestions given above are implemented in right earnest they will certainly contribute significantly to having empowered women. The empowered new Indian women should discover ways of blending religious commitment, cultural traditions and family obligations with new work styles and leadership in various areas. That envisages flowering of an individual, strengthening of community, building institution and strengthening our country.

Hence, our slogans are

> "Eliminate Inequality, not Women", "Destroy Dowry, not Daughters", say "No" to Sex Discrimination, say "Yes" to Gender Justice.

REFERENCES

Assocham, An Industry Body (2007): "A Study", *The Economic Times*, 8 March, Kolkata Edition.

Janaki, D. (2005): "Universities as Boundary Breakers for Empowerment of the Socio-economically Weak in India", *University News*, Vol. 43, No. 47, November 21-27, p. 122

Singh, Kalpana (2006): "Conceptual and Critical Issues Relating to Gender and Development—An Analysis", Conference Volume, *Indain Economic Journal*, Kurukshetra University.

Sinha, Mithilesh Kumar, Kumar, Neeraj and Singh, Chandra P. (2006): "Gender Inequality: Some Issues", Conference Volume, *The Indian Economic Journal*, Kurukshetra University.

Rajaraman, Indira (2007): "Women in the Eleventh Plan", *The Economic Times*, March 19, Kolkata Edition.

Women Empowerment: Stress and Mental Health

Anjali Prasad and Jyoti Prasad

INTRODUCTION

Mankind experience over the millennia of his life on the planet reveals that women have lived in two parallel worlds ever since the first community habitation, shelter or village. They have occupied positions of eminence and authority, even gone into battle. They have also been objects of repression, uncalled for violence and petty tyrannies of the male bread earner. An enigma to be desired mankind has ever been willing to give women everything but equal status. Today a stage has arrived where she is almost an equal partner in the voyage of life.

WOMEN EMPOWERMENT: A CONCEPTUAL FRAMEWORK

Empowerment is a multidimensional social process that helps people to gain control over their own lives, communities, and their society, by acting on issues that they decline as important. Empowerment occurs within sociological, psychological, economic spheres and at various levels and challenges our assumptions about the *status quo*, asymmetrical power relationships and social dynamics. Empowerment of women involves economic opportunity, property rights, political representation, social equality, personal rights and so on. Many who argue for empowerment of women do so either with or without a full understanding of the conflicts between the historical and contemporary status of women in the patriarchy and the goals of empowerment. Changes that have occurred in the direction of change in the status of women in India, but women have yet to achieve many of the ideal stages of empowerment. Empowerment may be defined as a process rather than an end point.

The process of empowerment is taking place at so many levels that it is quite difficult to gauge the actual nature and extent of empowerment in improving the status of women. The realities of women, most of the times, are even deprived of some of the fundamental human rights and this denial is often justified in the name of tradition. Without the power to work and earn a good income, their voices are silenced, as they are economically dependent and have no capacity to work and earn a living for themselves.

As more women enter the world of work the significant majority of them basically consider their job as an integral part of their lives, where they look forward to advancing in career. Work is no longer a way in which men or women must earn his or her living and provide himself or herself with physical well being, but it brings a basic change in the ability of the individual's energy, thus becoming a way of life by which an individual finds his or her identification. The increasing number of women in work force is indicative of the fact that they are sucked up into the labour force by expansion of the sectors of economy that rely heavily on women workers. The implications of employment ranges from negative to positive depending upon working women aspirations, involvement with the occupations and obligations for the family which are in turn dependent on their educational level and marital status. They can also regard their work as extension of their housework and thus having an integrated attitude towards both.

THE NATIONAL POLICY OF EMPOWERING WOMEN

In a society where men control the destiny of women how is it possible to empower women and take care of their mental health and stress. The National Policy of Empowerment of Women has set certain clear cut goals and objectives.

1. Creating an environment through positive economic and social policies for full development of women to enable them to realize their full potential.
2. The *dejure* and *defecto* enjoyment of all human rights and fundamental freedom by women on equal basis with men in all spheres.
3. Equal access to participation and decision-making of women in social political and economic life of the nation.
4. Equal access to women to healthcare, education quality at all levels, career and vocational guidance, employment, equal remuneration, occupational health and safety, etc.
5. Strengthening legal system aimed at elimination of all forms of discrimination against changing social attitude and community practices by active participation and involvement of both men and women.
6. Ministering a gender perspective in the development process.
7. Elimination of discrimination and all forms of violence against women and the girl child; and
8. Building and strengthening partnerships with civil society, particularly women's organisations.

In order to meet these goals the policy suggests the following measures:

1. Legal-judicial system will be made more responsive and gender sensitive to women's needs. New laws will be enacted and existing law reviewed for quick justice.
2. The policy would aim to encourage changes in personal laws such as those related to marriage, divorce maintenance and guardianship so as to eliminate discrimination against women.

3. The policy will aim to encourage changes in law relating to ownership of property and inheritance by evolving consensus in order to make them gender just.

The question of female employment has gained prominence as a world-wide phenomenon. Working women's role has significant and wide implications for the society and family which does not have any role model from the past. Professional women and stress go together. Women are accordingly more prone to stress due to their active dual role and competing in a male dominated environment.

The term stress has been borrowed from physical science where it is used to mean force, pressure or strain applied on an organism which resists this force and struggles to maintain its original position. Hans Selye (1946) observed the reactions of his arrival subjects to a variety of stimuli and proposed three stages in the "General Adaptation Syndrome (GAS)" model to explain the stress phenomenon.

- Alarm Reaction Stage
- Resistance Stage
- Exhaustion Stage

Stress is a dynamic condition in which an individual is confronted with an opportunity, constraint or demand related to what the individual desires and for which the outcome is perceived to be both uncertain and important. Hence stress involves an interaction between the individual and the environment. However, stress is essentially a psychological and internal phenomenon and its level is subservient, to many factors like perception of the individual, his capacity to deal with the situation and the importance of the possible outcome thereof, etc.

Surveying the definition of stress Tom Cox (1978) has described three clauses of stress (i) as a response, i.e. to an external stimulus, (ii) as a stimulus, i.e. as a stressor itself, and (iii) as an intervening variable.

The ways in which stress is understood and dealt is heavily influenced by role conflict or role stress which is often used interchangeably when talked about the mental health of professional women. Given are the potential sources of possible stresses for a working women.

1. *Role Ambiguity*—Professionals' lack of confidence and knowledge that they knew what others thought and expected of them.
2. *Work Amount*—Time pressures related to having a great deal of work to do.
3. *Available Time*—Not having the available time to devote to desired professional activities.
4. *Invested*—Professional feels that most important things that happen to her involve her job.
5. *Work Conflict*—Feeling not like by work colleagues and feeling of conflicting values with them.
6. *Work Imposing on Family* (*WIF*)—Occurrence of situations in which professionals have to miss out on family or household activity due to work.
7. *WIF Strain*—Diminished enjoyment of family activities due to thoughts of work responsibility.
8. *Family Imposing on Work Stress* (*FIW*)—Occurrence of situation in which professional work is curtailed due to family situations.
9. *FIW Strain*—Diminished enjoyment of work-related activities due to thoughts of family or home responsibilities.
10. *Work Imposing on Relaxation* (*WIR*) *Strain*—Diminished enjoyment of relaxations time due to thoughts of work responsibilities.
11. *FIR Strain*—Diminished enjoyment of relaxation time due to thoughts of family responsibilities.
12. *Work Affects Husband* (*WAH*) *Negatively*—Degree to which professional career leaves her exhausted and not left with time to enjoy with husband and provide support for which career.
13. *Family Affects Work* (*FAW*) *Negatively*—Degree to which having a family is perceived as slowing down career development and hindering performance at work.
14. *Work Affects Children* (*WAC*) *Negatively*—Degree to which professionals perceived having career deprived them of

rewarding aspects of parenting and causing them to treat children less patiently and devote less time to them than desired.

15. *Overall Suffering*—Degree to which performance in career suffered due to her family responsibilities, relationship with husband and children suffered because of career.

Mental Health

Sociologist and Psychologist have been concerned with how women's well-being is influenced by her involvement in different roles. The more roles one occupies, more obligations one faces; since the social structure normally creates overly demanding role obligations. Exploring the conceptual clarity, mental health has been defined as absence of mental illness to the extent that one is free from anxiety, depression, negative effect, psycho-physiological symptoms, etc. One is considered to be in good mental health. During the last two decades, mental health has come to be defined in terms of psychological well-being which includes happiness, life satisfaction and self esteem.

Stress and Working Women

The women of today have opted for new horizons and paths to satisfy her quest for self-expression and creativity. She strives to be economically, psychologically independent and attain her own social status, leading to harmonious family existence. This ultimately takes her towards acquisition of everything that her mail counterparts could think of achieving for themselves. With the influx of women into the employment market in India there have been definite changes with regard to the established norms regarding the position and status assign to them. As part of international phenomena women of all cast, creeds progressed and reached new paradigms. Women are taking extra role of self-expression, exercising creativity wherever and in whichever field they are striving hard to achieve the objective of self-role. This new role is in addition to the age old assigned role of bearing and rearing a child and management of domestic and household responsibilities.

At the level of reality, the woman of today is confronted with at least a few significant questions; Firstly, to work towards her work and career goals and assign time and effort to them;

Secondly, to sort out and fulfill the expectations of her assigned roles as wife and mother and to devote time and effort for it; and

Thirdly, to manage the problems arising out of meeting the obligations and requirement of these two separate sphere.

GENDER EQUALITY

Gender equality and empowerment of women is recognized globally as a key element to achieve progress in all areas. Gender equality means equal opportunities for men and women in all meals of life. In equality between men and women is one of the most crucial disparities in Indian society. Both inside and outside the household women are excluded from positions of power. They are denied opportunities to participate in the decision-making process, even when decisions are to affect their well-being. The primary challenge facing women today is to increase their participation to that they get hold of situation and become activity involved in the process of decision-making. Active participation in social, economic and political spheres would help in enhancing the process of empowerment and it would also give women the deceased self-respect and social dignity which are the pre-requisites of empowerment.

India with its vision of a new-economic regime has an urgency to guarantee the spirit of equality and social justice envisioned in the constitution. As per the 2001 census, women constituted about 48% of the total population of the country. Women suffer many disadvantages as compared to men in the areas of educations, labour participation rate and earnings.

The most glaring example of discrimination against women in India, is the literacy rate, which as low as 33% in Bihar to 54.16% for the country as a whole as per census 2001. The largest chunk of illiterate women in the world is in India. As shown in Table 1, as per Census, 2001 female literacy rate is 54.16% as against 75-85% for males. The so-called past "gains" in women's education is reflected in the female literacy rate shows an increase from 29.76% in 1981 to 54.16% in 2001.

TABLE 1

Literacy Rate (1951-2001)

Year	*Female*	*Male*	*Male-female gap in literacy rate*
1951	8.86	27.16	18.30
1961	15.34	40.40	25.06
1971	21.97	45.95	23.98
1981	29.76	56.38	26.62
1991	39.29	64.18	24.89
2001	54.16	75.85	21.69

Source: Census of India of respective years Govt. of India, New Delhi.

It has been revealed by the 2001 census for the first times the absolute under of female illiterate has come down from 200.07 million in 1991 to 189.6. As shown in Table 2 the number of women in higher education which includes colleges, universities, professional colleges of engineering, medicine, technology, etc. has also increased from 1.32 million (33.0%) in 1990-91 to 3.03 million (39.8%) in 1999-2000. The number of women enrolled has shown an increase in both absolute and relative terms.

Issues

The work and family life of individuals cannot be dichotomized and studied in isolation. The concept of role possesses a pivotal position in the life of a working women in the recent phenomenon. In the modern world material goods and standards of living determine social status to a great extent than family, education, etc. Gone are the days when aristocracy was based on birth in a certain family and such aristocracy was self-fulfilling.

Housework

Traditionally women are expected to work at home. This has been considered most essential for the subsistence of the family. The Indian women in majority wherever may go in pursuit of her cherished goals is dominated by rigid traditional beliefs, norms and values which make her prone to problems. She is faced with the dilemma of fulfilling the traditional expectations of her role and as a wife and dutiful daughter-in-law. The professional women give ample importance to the household work which needs to be managed. The extent of household works is demanding on their time, energy and required efforts. Work imposing on managing the household stress is quite widespread as most of the professionals experienced it. The traditional societies that assigned the role of home-maker to women were judicious in their approach as women were expected to perform one role that was commensurate with their interest and background. There was little discrepancy between what women understood to be there for most duties and responsibilities and the expectations of others and society at large. Hence what women wanted to do and be, was congruent with the expectations of the husband, children and other members.

TABLE 2

Enrolment of Girls in Graduation/Post Graduation/ Professional Courses (1990 to 2000)

Figures in million *Level*	*1990-91*		*1996-97*		*1999-2000*	
	Women	*Total*	*Women*	*Total*	*Women*	*Total*
Graduate (B.A./B.Sc./B.Com)	1.14 (34.7)	329	1.82 (37.2)	4.87	2.66 (40.9)	6.51
Post-graduate (M.A./M.Sc./M.Com)	0.12 (32.8)	0.35	0.17 (30.5)	0.54	0.22 (39.6)	0.55
Ph.D/D.Sc./D.Phill	0.01 (26.2)	0.03	0.01 (29.2)	0.04	0.02 (35.4)	0.05
B.E./B.Sc. (Eng.) B. Architecture	0.03	0.24 (10.9)	0.05	0.33 (14.9)	0.08	0.36 (22.0)
M.B.B.S.	0.03 (34.3)	0.08	0.04 (35.4)	0.12	0.05 (37.8)	0.14
Total	1.32	3.99 (33.0)	2.09 (35.3)	5.90	3.03 (39.8)	7.16

Notes: Figures within parentheses indicate percentage to total.
Source: Selected Educational Statistics for respective years, Department of Education, Ministry of Human Resource Development, GOI, N. Delhi

Child Care

Education and employment have contributed immensely in

shaping women's perceptions and expectations. They have facilitated changing norms and challenging values. The highly educated women are presumed to be most equal to men on all respect. But the mental stress she undergoes is incomparable when it comes to child care. Child care for several reasons remains major concerns of mothers. This is more when the child is small and needs the attention and the care prior to school going age. The working mothers are considered by others and also themselves bear the major responsibility of their children. The assumption of parental role usually magnifies certain gender linked expectations. With the presence of children, the equitable balance of task and responsibilities gets disturbed and there is a felt need for re-structuring of the relationship.

In a joint family elder person can take care of the child, posing lesser problem for the working mother as compared to mother in a nuclear family who have to rely upon other sources. Traditionally, in forced work arrangements, alternative pattern of parental role reversal based on spouse preferences or attempt to shared parenting experiment under strong social pressures and expectations. In area of child rearing societal norms and expectations work against dual career marriages.

The role strain of the wives involve fatigue, emotional depletion and in some case guilt. "A prestigious prize was bestowed to a professor in psychology for her pioneering work. During the ceremony she looked a little depressed when asked about the reason, she stated "she would have been much happier if her children had fared well academically rather than her being selected for the award". Work affecting children negatively, stress among professional women as it affects their children's academic performance it leaves to miss out on some of the rewarding aspects of being a parent or it causes to be short tempered, irritated with children. Thus the role conflict and stress undergone in terms of children and work depends upon the way a woman handles the situation and what the situation means to her.

Well-being

Importance should be laid on the conditions under which benefits of multiple roles out way its costs for the conservations of mental health. Women with marriages and career are better equipped to handle life changes. Steward and Salt (1981) found that young women with multiple role involvements showed fewer physical and psychological stress responses when faced with life changes, than their counterparts, who were involved with fewer roles. Within the institution of marriage a woman's powers or alternatively the influences she exercises in relationship with her husband, in relation to decision-making and receiving support for household management and childcare determines her well-being.

Another dimension of women's well-being is related to the unequal distribution of work and leisure according to gender. Women work longer hours then men and after carry a disproportionate share of the burden of coping with poverty. Usually women spend on an average 20% more time than men in rural areas and 6% move in urban areas because of their reproductive roles, their responsibilities relating to rearing of children and serving the aged persons in the family, their greater responsibility for agriculture work in family owned farms and barriers to their entry in labour markets.

Total work time in India is 391 minutes per day for men and 457 minutes per day for women. On an average women spends about 35% of their work time on market-related activities as against 92% by their male counterpart. Men spend only 8% of their work time in non-market activities while women spend about 65% of their total work time on non-market activities as shown in Table 3.

TABLE 3

Average Total Work Time of Men and Women and its Allocation in India, 2000 (Percentage)

Activities	*Total work time spent*		*All persons*
	Women	*Men*	
Market activities	35	92	61
Non-market activities	65	8	39
Total	100	100	100

Source: UNDP (2005); Human Development Report, 2005, Oxford University Press.

Marital Satisfaction

The dynamic of work-home interface stress can be rightly

understood in the light of husband-wife relationship. On the one hand, there are couples who seem to cope with both partners working with so much ease that others are almost compelled to emulate them. At the other extreme there are couples for whom the very mentions of the wives career are taboo. In between these two extremes are those who are in double mind: they don't want to give up the luxury which the dual packet brings but find coping on both fronts and sharing each other's role extremely stressful.

Not every dual career family is stressful; it depends upon the compatibility in a relationship. Charls Handy (1978) used four-fold model to understand husband wife relationship.

I. *The thrusting husband and the caring wife*: No cause for stress because life is structured and predictable.
II. *Both husband and wife are thrusting*: A lot of stress can be seen because the husband tries his best to get the wife to adopt her traditional role.
III. *Two involved people both high achievers; not only are they enjoying own careers but also understanding each other*: The stress level is very high because both are basically thrusters, though tempered down by caring attitude.
IV. *Involved husband and a caring wife*: Husband is likely to be under considerable stress he wants to realize his ambitions without hurting others.

Negative conditions at work for women (work overload, unpleasant social environment, and lack of authority) have related to their perception of increased stress at home and low material satisfaction. According to Sears and Grahambos (1992) women's work experience spill over into their marital adjustment through their feelings of work stress and global stress.

Inter-Personal Relationship and in-Laws

In the Indian set-up of family, inter-personal relationship within the family are of great significance. A women professional along with pursuing a full time job or career, taking care of home and children is also confronted with the task of maintaining satisfactory relationship with other member of the family. This is true in a joint family. Her difficulty is experienced more in joint family as compared to nuclear family.

Commuting

The daily distance traveled by the professionals from their residence to place of work assumes significance in metropolitan cities where traveling long distance are mandatory. This fatigue associated with traveling could be source of physical and mental strain. It is not always possible for both the partners to find a suitable employment in same place. It is generally observed that husband's career takes priority while the wives career is accorded secondary status. In keeping with tradition she can not complain but one can hardly pre-suppose a lack of frustration and consequent stress.

At Work

The working women of today lives in the mental stress of coping with her dual responsibilities. The problems could be of a practical or emotional nature. How will she manages this depends on so many significant factors. The consequences of women going out to work has its own implications at different level. Lack of availability of women in the household has most obvious implications, her being in employment mainly depend on at least three factors:.

(i) The economic aspect, whereby how important one considered her financial contribution to the family;
(ii) The ideological orientation of the husband towards her role acceptance; and
(iii) Supportiveness extended both emotional and practical.

How significant she considered the work for her own self-esteem? The real dilemma for most women is that both the roles are dear to her. It is painful for them to sacrifice any of them or to take short cuts. And that is precisely how they remain in a state of conflict all through. It is not difficult to see, why males do not suffer from any such pull or push and they are only concerned about their performance at one role and that is, one of a bread earner.

In dual roles two spheres overlaps the lives of professional she is expected to make the sense of the coping skills to enact the roles to her own satisfaction and that is the significance of others surrounding her. Her dilemma is the one involving pressure in order to confirm or choose between options to reject and to enact. Additional depression is the time constraint between the personal goals *vs.* other goals. Significant is the question of process of rejection and acceptance in terms of satisfaction/dissatisfaction thereby affecting her mental health and adjustments.

The tools that are at her disposal are her personal competence and skills. In the process the women may respond with great pressure upon her physical and mental health in trying to meet all obligations with dignity and perfection. Stress does not affect the individual's motivation to work. It has negative relationship with job satisfaction which is not very significant. It also affects job involvement negatively. Career orientation bears a positively significant relationship.

Work done by women in homes is not accounted for the estimation of National Income. Similarly, work performed by women out of the preview of income generating activities also remains unaccounted. As shown in Table 4 the female work participation rate increased from 14.22% in 1971 to 25.7% in 200, still it is much lower than the male work participation rate in both rural and urban areas.

TABLE 4

Work Participation Rates by Sex (1981 to 2001)

(in per cent)

Census	*T/R/U*	*Female*	*Male*	*Persons*
1971	Total	14.2	52.7	34.2
	Rural	5.9	53.8	35.3
	Urban	7.2	48.9	29.6
1981	Total	19.7	52.6	36.7
	Rural	23.1	53.8	38.8
	Urban	8.3	49.1	30.0
1991	Total	22.3	51.6	37.5
	Rural	26.8	52.6	40.1
	Urban	9.2	48.9	30.2
2001	Total	25.7	51.9	39.3
	Rural	31.0	52.4	42.0
	Urban	11.6	50.9	32.3

Source: Census of India, 1991 and 2001, GOI, New Delhi.

The occupational pattern of work force shows that while male workers are engaged in jobs like cultivators, industrial workers and in service sectors which are of more stable nature, female workers are engaged as agricultural laborers in household industries and in less remunerative jobs.

Table 5 depicts the occupational pattern of India during the last census. This difference in occupational structure of Indian population makes women less self-reliant and less empowered.

TABLE 5

Occupational Pattern of Workforce in India, 2001

Category	*Share of male and female workers in various occupation*			*Share of male and female workers in each category*		
	Male	*Female*	*Total*	*Male*	*Female*	*Total*
1	2	3	4	5	6	7
Cultivation						
Total	32.59	34.8	33.10	75.53	24.46	100.00
Rural	45.20	41.46	44.22	75.42	24.58	100.00
Urban	2.57	3.58	2.72	79.93	20.07	100.00
Agricultural labourers						
Total	17.12	30.71	20.28	64.75	35.24	100.00
Rural	19.68	35.60	26.41	64.65	35.24	100.00
Urban	2.79	7.75	3.55	66.75	23.25	100.00
Household ***Industry workers***						
Total	3.13	6.44	3.90	61.52	48.48	100.00
Rural	4.92	5.48	30.63	60.45	39.55	100.00
Urban	3.48	10.98	4.62	63.85	36.20	100.00
Other Workers						
Total	47.16	28.02	42.71	84.73	15.27	100.00
Rural	28.68	17.47	25.74	60.45	39.55	100.00
Urban	91.15	77.68	89.10	63.81	36.19	100.00
Total Main Workers						
Total	100.00	100.00	100.00	76.72	23.28	100.00
Rural	100.00	100.00	100.00	73.78	26.22	100.00
Urban	100.00	100.00	100.00	84.76	15.23	100.00

(Contd.)

TABLE 5 (*Contd.*)

1	2	3	4	5	6	7
Percentage share of main workers to total workers						
Total	87.32	57.27	77.80	76.72	23.28	100.00
Rural	85.04	54.07	73.94	73.78	26.22	100.00
Urban	93.27	79.31	90.83	84.76	15.230	100.00
Percentage share of marginal workers to total workers						
Total	12.68	42.73	22.20	39.03	60.97	100.00
Rural	14.96	45.93	26.06	36.82	63.18	100.00
Urban	6.73	20.56	9.17	60.62	39.38	100.00

Source: Census of India, 2001, Series I, Registrar General of India, New Delhi.

Women share in various segments during census might be showing, a low degree of participation, however in practice, women hold substantial share in the workforce of various sectors, i.e. 90% in informal sector, 70% in agriculture sector, 35.53% in its allied sectors, 46.1% in Khadi and Village industries, 65.5% in Handloom and Sericulture, etc. In urban areas women workers are concentrated more in occupations like production and related works, domestic services, construction work, retail trading street vending and helping, etc. Similarly, women's employment in the public sector has also increased from 1.5 million (9.7%) in 1981 to 2.8 million (14.5%) in 1999. However, it is still much lower than that compared to men as is evident from Table 6. So far as women's share in organized sector is concerned it has steadily increased from 11.0% in 1971 to 17.2% in 1999. As Table 7 shows women's share is still very low in the organized sector.

TABLE 6

Women in the Public Sector (1981-99)

(*in million*)

Year	*Women*	*Men*	*Total*
1981	1.5	14.0	15.5
	(9.7)	(90.3)	(100.0)
1991	2.4	16.7	19.1
	(12.3)	(87.7)	(100.0)
1999	2.8	16.8	19.4
	(14.5)	(85.5)	(100.0)

Note: Figures in parenthesis indicate percentage to total.

Source: Director General of Employment and Training, Ministry of Labour, GOI, New Delhi.

TABLE 7

Women in Organized Sector (1971-99)

Year	*Public Sector*		*Private Sector*		*Total*	
	Women	*Men*	*Women*	*Men*	*Women*	*Men*
1971	8.6 (8.0)	98.7 (92.0)	10.8 (16.0)	56.8 (84.0)	19.3 (11.0)	155.6 (89.0)
1981	14.99 (9.7)	139.85 (90.3)	12.95 (17.5)	61.01 (82.5)	27.93 (12.2)	200.52 (87.8)
1991	23.47 (12.3)	167.1 (87.7)	14.34 (18.7)	62.43 (81.3)	37.81 (14.1)	229.52 (85.9)
1997	26.11 (13.8)	162.57 (86.2)	17.77 (20.4)	69.20 (79.6)	43.88 (15.9)	231.77 (84.1)
1999	28.0 (14.5)	166.0 (85.51)	20.0 (23.0)	67.0 (77.0)	48.0 (17.2)	233.0 (82.8)

Note: Figures in parenthesis are percentage.
Source: DGE&T, Ministry of Labour, GOI, New Delhi.

CONCLUSION

Women in India are being discriminated in the family, society, government and business organisations, in a big way. Intra household distribution of food and nutrients and allocation of resources makes the position of women worst. Gender inequality and poverty have a closed and director relationship affecting each other. General and stereotype measures for the upliftment of women fail to provide desired results. Hence, an area specific, sector specific and participatory approach is required to bridge the gender gap and bring the women at par with men.

Problems could be of practical or emotional in nature. How well she manages this depends on so many factors. Employment enhances the self-esteem and provides satisfaction of various needs of working, but, being with it its resultant stress surrounding the work and family. "It is better to pray for a stronger back than lighter cross" according to Rani Raute (1995), a practicing psycho-therapist each one has to face and straggle with some imperfect or non-optional condition. The list is never ending. No matter how we try, we all have to carry our cross. The only difference is in the size of the cross. Which is the only consideration? The problem is the task of strength needed to carry it. Thus life can be made much less stressful by simply trying to increase our internal resources for coping both qualitatively and quantitatively. Since stress is inevitable, learn how to cope with it rather than weighing a life stress. Former president A.P.J. Abdul Kalam said, empowering woman was a prerequisite for creating a good nation, "when women are empowered, society with stability is assured. Empowerment of women is essential as their thoughts and their value system lead the development of a good family, good society and ultimately a good nation."

References

Agrawal, Rita, *Stress in Life and at Work*, Saga Publication, New Delhi, 2001.

Arora, Poonam, *Professional Women—Role and Conflict*, Manak Publisher, New Delhi 2003.

Business Line, July 12, 2006, N. Delhi .

Cox, Tom, *Stress*, University Park Press, Hong Kong, 1980.

Dhaneja, S.K.: *Women Entrepreneurs*, Deep & Deep Publications Pvt. Ltd., New Delhi, 2002.

J. Bhagyalakshmi: "Women Entrepreneurs Miles to Go", *Yojana*, Vol. 48, Aug. 2004, p. 38.

Kaur, Amarjeet, "Poverty, Women and Heir Empowerment" in Pramilla Kapur (ed.) Empowering the Indian Women, Publication Division, GOI, New Delhi (2001).

Mishra, Laxmi, *Women Issues*, Northern Book Centre, New Delhi, 1992.

Philip, Tomy, Impact of Women Employment on Family and Marriage, *Social Change*, Vol. 32, No. 12, March-June, 2004.

Shah, Farooq A., Role of Stress in Indian Industry, *Indian Journal for Industrial Relation*, Vol. 38, No. 3, Jan. 2003.

Singh, Chandra Bhan Raj, "Women's Empowerment for Gender Equality—A Functional Analysis," *Kurukshetra*, Vol. 49, No. 11, Aug. 2001.

UNDP (2006), Human Development Report, 2005, Oxford University Press, New York.

Valsamma Antony: "Education and Employment—The key to Women Empowerment," *Kurukshetra*, Vol. 54, No. 4, Feb. 2006.

WOMEN AND EDUCATION IN INDIA

TALAT JABEEN AND MURSHID ALAM

INTRODUCTION

Education is prime factor for Women's Development and Empowerment. Through education it is possible to improve women's opportunities for participation in the various fields of life. Due to illiteracy women are deprived of their rights. For women empowerment women literacy is a key factor. Through achieving high female literacy rate it is possible to achieve women empowerment. For improving skills, the bare minimum is literacy. The relationship between educational attainments and awareness of hygiene, improvement in family health, child health, girl's education and general family welfare is well established, formal education delays marriage, kindles a desire for a small family, increases the chances of survival of children and has thus a positive effect on fertility reduction. It increases a women's earning capacity and the potential for empowerment. It is one of the most important tools of expanding social opportunity. But in India and the global level, gender inequalities are the barriers in the women literacy and women empowerment. 'Gender inequalities continue to limit girls' education. Policy planners and educationist have realised that without promoting education of women which is important section of humanity, growth and development of the society cannot take place. Women are almost one-half of the world's population. Since years women have been suffering from the social injustice. Gender in the present sense is not the biological difference between men and women but the power difference created by the society. Socio-cultural, economic political dimensions have bearing a women's education. The important hurdle is the attitude and behaviours, that is consciously inherent gender bias in our society. Education has long been one of the most decisive of our life-choices, the key to equal opportunity and the ladder to advancement. Without education, and especially without equal educational opportunities or skills and qualifications, men and women alike of certain classes and social groups have over the years been condemned to inferior status, women specially in their personal development, in their power to influence government leadership and decisions. Education conceived as organised instruction is part of the development process. Theoretically, education must enable persons to capture knowledge and necessary skills. Thus knowledge and skills should further enable them to compete for and acquire better occupational status or higher social status in life. Thus, education should lead to social and economic productivity of the individual and, as a corollary, of the society. These are some basic assumptions about education is an open and competitive society.

IMPORTANCE OF WOMEN EDUCATION

It is universally recognised that "mother is the first school of the child". In particular, education has come to be considered more important for women than men at least in theory. University Education Commission (1949) remarked: "There can be educated people without educated women. If general education had to be limited to men or the women, then opportunity should be given to women, from them it would more surely be passed to the next generations."

Jawaharlal Nehru very rightly observed, "Education of a boy

is the education of one person, but the education of a girl is the education of entire family."

The Kothari Commission (1964-66) stated, "For full development of human resources, the improvement of human beings and for moulding the character of children during the most impressionable years of infancy, the education of women is of great importance than that men."

Women play a prominent role in the cultural, economic, political, religious and social life of a country. Swami Vivekananda has emphasised, "If you do not raise the women who are living embodiment of the divine mother, do not think that you have any other way to rise."

PROBLEMS OF WOMEN EDUCATION IN INDIA

Committee on the status of Women in India, National Plan of Action for Women, National Policy on Education-1986 and National Perspective Plan-1990 studied and analysed that there is poor progress in girl's education/women education. Studies reveal that women of modern India are playing role in different fields which were earlier monopolized by men. For instance, politics, Science and Technology, Journalism, Administration, etc. In certain areas women have proved better than men e.g. medicine, teaching, nursing, social work, etc. The progress in the education of women in modern India is slow. The major problems related to women education in India are given below:

1. Domestic Duty

(a) Girls are required to devote time in domestic works at a very young age.

(b) In poor section of society, girls even perform such duties as bringing potable water, taking food to fields for parents engaged in work and looking after their young siblings.

(c) Girls in poor sections of society are required to work as paid and unpaid workers.

(d) Parents do not understand the importance of education of daughters. They give preference to boys as compared to girls.

2. Social Problems

Marriage of girls especially early marriage is one of the important factors/problems of women/girls education. It is serious problems in certain states in India, e.g. U.P., M.P., Bihar, Rajasthan and Gujarat.

3. Inadequate Facilities

There are many villages where there are no schools. In case the schools are there they lack physical facilities or infrastructure facilities like school building, sufficient and trained teachers. According to an estimate 44 percent of the primary schools do not have pucca building. Fifty-nine per cent schools do not have drinking water supply.

4. Sex Bias in Curricula and Policies

The curricula cover topics which show role of women as home-makers, wives and mother. Women should be held in curricula in modern roles. Contents in books sometime pose women as non-achievers, timid and dependent.

5. Economic Problem

The economic backwardness is an important barrier in the process of women education in India. The poor families cannot afford to pay high education fees. This problem is more severe in the rural areas. Because the percentage of rural poverty is more.

6. Dropouts

The high rate of dropouts in the rural areas is the principal factor for to low female literacy rate. There is evidence to show that physical inaccessibility, irrelevance of curricula, repeated 'failure' and even harsh treatment in schools contribute to children dropping out or never enrolling in school. It has been seen that in the case of girls the influence of these factors is even more acute.

FACTOR RESPONSIBLE ILLITERACY AMONG FEMALES SPECIALLY IN RURAL AREAS

1. Inadequate School Facilities

Many states do not have enough classrooms to accommodate

all school-age children. And the classrooms that are available often lack basic necessities such as sanitary and water.

2. Lack of Qualified Female Teachers

Girls are more likely to attend schools if they have female teachers. Girls are more comfortable and vocal with female teachers—this actively focusing and participating in the learning processes. Also, parents especially in rural areas are hesitant to send their girls to school that have only male teachers.

3. Lack of Transport Facilities

Particularly in rural areas, transportation is needed for girls to attend middle and secondary schools, which are often far away from their homes. Primary education is often accessible much closer, but secondary education facilities assume that children will dropout as they age, and therefore fewer schools are established to cater to older children.

4. Lack of Hostel Facilities for Girls

Many girls desirous of pursuing education above middle level, facilities for which are available away from their homes can not avail themselves of these facilities due to lack of hostel arrangements. Girls, particularly those belonging to scheduled castes and Scheduled Tribes would continue their education at middle and above levels if they could find free or inexpensive residential facilities nearer the educational institution.

5. Fear of Sexual Harassment

Parents often complain about insecurity for girls attending schools. Instances of abduction, rape and molestation of girls dampen the enthusiasm of parents and girl students in pursuing education beyond a certain age, thereafter they remain bound to their homes.

6. Fixed Schooling Hours

Fixed schooling hours do not suit girls in rural areas, as they are needed for domestic work at home or in farms and fields during these hours. This is one of the causes of lower participation rates of girls in education. The enrollment rate of girls and their retention can be improved if educational facilities are made available to girls during periods suitable to them when they are free from domestic chores.

These factors combine to produce unattractive environments in which girls must run the gauntlet of difficulties to remain in schools, as a result of which their learning is severely compromised even if they do remain. Countries that provided education for girls as well as boys experienced higher economic growth rates than those did not. Gender inequality in education also produced a moderate negative effect on economic growth and provision for basic needs. Many countries still do not have equality of education. There are many reasons for this including limited economic opportunities for girls; religious, societal and financial constraints; and parental concern for girls' safety arising from cultural traditions. Parents see the cost of their son's education as an investment because they will care for them in their old age. They may be unwilling to bear the educational cost of their daughters, because the girls normally will take with them the benefits to their husband's family.

STEPS TAKEN FOR UPLIFTMENT OF WOMEN EDUCATION IN INDIA

Realising the significance of vitality of human resource development, the Government at the centre and states have initiated several policies and programmes that have encouraged the participation of girls and women at all the levels of education (i.e. primary, upper primary, middle, higher secondary and the university levels). Some of the significant steps taken are as follows:

1. Education is made free for all girls upto the higher secondary stage, in most of the states have made girl's education free upto the university level.
2. Government provides assistance to boarding and hostel facilities for girl students of secondary and higher secondary schools. In this context Kasturba School has been open by the Central Government.
3. Government has opened special Women's study centres and cells in selected universities and colleges.

4. The University Grants Commission has also succeeded in creating the posts of part-time Research Associateship for women in Science and Humanities, including Social Sciences, Engineering and Technology.
5. Opening of Distance Education System and open universities have made higher education more accessible to all girls and women in urban areas, small towns and even in rural areas.
6. Conscious endeavour to improve the content and process of education from gender bias and sex stereotyping, and making the curriculum at all levels of education gender sensitive and gender friendly, so that gender justice, gender harmony and gender peace are achieved.
7. Efforts are consciously made by the government to encourage the involvement of girls in vocational and technical programmes. Steps are especially taken so that girls learn new skills and technology. In this connection the National Vocational Training Institute provides advanced skills in selected trades with high employment potentials. A new scheme, 'Technology for Women' was introduced in the universities during 1998-99 for providing financial assistance for the introduction of undergraduate courses in Engineering and Technology. Also, the strength of Industrial Training Institutes are being augmented—hundred new ITIs and Women's Wings are being set-up.

OBSERVATION

Positive initiatives of the govt. have helped in improving the participation of girls at all levels of education especially higher education since the post-independent period. During the last five decades the participation of girls has increased in Primary, Middle, Secondary/Higher Secondary stages, and higher education from 28.1% to 43.7%, from 16.1% to 40.9%, from 13.30% to 38.6% and from 10.0% to 36.89%, respectively. However, the participation of girls is still below fifty percent at all stages of education. Table 1 clearly show.

TABLE 1

Percentage of Girls' Enrolment of the Total Enrolment by Stages

Year	*Primary I-V*	*Middle VI-IX*	*Secondary/Higher Secondary 10+2/ Intermediate*	*Higher Education*
1950-51	28.1	16.1	13.3	10.0
1955-56	30.5	20.8	15.4	14.6
1960-61	32.6	23.9	20.5	16.0
1965-66	36.2	26.7	22.0	20.4
1970-71	37.4	29.3	25.0	20.0
1975-76	38.1	31.3	26.9	23.2
1980-81	38.6	32.9	29.6	26.7
1985-86	40.3	35.6	30.3	33.0
1990-91	41.5	36.7	32.9	33.3
1991-92	41.9	38.2	33.8	32.3
1992-93	42.6	38.8	33.9	33.2
1993-94	42.7	39.1	34.3	33.5
1994-95	42.9	39.3	35.9	34.0
1995-96	43.1	39.5	36.1	37.2
1996-97	43.4	39.8	36.2	38.2
1997-98	43.6	40.1	37.1	34.8
1998-99	43.5	40.5	37.8	38.8
1999-2000	43.6	40.4	38.9	39.9
2000-01	43.7	40.9	38.6	36.9

Source: Selected Educational Statistics—2000-01, p. 14.

FEMALE-MALE LITERACY RATE IN INDIA

The female-male literacy rates in India for the period 1951-2001 are shown in Table 2.

Table 2 indicates the female-male literacy rates in India for the period 1951 to 2001. In the year 1951 the female and male literacy rate was 8.86 and 27.16 percent respectively. The total literacy rate was 18.33 percent during the same year. In the year 2001, the total literacy rate reached to 65.38 percent. During 2001 the female and male literacy rates were 54.16 and 75.85 percent respectively. It is clear from the above data in Table 2 that the decennial increase in the female literacy rate was less than the male literacy rate for the period 1961 to 1981. However, during

TABLE 2

Female-Male Literacy Rates in India (1951-2001)

Year	Total Literacy	Female Literacy	Male Literacy	Female Literacy (decennial increase) (%age)	Male Literacy (decennial increase) (%age)	Difference between female-male Literacy rate
1951	18.33	8.86	27.16	—	—	18.30
1961	28.30	15.35	40.40	6.49	13.24	25.05
1971	34.45	21.97	45.96	6.62	5.56	23.99
1981	43.57	29.76	56.38	7.79	10.42	26.62
1991	52.21	39.29	64.13	9.53	7.75	24.84
2001	65.38	54.16	75.85	17.87	11.72	21.69

Source: India 2002—Information and Broadcasting Ministry, Govt. of India, New Delhi.

the year 1991 to 2001 the decennial percentage of female literacy rate was more than the decennial percentage of male literacy rate. This is the show the gender literacy gap is closing gradually. The female decennial literacy rate was 6.49 percent, which reached to 14.87 percent in 2001. During 1951 to 1981 there was widening gap between female literacy rates. The difference between the female-male literacy rates has decreased after 1991. In 1991, the difference between female-male literacy rate was 24.84 percent which declined to 21.69 percent in 2001. The gender gap in education is closing gradually, which may help for women empowerment in future in India.

The Enrolment of Girls in Various Courses at Higher Levels

Table 3 show clearly the enrolment of girls in various courses at higher levels which is given on next page.

Table 3 clearly depicts that girls have now started participating in higher and professional courses. The emerging courses that girls are now entering into are M.Com, B.Sc., B.Sc. (Hons), B.E., B.Sc., B. Arch., M.B.B.S. and so on. This is encouraging. It depicts that parents, especially from urban areas and from relatively good socio-economic backgrounds, are keen to send their daughter to higher education/professional courses. Participation of women in non-traditional courses has gradually eroded the myth of gender bias and sex stereotyping in courses and professions. This encouraging phenomena also explains why there is a gradual change in the status of women from ascribed to achieved status. However, this change is confined to urban areas only and among the educated classes. Girls belonging to the urban slum and rural areas continue to leg behind.

TABLE 3

Enrolment of Girls by Stages: 2002

Sl. No.	*Course*	*Boys*	*Girls*	*Total*
1.	Ph.D/D.Sc/D.Phil	29149 (64.8)	15855 (35.2)	45004
2.	M.A.	264262 (63.4)	152444 (36.6)	416706
3.	M.Sc.	70408 (55.5)	56365 (44.5)	126773
4.	M.Com.	64689 (62.3)	39170 (37.7)	103859
5.	B.A./B.A. (Hons)	2690712 (61.9)	1657325 (37.7)	4348037
6.	B.Sc./B.Sc. (Hons)	876722 (62.5)	525346 (37.5)	1402068
7.	B.Com./B.Com. (Hons)	964952 (64.6)	529858 (35.4)	1494810
8.	B.E./B.Sc./B.Arch.	324914 (77.7)	93279 (22.3)	418193
9.	B.Ed./B.T.	69625 (57.2)	52108 (42.8)	121733
10.	M.B.B.S.	88396 (59.4)	60303 (40.6)	148699
11.	Intermediate/ Jr. College/Pre-Degree/Pre-University	1583392 (65.4)	838680 (34.6)	2422072
12.	Higher Secondary (10+2 New Pattern XI-XIII Classes)	4493390 (60.5)	2935829 (39.5)	7429219

Source: Selected Educational Statistics—2000-01, pp. 15-18.

The growth in the number of women students in higher education since independence has been phenomenal while women constituted only 9.3 percent of all students in institutions of higher education on the eve of independence the percentage of women students enrolled in all colleges and universities was 34.1% in 1995-96. The pace of growth has been particularly faster in the last two decades, or so. The number of women enrolled, per hundred men, registered a four-fold increase during the period 1950-51 to 1995-96. Noteworthy factor of the general increase in the number of girl students in higher education is the uniformity in their enrollment at all levels of education faculty-wise. Arts stream accounts for the highest, followed by Commerce, Science, Education, Law, Engineering and Technology. The number of women colleges in the country has recorded substantial increase. It increased from 780 in 1986-87 to 1146 in 1995-96. It is significant that the University Grants Commission has a programme for promoting women's studies wherein it gives assistance to universities for setting up centres/cells for women studies. As on 31st March, 1996 the UGC had provided assistance to 33 universities and colleges for setting up such centres/cells (22 centres and 11 cells). At the time of Independence in 1947 we had only 20 universities and 500 colleges. The number of students and teachers in higher education system was very small. At the beginning of 1996-97 we have 209 universities and there is a tremendous increase in the number of colleges, i.e. from 500 to 9278 in which the number of women college is 1146. The women universities in the country (5), the number is very small, could take a lead in this matter in association with the UGC and the women study centres. They could specifically examine the issues and recommend to the government and the corporate sector the needs of girl students, desiring and deserving and to at least render financial and motivational assistance to those who go in for higher education.

STATE-WISE FEMALE-MALE LITERACY IN INDIA (2001)

Table 4 reveals high disparity in the literacy rate among all the states and union territories in India "The female and male literacy rates and overall literacy rate were highest in Kerala and lower in Bihar" in 2001. The disparity in the overall literacy rate among all the states in the country was 54.29 and 33.88 percent respectively. It is clear that there is still more disparity in female literacy rate than the male on overall literacy rate in India. There was also more disparity in the female and male literacy rates within the states. In Mizoram, there was lowest disparity (4.56%) between female-male literacy rates and the highest disparity (32.12%) was in Rajasthan state.

TABLE 4

State-wise Female-Male Literacy in India (2001)

Sl. No.	State/Union Territory	Total Literacy Rate	Male Literacy Rate	Female Literacy Rate	Difference between the female & male literacy rate
1.	Kerala	90.92	94.20	87.86	6.34
2.	Mizoram	88.89	90.69	86.13	4.56
3.	Lakshadweep	87.52	93.15	81.56	11.59
4.	Goa	82.32	88.88	75.51	13.37
5.	Delhi	81.82	87.37	75.00	12.37
6.	Chandigarh	87.76	85.65	76.65	9.00
7.	Pondicherry	81.49	88.89	74.13	14.76
8.	Andaman and Nikobar	81.18	86.07	75.29	10.78
9.	Daman and Diu	81.09	88.40	70.37	18.03
10.	Maharashtra	77.27	86.27	65.71	18.76
11.	Himachal Pradesh	77.13	86.02	68.08	17.94
12.	Tripura	73.66	81.47	65.41	16.06
13.	Tamil Nadu	73.47	82.33	64.55	17.78
14.	Uttranchal	72.28	84.01	60.26	23.75
15.	Gujarat	69.97	80.50	58.60	21.90
16.	Punjab	69.95	75.63	63.55	12.08
17.	Sikkim	69.68	76.73	61.46	15.27
18.	West Bengal	69.22	77.58	60.22	17.36
19.	Manipur	68.87	77.87	59.70	18.17
20.	Haryana	68.59	79.25	56.31	22.94
21.	Nagaland	67.11	71.77	61.92	9.85
22.	Karnataka	67.04	76.29	57.45	18.84
23.	Chattisgarh	65.18	77.86	52.40	25.46
24.	Assam	64.28	71.93	56.03	15.90
25.	Madhya Pradesh	64.11	76.80	50.28	25.52
26.	Orissa	63.61	75.95	50.97	24.98
27.	Meghalaya	63.31	66.14	60.41	5.73
28.	Andhra Pradesh	61.11	70.85	51.17	19.68
29.	Rajasthan	61.03	76.46	44.34	32.12
30.	Dadar & Nagar Haveli	60.03	73.32	42.99	30.33
31.	Uttar Pradesh	57.36	70.23	42.98	27.25
32.	Arunachal Pradesh	54.74	64.07	44.24	19.83
33.	Jammu & Kashmir	54.46	65.75	41.82	23.93
34.	Jharkhand	54.13	67.94	39.38	28.56
35.	Bihar	47.53	60.32	33.57	26.75
	India (Total)	65.38	75.85	54.16	21.69

Source: Government of India (2002), Information and Broadcasting Ministry, New Delhi.

CONCLUSION

Now it is a well-established fact that education is the most significant factor that has highest degree of positive correlation with social and economic development. The present study on gender disparity in literacy rate reveals widely differing trends. These trends however, conclude that with the gender increase in the literacy rate of females, the gender gap is fairly large, since the number of non-literate females is 189.6 million against 106.7 million non-literate males, that is, there are 83 million more non-literate females. The difference between the female-male literacy rates has decreased after 1991. In 1991, the difference between female-male literacy rate was 24.84 percent which declined to 21.69 percent in 2001. The growth in the number of women students in higher education since independence has been increased from 9.3 percent to 34.1 percent in 1995-96. The participation of women in every field of education has also been increased. The disparity in the overall literacy rate among all the states in the country was 54.29 and 33.88 percent respectively. It is clear that there is still more disparity in the female literacy rate that the male on overall literacy rate in India. Therefore, sincere efforts must be made on increasing the literacy rates especially among women. The worst performing States/UTs, Orissa, Chhatisgarh, M.P., Bihar, U.P., Jharkhand, Dadar and Nagar Haweli and Rajasthan need more attention.

SUGGESTIONS FOR IMPROVING GIRLS/WOMEN EDUCATION

For improving the women education the following steps should be taken:

1. Use of media for promoting awareness among masses for Women Education/Girls Education. Media can play a significant role in developing awareness among masses regarding the education of women/girls.
2. Assistance in the form of cash or kind for primary education. Following steps can be useful for promoting girls/women education:
   (a) Some compensatory economic assistance should be

given to parents for sparing their girl children for education.

(b) Social service agencies or Government may extend assistance in the shape of cash and kind to the girls of poor families. There is a scheme in Maharashtra known as 'Savitribai Phule Foster Parent Scheme'. Under this scheme, poor families are economically helped for the completion of primary education of their daughters.

3. Educated women should be provided opportunities of employment in various sections of the society.
4. Environment, quality of teachers should be improved. Their qualification and competencies should be better. The teaching-learning environment should be good so that students may like to attend school and develop interest in studies.
5. Contents covered in text books should not deal with reading material which shows sex bias. The curricula should be revised accordingly.
6. Every primary school should have at least two all weather rooms, a second teacher preferably a female teacher in single teacher schools and essential teaching and learning materials.
7. To create more non-farm employment opportunities for women especially in the rural areas so that income level of the rural families can be increased.
8. The Government should provide more attention towards the compulsory education programme. It will help in improving the female literacy rate.
9. The Government should promote higher and technical educational facilities in the rural areas. There should be special incentive package for women education.
10. It is necessary to develop infrastructure facilities in the rural areas. It will help to accelerate the education process.
11. The Anti-Dowry Act should be strictly implemented.
12. It is necessary to ensure registration of marriages to arrest marriages below the age, which is legally permissible. The tradition of early marriages should be prohibited.

13. To create more awareness about women education in the rural areas.
14. The network of distant education should be developed in the rural areas.
15. It is essential to focus special efforts towards rural women.

REFERENCES

Government of India, Economic Survey, 2003-04.

Human Development Report (UNDP), 2005.

Kurukshetra, A Journal on Rural Development, Vol. 55, No. 1, November 2006.

University News, 41 (11), March 17-23, 2003.

Development of Education System in India, by Tara Chand (2004), Anmol Publications Pvt. Ltd., New Delhi.

Anand, Sudhir, and Amartya Sen (1995), "Gender Inequality in Human Development: Theories and Measurement", Occasional paper 19, United Nations Development Programme, Human Development Report Office.

Anandalakshmy, S. (ed.) (1994): "The Girl-child and the Family: Department of Women and Child Development, MHRD, Government of India, New Delhi.

The Indian Economic Association, 89th Annual Conference Volume, 27-29 December, 2006, Part II.

Third World Impact, April-June 2006.

WOMEN: EDUCATION AND HEALTH

RAJESH SHUKLA, RANJANA SHUKLA AND RAJESH RANJAN

Ours is a traditional society. Every aspect of our life is deeply steeped in values. Looking at the things in this perspective, theoretically the position of a woman in our society is considered as very high but practically it is not so. The general subordination of women assumed a particularly severe form in India through the powerful instrument of religious traditions which have shaped social practices. A marked feature of Hindu society is its legal sanction for an extreme expression of social stratification in which women and the lower castes have been subjected to humiliating conditions of existence.[1] On the one hand, she is an embodiment of all powerful goddess Durga, a symbol of Shakti, but on the other, is always an effeminate figure, controlled by male counterpart. Although, she represents all good things happening on the earth and is considered as the beauty interwoven in poetry of life but unfortunately, she loses her individuality, as she is to be protected by her father in her youth, by her husband after her marriage and is looked after by her son in the old age. What is worse is that in spite of hard work, inside home or at the workplace, her contribution is not rated properly, rather she is sacrificed at alter of chauvinistic male world, every now and then. The subordination of woman is a common feature at almost all stages of history, and is prevalent in large parts of the world. Certainly, the extent and form of that subordination has been conditioned by the social and cultural environment in which women have been placed and the role of education and health are the parameters on which their status in the society is dependent.

If we look back into the early period of our history, it is found that even during the early patriarchal Vedic age, a woman; only in the capacity of an obedient daughter and a sincere wife, is admitted to the privileges of higher education. Although she was equally entitled for the sacred thread ceremony (Upanayana) and resided with the family of the teacher or Guru for several years in the gurukul along with the male students, but had to maintain complete celibacy to complete her Vedic studies. Women who dedicated their lives to the cause of education were called brahmavadini, and those who chose to enter the family life after completion of their studies were called sadyovadhu. The early Vedic literature is full of many instances where education of the time received great contribution from women scholars like Vishwavara, Lopamudra, Aitreyi, Apala, Ghosha, Siphal and so on. In the Later Vedic age also, we come across several learned ladies like Maitreyi, Gargi, Sachi and others. During the Vedic period, flourished a number of women teachers who taught philosophy and rituals. Those teachers were designated as Acharya, Upadhyaya, and Audhamedhya. The term gandharvagrhita, meaning married to the Gandharavas, was in vogue particularly for unmarried women teachers. In fact, in the later Vedic traditions also it is mentioned explicitly that getting a husband by virtue of brahmacharya (celibacy) and complete education is highly appreciable.

In the post-Vedic period, Jayanti and Sahasranika contributed a lot to Jain literature in the fifth-fourth centuries B.C. Sanghmitra, daughter of Emperor Asoka propagated Buddhism in Sri Lanka. The Therigatha comprised poetry of fifty nuns, who were great scholars of Buddhist ideology. Subha and Anupama wrote extensively on philosophy.[2]

The Epic period as referred to in the literature of the age; and as mentioned in the Epics, about the remarkable achievements of the women in the field of education. The Ramayan lays down that Kaushalaya and Tara were well versed in the incantations and Kaikeyee was specialist in the field of military science. The Mahabharata at several places extols that Draupadi was an enlightened lady and Uttara excelled in fine arts. Bhasa, a great Sanskrit scholar of the first century describes Vasavadatta as a great diplomatic lady. The Puranic literature of the early period mentions Bhavana, Aparna, Ekaparna, Ekapatala Mena, Dharini, Sanati and Shatarupa as experts in metaphysics. Epigraphic sources reveal that Naganika of the Satavahana dynasty and Prabhavatigupta of the Vakataka dynasty and Akka and Bhailadevi of Chalukya dynasty of Gujarat were successful rulers, warriors and well-versed in administration.[3]

During the golden age of the Gupta period, literary and cultural education was imparted to the girls in the well-to-do families and several women like Sil, Bhattarika, etc. figure as authoresses and poetesses, in the age. In the later part of the Rajput period, the women seem to have received proper education, cultivated the fine arts and sciences and into debates and discussions with the great scholars of the time. The great Sankaracharya, a passionate propagator of the Hindu philosophical thought in all the directions, is said to be defeated, on one occasion, by a poor Brahmin lady called Bharti, the wife of Mandan Mishra, Avanti Sundari, the wife of the famous poet Raja Shekhar, was renowned for her scholarship. Indulekha, Marula, Morika, Vijjika, Shila, Shubhadra, Padmasri, Madalsa, Lakshmi, etc. were well-known poetesses of Sanskrit of the period under review.

Later, in the Mughal period, the great ruler Akbar established a girls' school in his palace at Fatehpur Sikri. Actually, Mughal rulers were great patrons of education. Although, women due to purdah system could not attend public institutions but in nearly every nobleman's establishment, a school mistress or governess was kept and Mughal rulers employed learned Persian women to teach their girls. The ladies studied the humanities in preference to theology and Persian rather than Arabic. They also had to take the religious teachings through holy Koran. Many Muslim women were patrons of literature and themselves writers. The memoirs of Gulbadan Banu Begum, the talented daughter of Babar, are well-known, and Akbar's foster mother, Maham Anaga, endowed a college at Delhi. Some of the Mughal princesses—Salima Sultana, Akbar's wife, Nur Jahan, Mumtaz Mahal and Jahan Ara Begum, the daughter of Shah Jahan, and Zeb-un-nisa, the daughter of Aurangzeb distinguished themselves in literature.[4] In fact, the royal patronage of the times saw that education is imparted to the elite women of the society.

In spite of the great saga of the women, education in general for women began to deteriorate in the later Vedic period only. It was to be so because of growing orthodox caste system in the post-Vedic society. It was quite apparent that while the Kshatriyas made their sway over mahajanapadas by acquiring sovereignty while the Brahmanas kept general populace under their own sway through strict control of the Vedic and ritualistic performance. Growing importance of male child as a descendant in the property also contributed in the weakening of the social and economic condition of women. The Dayabhag mentions that the Sati system intended to snatch the property of the widows. Probably, it aimed at formally acknowledging and strengthening the right of lineal male descendants to inherit their property. The life of widows was miserable and they began to be considered to have incurred heavy sins, hence the system. The Sati, child marriage and a number of anti-social customs began to prevail in our society and affected women education badly. Coming down to the Gupta period, women were almost deprived of proper education barring a few examples to those of much limited royal families—kingly and bureaucratic but there too limited subjects. During the Rajput period in the Indian history women are seen as the most loyal, sincere better half, who had no choice or freedom to lead her life after the death of her husband. She had to perform Jauhar, in the name of safeguarding her self-respect. More often than not, it was committed in bulk, to protect her chastity from the marauding invaders. Even Sati and girl child killing (infanticide) was prevalent in many parts of Rajasthan. In fact, all these social banes strongly indicate towards the lack of education among the woman folk. During the Sultanat and Mughal period, women education was confined to the privileged few—it was mostly closeted to the royal harem and ladies. Both for Muslims and Hindus, education was mostly a private concern, interwoven certainly with religion. Actually, at the primary level, every mosque had a maqtab, a primary school, where girls and boys from neighbourhood received elementary education. Only very advanced ones went to the madrasas or colleges and that too for studying mainly theology.

During the 15th and 16th century India, we see the entire country dotted with migratory Sufi and indigenous Bhakti saints, who spread the message of love and devotion to God through their preaching all over country. They treated men and women as equals.

But same is not the condition of women in the 19th century India, as we see the social reformers of the time raising the question of unequal status of the women in the society. To begin with; Raja Rammohun Roy, Ishwar Chandra Vidyasagar, M.G. Ranade, Maharshi Karve, Jyotiba Phule, Dayanand Saraswati were quite concerned about the position of women in the society. Legislation brought by the British government of the times, of course at the behest of the liberal Indians played an important role in improving the role and status of women. The severe disabilities from which an Indian woman passed at the beginning of the 19th century were too numerous and drastic and were gradually removed through laws and successive amendments. Lord William Bentinck at the instance of Rammohun Roy abolished Sati System through a regulation in 1829. The Widow Remarriage Act, 1856, the Civil Marriage Act of 1872, The Married Women Property Act of 1874 and the Age of Consent Act of 1881 led to emancipation of the women in India. The Sarada Act of 1929 also came to rescue the girl child while it legislated on the marriageable age. Now, it has been amended to raise the marriageable age for boys and girls to 21 and 18 respectively. The Marriage Validation Act of 1892 and the Special Marriage Act of 1954 permitted inter-caste and inter-religious marriages. The Hindu Marriage Act of 1955 is a major social legislation covering all aspects of Hindu marriage and amended sometime back to liberalize the provisions in favour of women. The Hindu Succession Act of 1956 confers property rights on women. Similarly, The Hindu Adoption and Maintenance Act, 1956 as well as The Dowry Prohibition Act were brought to provide them much needed relief. During the freedom movement, Gandhiji had made the masses join the struggle against the mighty British imperialist force, which also included the women—Annie Besant, Sarojini Naidu, Kamladevi Chttopadhya, Vijayalaxmi Pandit, Renu Chakravarti, Indira Gandhi, etc. And after hard earned independence from the British rule, an Indian Constitution was adopted, which guaranteed equality to all its citizens, gave social, economic and political justice and recognized liberty of thought, expression, belief and worship. Now, men and women are considered equal in the eyes of law. In fact, with the constitutional safeguards, many types of problem faced by the women in our society were solved to some extent. The age old issue of discrimination, inferior social position and consequent subjects of health and education were met theoretically at a stroke but on a practical level lot of work has to be done in this field.

However, one must forget that there was a time in our lives when it was firmly believed that a girl does not need education and her role was just confined to look after the household affairs, more explicitly said; for housekeeping. One just cannot imagine her domain outside family. In fact, there was a strong belief that if a woman is educated she will become widow! However, the social reformers in the 19th century India were perhaps the firs. to visualize the value of education for women. Probably, they realized the potential of educated woman in reforming the contemporary Indian society. Actually, at that time education was looked upon as an emancipator from the age old traditional values, which have kept her in chains for so long. Gradually, it was fully accepted that women had more important role to play in the social development and also to perform outside the family limits.

In the mid-20th century, we can see perceptible changes in the condition of the women in all spheres of life. Moreover, the 'Women lib' became very active during this period and even our country witnessed a strong wave against all forms of 'patriarchy'. In the present world when the things are moving at very fast pace and the impact of globalisation can be seen on each and every aspect of our life, a woman cannot be kept on the sidelines. The impact on her status in general and on her health and education in particular is clearly visible. The women population consists of about half of the world population and human progress cannot be realized fully by ignoring them. Their participation in the desired field of socio-economic development and for the comprehensive welfare of the human beings has become a 'necessity' and not merely a 'wish' or a 'desire', as expressed by an individual, anywhere-anytime.

It is aptly said that 'if you educate a man, you educate an individual, while if you educate a woman, you educate the whole family.' Although, there has been substantial change from pre-independence India, the goal of primary universal education is far from realized and the phenomenon has Pan-India shades. On the global level, there are 86 countries in the world that have yet to achieve universal primary education. Every effort is being carried out so that both boys and girls will receive full course of primary schooling by the year 2015. In present conditions, 58 countries will still not have done so by 2015. But there are hopes rife that progress will be speeded up, with attention in the better performing countries now switching to quality of education and expansion of secondary schooling.

On current trends, the two indicators used to monitor progress in meeting the goal are the percentage of children enrolled in primary schools and those who complete this stage of education by reaching the grade five or "primary completion rate." Both developed and developing countries have put considerable effort into achieving the education goal, and the UNICEF report says there has been "substantial progress." If we look into a particular example of a sub-Saharan African state of Tanzania, it is on the course to achieve 100 percent primary participation by 2015 although as a whole the region will not be able to meet the target without more rapid progress over the next seven years. The United Kingdom has a 10-year ten billion pound programme for education in developing countries. According to the UNICEF report, more than 85 percent of primary school-age children are receiving a basic education though the figure drops to 70 percent in eastern and southern region of the subcontinent, and is just 62 percent in west and central parts. Between 2002 and 2005, the number of children out of school dropped from 115 million to 93 million, and of those without a school place, 41 million live in Sub-Saharan Africa and a further 31.5 million live in South Asia. Actual attendance rates tend to be lower than enrolment rates. In eastern Africa, for instance, fewer than three out of five children attend the school at the primary level and the UNICEF says that some of those pupils are of Secondary school age, which started their education late or are retaking grades. It further says that reaching the last 10 percent of children out of school is a "particular challenge". Another area which needs to be looked after is gender gap, empowerment of women, etc. The focus will certainly help the cause of women by filling the chasm between boys and girls receiving a primary education. In fact, the gap between both was narrowed from 8 per cent points to 3 per cent points during the years 1990 and 2005. But according to UNICEF the big gender disparity remains, particularly in West and Central Africa, West Asia and North Africa, and South Asia. Only 2/3rds of the countries met the target of gender parity in primary education by 2005, with only 1/3rd achieving that in secondary education. It is found that gender disparities are greatest in rural areas and among poor households. Here, also the target is fixed so that to eliminate gender disparity in primary and secondary education, not later than 2015. [5]

Whatever may be the plan and programmes of UNICEF, to meet the educational and health requirements of women all over the world, every care is being taken up for them, whether it is equality, liberty or any other social needs of theirs in the developed countries; but the same situation does not prevail for them in the developing world, what to say about the underdeveloped parts of the world. School drop-out rate is directly related with the development index which consists of the important parameters of health and education apart from others, i.e. women are more likely to complete fewer years in school than men. In fact, some socio-economic and educational factors affect the access or retention of a girl child in the schools. Firstly, the girls are considered to be useful as workers/helpers in the household matters; poorer families prefer to send their boy child to schools rather than the girls as the latter are needed to look after siblings or does some other work at home. Poor families and their economic needs, for even a meager sum as a contribution towards family kitty consider education up to some level for a girl child as unnecessary. Drop-outs from the school level can be seen among the girl child more because early marriage phenomenon or restriction on their movement and least decision-making power to her, also affect negatively. Although, literacy rates have climbed up in the recent years, women record a larger proportion of illiterates in the world. Even the World Bank rightly called the women's education the single most influential investment that can be made in the developing world. In fact, the women education is associated directly with the smaller family size and women with ten or more years of schooling have half the number of children as compared to that of women with no education at all! The disparity or gender bias is starker at the secondary level of education. Lower level of enrolment is due to different socio-economic and cultural factors. These also include reasons like high child mortality rate especially among the girl child as the preference for a boy child is practiced at the very outset, leading to all kinds of discrimination and differentiation. Early child bearing, child marriage, house-hold duties, etc. also do not help the cause of women. However, if we look at the higher education, scenario is slightly different. Despite regional variations, going to college is more an urban middle class phenomenon and is a preserve of the elite section of the society. As compared to the University going 5 percentage boys, the girl child constitute about 3 percent, which is not very rosy either. The data given here suggests that education is still a preserve of the elite section of the society and if the girls are able to break through the barriers of the prejudices against themselves, their forward march is easily possible.

At this point of time, a very relevant question that comes in our mind is about the basic objective of higher education for girls and women. In the background of elitist nature of education, the centres of higher education are not only considered as institutions of learning but as waiting place for girls, who wait for a few more years in the colleges with a wish to marry as soon as a suitable bridegroom is made available to them. Even the media, through all its apparatuses has projected it like that. Media, inadvertently, has created a negative image about women in the society and she is bestowed with the negative qualities like aggressiveness and undue assertion of her rights. With this kind of situation, the problem of adjustability arises. It is widely believed that more educated girls and women are less likely to adjust in their lives as compared to less educated ones, who will blindfold follow, the dictates of the male members of their family.

Even in present 21st century society, chastity of a woman is valued above all qualities; permanence of relationship is also valued highly in this age of Live-in relationship. (Which is however, legalized by the Court of Law recently, to provide legitimacy to the off springs of such relationships. But how much social acclamation will it get, is a matter of wide speculation!)

Widowhood, divorced or single status of a woman is still considered as a 'unique thing' in the otherwise egalitarian society. In our society, marriage is invariably accompanied by the despicable practice of dowry. The boys with high education and in the government jobs yearn for high dowry and even girls with high education and a job have to pay dowry to get married. Sometimes, the greed for dowry leads to the worst incident of bride-burning or dowry death in its other manifestation and before such thing takes place, harassment of all kinds are imposed on the victim or even on their parents. To add insult to the injury, when no relief comes to the hapless woman, she is driven to the hopeless situation and more often than not, takes her own life.

Education and health of women constitutes an important part of social welfare in our country. A national plan of action has been formulated for this purpose. The conventional literacy for adult women, condensed course of education and vocational training for adult women, hostels for working women, training centres for rehabilitation of destitute women and many other socio-economic programmes for women are being implemented by the successive governments. The supplementary nutrition programmes provided special nutrition for pregnant and nursing mothers from the weaker section of society. The government of India, at the fourth World Women Conference in Beijing (China), announced that it will spend about 6 percent of GDP on education, to frame a national policy and to appoint a commission for inquiring into oppressions on women by appointing a commissioner and also to device a suitable mechanism for monitoring of women's education and health. Unfortunately, these promises made by the government of India are yet to be fulfilled.

So far health of a woman is concerned it is firmly believed that only a healthy woman can give birth to a healthy child. In fact, they are getting equal attention but in some areas of the world, which lags in socio-economic fronts, the girl child mortality rate is very high. The year 2006 saw, that too for the first time, that overall child mortality dropped below 10 million a year, to 9.7 million. Similarly, the maternal mortality rate is very high. The ratio of maternal deaths is 1 to 48 in less developed world, while it is 1 to 1800 in the developed one. In our country the Planning Commission envisaging for 11th Plan period (2007-12) has fixed the target at 1 per 1000 live births.[6]

However, it has proved very difficult to get accurate figures for maternal death in the developing world. Many countries have no system to register deaths from diseases such as acquired immune deficiency syndrome (AIDS) or even malaria; and will not be added to the maternal mortality count even though they are made more likely by pregnancy. Every year, half a million women die in pregnancy or childbirth, almost all of them in sub-Saharan Africa and Asia. Having a baby is a very high risk proposition in southern Africa. According to a recent report published in the UNICEF report, a woman there has a one in twenty-two lifetime chance of dying in pregnancy or childbirth compared to one in eight thousand in countries such as U.K.

Experts believe that the global rate of maternal mortality did come down between 1990 and 2005 but only by about 5.4 per cent. But not even this small rate of progress is being achieved in sub-Saharan Africa. According to a report from the World Bank, the World Health Organisation, UNICEF and the UN Population Fund, the number of maternal deaths actually rose in sub-Saharan Africa from 212,000 a year to 270,000 over that period. More than a third of deaths are caused by haemorrhage and 16 per cent by blood poisoning and infections including AIDS. Skilled birth attendan s play important role to reduce deaths, but sub-Saharan Africa only managed to increase their presence at births from 43 to 47 per cent and south Asia from 31 to 40 per cent. Also prevention of unplanned pregnancies could cut deaths by a quarter, but only 23 per cent of sub-Saharan African women use any form of contraception.[7]

HIV/AIDS emerged as a major disease in this world. It took its toll all over the world especially in the Western World as the practice of free sex was more prevalent. Awareness about the dreaded was less in those parts of globe; and unfortunately it was least in the developing countries of the world. UNAIDS is a UN programme, which keeps tab of the spread of the disease all over the world. It found that the number of the diseased people peaked in the late 1990s, when it was more than 3 million a year. Although, the advanced skill of treatment and general awareness about the disease helped to fight it successfully and the survival span also increased significantly but still lot has to be done in the low and middle-income group countries, in making the people of those places to comprehensively understand AIDS and to take appropriate measures to check its spread.

Apart from these, prostitution, coercive sexual practices, gender violence, poor hygiene conditions also lead to numerous health problems for a woman. Throughout historical time-scale she has been an object, whose sexuality and sensuality—her feminine qualities—had been a subject of sensuous discussion. In this age of globalisation, she is considered nothing but a commodity, which is salable at any price and has a value tag attached with. She is destined to suffer—from womb of a mother (foeticide), as an infant (infanticide) and if survived these onslaught, later on, under the masculine power of the society or patriarchal system.

Hence, it is imperative to ensure an environment, which makes the world a conducive and safe for them to thrive and grow, so that they can contribute substantially for the society and make it a better place for human beings to live.

Notes and References

1. Chakravarti, Uma, Conceptualizing Brahmanical Patriarchy in Early India Gender, Caste, Class and State, VIIth Refresher Course In History (Dec. 2-22, 2005), Gender and History, Dept. of History, Patna University, Patna, p. 1.
2. Arya, Samrendra Narayan, Women and Education in Early Indian Patriarchal Society, VIIth Refresher Course in History, Gender and History, P.U. Patna, p. 44.
3. *Ibid.*
4. Luniya, B.N., Evolution of Indian Culture, Indian Culture and the Mughals, Laxmi Narayan Agarwal, Agra-3, Sixteenth edition, reprint, 2001, p. 389.
5. *Frontline*, How the Other Half Dies, January 4, 2008, p. 128.
6. *Hindustan Times*, Business, Plan Panel Sets 27 Targets for Inclusive Growth, Lucknow Edition, November 9, 2007, p. 11.
7. *Frontline, op. cit.*

Empowerment of Women and Education

Sanjeev Kumar Singh and Roma Rupam

Education is the prime factor for women's development and empowerment. Through education it is possible to improve women's opportunities for participation in the various fields of life. The National Council of Women's education emphasized the potential significance of the mass-media to generate public opinion in rural areas in favour of girl's education. It is a well-known fact that even under the conditions of the free education, least preference is being given to the education of a girl child. In our socio-cultural structure an educated son is "important" because he will be responsible for caring their aging parents but an educated daughter is viewed as an asset by her husband's family. The parents will not benefit directly from their daughter's education. This is a negative Parental attitude which can also be a barrier to a girl's education.

Lack of education forces millions of women to work on the fields, construction-sites or in occupations that hardly bring them insufficient income. These women also have to attend all the household duties because that is not supposed to be a man's duty and ending up with no time and energy for gaining self-confidence and self-development. The education is an important tool for individual development and for social progress. For the individual, education offers the opportunity to explore a wider set of ideas than in often available at home and in doing this it widens certain future possibilities. It promotes a scientific temper, enables every child to reach his or her maximum potential, empowers them with a tremendous strength of self-confidence.

Literacy and basic education is the key-factor that plays an important role to empower women. Empowerment of women refers to economic independence and their involvement in decision-making process. Men should given women opportunity and freedom to develop herself. It is an active process of enabling women to realize their identify and power in all spheres of their lives. The educated and the literate mother who lives and works with her children in the home is the best teacher in the world of intelligence. For the earlier years of schooling women are the natural teachers and for all the later stages of education they have their own place. In America meanly all basic school teachers are women while in our country they are mostly men. In a society made up of such homes children starting to school already have a background of information, understanding and culture which result in their getting more benefit from school then otherwise would be possible. If general education had to be limited to men or to women, that opportunity should be given to women, for then it would most surely be passed on to the next generation. Pandit Jawaharlal Nehru, the first Prime Minister of India, has rightly said, "when a woman moves forward, the family moves, the village moves and the country moves".

Access to education has been one of the serious demands for women's empowerment. The ideas of women empowerment have led to the surprising result throughout the world in recent times. It has emerged as an important issue in our social structure in recent years because they have long been neglected in their role as beneficiaries in the process of development. The spread of education is all that more important in a country where women emerged fifty percent of the population.

Another matter of concern for education is that literacy programmes have fallen off the government's priority list. Illiteracy remains a major problem and therefore, literacy programmes cannot be ignored or given less importance. India has the largest number of illiterate people in the world. For a country that has amended its constitution to make education a fundamental right and which is in the process of enacting legislation to provide the right to education to all its citizens.

The United Nations Educational Scientific and Cultural Organisation (UNESCO) report in New Delhi recently says that the efforts are on to improve this situation but they are too slow. The UNESCO is also trying to improve all aspects of quality of education and ensuring excellence of all so that recognised and measurable learning outcomes are achieved by all, especially in literacy, numeracy and essential life skills. The current Education For All (EFA) report marks the midway in the ambitious movement to expand learning opportunity to every child, Particularly girls and achieving gender equality in education by 2015. The present Prime Minister Manmohan Singh promised this during the release of the EFA Report.

The World Economic Forum (WEF) recently released annual Global Gender Gap Report and finds major gap between men and women in four critical areas mainly—survival, educational attainment, economic participation and political empowerment. The entire emphasis of the government in this connection has been yet only on enrolment, which no doubt has shown impressive results but the survival rate and the quality of education, too, are important and the government has not paid enough attention to these aspects. Quality of education is directly linked to the resources available and the government has to improve resource allocation to bring about qualitative changes in the field of education.

There are millions of women and young girls who silently suffer injustice just because they are born as women. They languish in an unhappy home or in the unorganized sectors where they are wilfully exploited. They are disadvantaged in every way in terms of literacy and developmental participation. Perhaps the highest form of violence against women is to deny life because of gender. Despite laws and an increase in educational and economic levels, female foeticide is increasing in certain regions. They are killed in the womb. There is the another trend reflected in rural areas where people are choosing sex-selective abortion. Our traditional attitude glorifies the male child for their "achievement needs" and daughter for their "affiliative needs". The Pre-natal sex-selection and female infanticide are much more common where female progeny is seen as an economic or social burden. We clearly find these social practices in rural areas in a form of early marriage, pressure to bear male child and disparities in access to education. This denial of women's rights including her equality, liberty and safety has permitted acts of inhuman forwards women and girls in India. As former UN Secretary General Koffi Annan has rightly stated, "Gender equality is more than a goal in itself. It is a pre-condition for meeting the challenge of reducing poverty, Promoting sustainable and building good governance".

The impact of new technologies and globalisation have provided jobs only to the urban elite group of women whereas it has failed to provide jobs to the rural group of women as most of these are unskilled and untrained to work in elite industries. Rural group of women have been still contributing largely to the unorganized sector which is mainly agriculture-based. It is apparent that the organized sector cannot absorb even a fraction of these under skilled women. To improve the position of rural women work force it is important to treat them as economically independent, not as dependent on her family. It will free every woman from the shackles that they have been traditionally suffering from time immemorial. They have to be encouraged to acquire the skills and finance to start their own small enterprises. That's how Mahila Griha Uddyog (Lijjat Papad) started in a small way with a small group of women. This also provides a livelihood to a lot of men Social mobilisation through Grih Uddyog, Self-Help Groups or Co-operatives is enevitable for economic empowerment and poverty alleviation. There is a need to stress on extensive awareness campaign for the development of SHGs and Co-operatives through Banks, NGOs and other financial resources with the growing emphasis on the idea of the empowerment of women a lot of hope depends on local business, health care, multinational corporations, teaching, etc. Political influence and economic strength within and across the nations much more progress can be made in this regard.

The Government of India in her Industrial Policy (1991) advocates for conducting special entrepreneurship development programmes for women entry into industries. But the growth rate of Participation of women was not so impressive. Now in this era of globalisation we are still suffering from very less utilisation of this important human resource. Even though government and their agencies have been busy for a long time but they have not been able to make any significant headway that exist between urban and rural areas. This is because of the government's inefficiency and lack of motivation of the agencies. This ultimately poses serious obstacle to national efforts to achieve education for all and eradicate poverty. The government has to understand that even in this era of neo-liberal economic policies and in the rush to involve private participation in all spheres of education, there is no way the state can ignore its own role and responsibilities. The Nobel laureate Amartya Sen at a recent Seminar in New Delhi said in this regard that "No Country in the World has been able to educate all its children without state intervention. Even if children went to terrible Schools, it had an impact".

Keeping in view of the difficulties of the girls of rural remote area, the Government of India, recently decided to set-up 750 Kasturba Gandhi Balika Vidyalaya. This is block-based schools with boarding facilities. The blocks have been selected on the basis of SC/STs population. The objective of the government is to enhance the self-image and self-confidence of the rural and the backward area girls and to create an environment where they can seek knowledge and information which empowers them personally. Sir Winston Churchill once said about this "... the empires of the future will be the empires of the mind."

References

Annual Report, 2004-05 of Department of Women and Child Development, Government of India.

Empowerment of Women and Educations.

Kurukshetra, March 2007, pp. 30 and 41.

Kurukshetra, May 2006, p. 22.

Samantha, R.K., They Reap Less Than They Sow, *The Hindu*.

Sharma, Sheetal, Educated Women, Empowered Women.

Sinha, Champa, Educational Empowerment.

Yojana, March 2006, p. 35.

Economics of Women Education: An Overview

R.U. Singh

Education is the engine of economic growth and social change. It creates motivation for progress and brings revolution in the ideas necessary for the progress of the country. It teaches honesty, inspires patriotism, educated social prestige and promotes economic development. When people are educated, we not only get teachers, professionals and executives but more importantly citizens who are aware, sensitive and responsible. It makes people place social good above personal gains. Not only this, it transforms a human being into a wholesole whole, a noble soul and an asset to the universe (*Kalam, APJ Abdul, 2004*).

History proves that greater progress has been achieved in those countries, where education is widespread. During the 19th Century, nothing occupied a more prominent place among the requirements for economic and social change than public education and population enlightment (Galbraith). Today also, among the areas of the prime concern are the runway growth of population in the developing world, the threat to our natural environment and the role of the educational process in dealing with our present situations (Singh, Dr. Karan, 2002).

People are the capital of a knowledge drive society. Therefore, a constant development human capital with thrust on skill upgradation, generation, assimilation, dissemination and use of knowledge needs emphasis. India is in the process of transforming itself into developed national by 2020. Yet we have about 350 million people who need literacy and many more who have to acquire employable skills to suit the emerging modern India and the globe. It is essential that we enlighten and create wider spread awareness of education among all sections of society particularly in rural areas and among urban poor. We should use of technology for this important social purpose, mobilize resources and allocate them properly for full literacy and quality education and for this, not only the government (Central and States but the corporate sector, the NGOs and other social and philanthropic institutions, etc. have to come forward for creation of awareness, mobilisation of resources and overall development of educational facilities having formal and informal, technical and non-technical, professional and general as well as quantitative and qualitative aspects. In creating awareness among the masses, media has also an important role to play.

No doubt, our plan efforts have yielded good results. Expenditure on education has increased multiple times, number of schools, colleges and universities and other institutions both technical and non-technical have gone up several times and the literacy ratio has risen sharply from 18.3 per cent in 1951 to 64.8 per cent in 2001 (Economic Survey, 2005-06a, p. 210). Nevertheless, India continues to lag behind several other developing countries in the region such as China (86 per cent) and Sri Lanka (92 per cent) Not only this, there are inter-regional and intra-regional disparities in the country itself. Likewise, the enrolment ratio has gone up progressively from 32.1 in 1950-51 to 84.91 in 2003-04 [Economic Survey, 2005-06b, S. (112)] but the drop-out ratio, even after a declining trend, still continues to be higher, being 31.4% at the primary level (Class I to V). The number of Children (in age group of 6-14) out of school has sharply declined, but still in October 2005 it stood at about 95 lakhs (Economic Survey, 2005-

06c, p. 210). Several schemes/programmes for universal and quality education are in operation and we have high hopes from them in near future, but still there are some problems which must be diagnosed properly and cured so that we can have the better results. The present paper tries to analyse some of these aspects.

STATUS OF EDUCATION IN BIHAR

(a) Access to Education: Bihar

Access to education increases the self-esteem and social dignity of an individual, reduces deprivation as enumerated by Chambers (1995). Male, Female rate of Education in Bihar can be seen from Table 2.

TABLE 1

Sl. No.	*States/U.T.*	*1951*	*1961*	*1971*	*1981*	*1991*	*2001*
1.	Bihar	13.49	21.95	23.17	32.32	37.49	47.00
2.	Manipur	12.57	36.04	38.47	49.66	59.89	70.53
3.	Mizoram	31.14	44.01	53.80	59.88	82.26	88.80
4.	Tripura	NA	20.24	30.98	50.10	66.44	73.19
5.	Meghalaya	NA	26.92	29.49	42.05	49.10	62.56
6.	Daman & Diu	—	—	—	—	71.20	78.18
7.	Goa	23.48	35.41	51.96	65.71	75.51	82.01
8.	Lakshadweep	15.23	27.15	51.76	68.42	81.78	86.66
9.	Kerala	47.18	55.08	69.75	78.85	79.81	90.86
10.	Tamil Nadu	—	36.39	45.40	54.39	62.66	73.45
11.	Pondichery	9.00	43.65	53.38	65.14	74.74	81.24
12.	Andaman & Nicobar Islands	30.30	40.07	51.15	63.19	73.02	81.30

Source: *Quoted in Economic Survey*, Government of India, 2005-06 S-114.

Table 2, shows that in Bihar level of literacy is low in comparison to Jharkhand and all India level. According to 2001 census, the overall literacy rate in Bihar including men and women is lowest, i.e. 47.53 of the total population, 60.3 of men and 33.6 of women much below the national average and 54.16 respectively. It is highest in Kerala, i.e. 90.92, 94.20 and 87.86 respectively.

TABLE 2

Year	Bihar			India		
	Literacy Rate	*Male*	*Female*	*Literacy Rate*	*Male*	*Female*
1951	12.20	—	—	18.30	27.20	8.90
1961	21.80	35.20	8.20	28.30	40.40	15.30
1971	19.90	—	—	34.50	46.00	22.00
1981	26.20	38.1	13.60	41.40	53.40	28.50
1991	38.50	51.37	21.99	52.20	64.10	39.30
2001	47.53	60.30	38.60	65.38	76.00	54.16

Although enrolment ratio in Class I to V is not very bad in the state of enrolment ratio in Class VI to VIII is very bad. Gross enrolment ratio in Bihar during 2001-02 can be seen from Table 3.

TABLE 3

Cross Enrolment Ratio: Primary and Upper Primary Education in Bihar, 2001-02

	Bihar	*India*
Boys	95.45	105.29
Girls	61.19	86.91
Total	78.70	96.30
Boys	38.22	67.77
Girls	21.07	52.09
Total	30.07	60.20
Boys	72.72	90.69
Girls	45.78	73.56
Total	59.69	82.35

Table 3 shows that the gross enrolment ratio of both boys and girls are very low in upper primary (VI-VIII) level in the state.

According to third annual study of Indian States published in the *India Today* (August 15, 2005) Bihar maintains its overall bottom position ranking 20th among the big states as regards to primary education. Jharkhand occupies the 18th position, just two steps above Bihar. Only 23 per cent of children over 10 have completed primary education in Bihar.

Another significant study made by the National Council of Applied Economic Research—March 2005 published in the *Hindustan Daily* News Paper on 9th August, 2005, reveals that 84 per cent of girls at the age of five-nine in rural Bihar are neither in school in school nor at any work. In urban area, it is 59 per cent. 74 per cent of boys at the same age in rural area are neither in school nor at any work. In the urban area, it is 52 per cent.

Sixty-five per cent of girls in the age of 10-14 in rural Bihar are neither in school nor at any work. In urban area, it is 31 per cent. 33 per cent of boys at the same age are neither in school nor, any work. In the urban area, it is 17 per cent.

Thus, with regards to children's participation in education in Bihar, there is a large concentration of out of school children in the state.

The reasons for such a high drop-out rate can be identified with poverty, lack of adequate income of the parents, poor school facilities like mismanaged mid-day meals, no facilities of urinal for girls, poor method of teaching and above all administrative inefficiency is the most important factor for this vicious cycle.

CONCLUSION

It appears from the above discussion that education, the engine of growth is in a poor condition in the country both quantitatively and qualitatively, whether it is at the elementary level or at the secondary or higher level. 35% of our adult population are yet to achieve literacy. The expenditure of education is still much below the accepted international standards, near about 4 per cent of the GDP as against the accepted and declared goal of 6 to 7 per cent of GDP which is required for 100 per cent literacy. The quality of education is so poor especially in government schools and rural areas that even teachers in these schools are managing to send their children in better quality private schools even at distant place with higher fee structure. The rural rich and elites are also moving on the same path. The residual clients of these poor village schools happen to be poorest of the poor, economically and socially. Ultimately, the stakeholders of these schools being weak and vulnerable, cannot ensure accountability of the system for quality education. Whatever number of schools we have, most of them are in the government sector and majority of them lack the infra-structural facilities and quality teachers. There is also the problem of syllabus followed in the schools. Here it may be mentioned that job opportunities being national, the syllabus that job opportunities being national, the syllabus should be structured in such a manner that it should meet the changing societal needs, fulfil the needs of the occupation and inculcate high moral values among the students in addition to learning skills. The delivery of quality education is possible only through quality teachers. The teacher has to be a committed teacher who loves teaching and children. And also the teacher has to be equipped with all the knowledge required for effective teaching. The self-esteems of the teacher must be high and the teacher must have the quality to become a role model for the children. Some element of competition rewarding is to be done based on performance. This competency has to be built up throughout the country through a massive teacher education programme delivered through a tale-education system and continuously updated. This can be funded and implemented a consortium of government, educational institutions with the corporate sectors providing value added services.

There is also an urgent need that every school should have basic amenities, such as good building equipped with ventilated, lighted, airy and spacious class room besides library, laboratories, including the latest I.T. tools and infrastructure, safe drinking water, clear toilets and play ground. This is possible by making additional investment in education and increasing expenditure upto 6-7 per cent of GDP in this field. The state governments should take a lesson from on going practices from Kerala where the government subsidies for education through private quality school by compensating expenditure on fees and provision of scholarship, etc. The awareness in Kerala is so high that even the people below the poverty line spend about 30 per cent of their income on childrens' education (Thangamuthu, G., 2001).

Further, it is reported that about one-third of children dropout from schools after studying upto Vth class and more than 50 per cent dropout after studying upto 8th class. This situation needs remedial action, especially since assent has been accorded for the 86th Constitution Amendment Act (Right to Education) Bill for children between age group of 5 to 14 years. But an Act alone cannot achieve the goal unless the education is delivered in a manner, which will take into account the socio-economic reality and perception of people to whom it is address. Apart from attracting the children to the schools, the education system should be able to provide nourishment and inject creativity among the children. Also the aim of education system should be to build character, human values, enhances the learning capacity through technology and build the confidence among the children.

It may also be suggested that on experimental basis, where possible, the management of schools and colleges may be handed over to reputed NGOs established educational agencies, industries, and such other bodies. These schools, however, would be aided schools but managed privately. The tuition fees if any shall be compensated through scholarship.

It may also be suggested that providing teachers with learning materials and encouraging parents to get more involved in the schooling of their children are more effective than a school feeding programme in reducing dropout rates and increasing learning.

References

Kalam, A.P.J. Abdul (2005), President's Address to the Nations on the Eve of Independence Day, 2004, Published in *Yojana*, September, p. 2.

Kulandaiswamy, V.C. (2005), Reconstruction of Higher Education, *Yojana*, Vol. 49, September, pp. 29 and 30, *Ibid*.

Singh, Dr. Karan (2002), *Yojana*, September, p. 6.

Government of India (Planning Commission), Economic Survey, 2005-06.

PART III

GENDER DEVELOPMENT AND EMPOWERMENT

Women's Empowerment Through Gender Budgeting: A Review in the Indian Context

Rashmi Akhaury

"Gender Budgeting" is now recognized as a tool for empowering women. This paper gives a broad overview of the gender budgeting initiatives in India, highlighting certain related issues that need to be addressed for making gender budgeting an effective tool for women's empowerment, in the Indian context. It explores the query—*how effective has gender budgeting been as a tool for women's empowerment, in its present form, in the Indian context.*

Gender budgeting, a relatively new concept, aims at bringing in gender equality in the allocation of public funds through recognition and identification of its implications for women and girls in a country. This process does not strive to create separate or special budgets nor requires more monetary allocation for women. Here, the aim is to ensure a fair, just and efficient distribution of public resources for the all-round development of the society.

Gender Responsive Budget Initiatives (GRBI) are an outcome of a collaborative effort of the United Nations Development Fund for Women, the Commonwealth Secretariat and International Development Research Centre, Canada. Gender budgeting is now practiced by many countries with an objective to support government and civil society in examining national, regional and local budgets from a gender perspective and applying the study results for the formulation of gender responsive budgets. The ultimate stated goal of gender budgeting, in a country is, therefore, to bring gender quality in the allocation of public funds and to enhance women's participation in the decision-making processes that shape their lives.

DEFINITION AND CONCEPT

The tem "gender budgeting" has become a catch all phrase to describe various government initiatives that seek to address gender issues in the domain of public expenditure and policy.

" 'Gender-sensitive budgets', 'gender budgets', and 'women's budgets' refer to a variety of process and tools aimed at facilitating an assessment of the gendered impacts of government budgets. In the evolution of these exercises, the focus has been on auditing government budgets for their impact on women and girls." (Sharp, Rhonda; 1999)

"Gender budget initiatives analyze how governments raise and spend public money, with the aim of securing gender equality in decision-making about public resource allocation; and gender equality in the distribution of the impact of government budgets, both in their benefits and in their burdens. The impact of government budget on the most disadvantaged groups of women's is a focus of special attention."(IDRC, 2001)

The above definitions underline the fact that gender budgeting is now seen as a socio-economic tool for ensuring gender equity in the development process and lays a strong emphasis on engendering public expenditure and policy. Critical activities constituting the gender budgeting exercise would include:

(a) Addressing gap between policy commitment and allocation for women through adequate resource

GENDER BUDGETING—AN ACTION PLAN

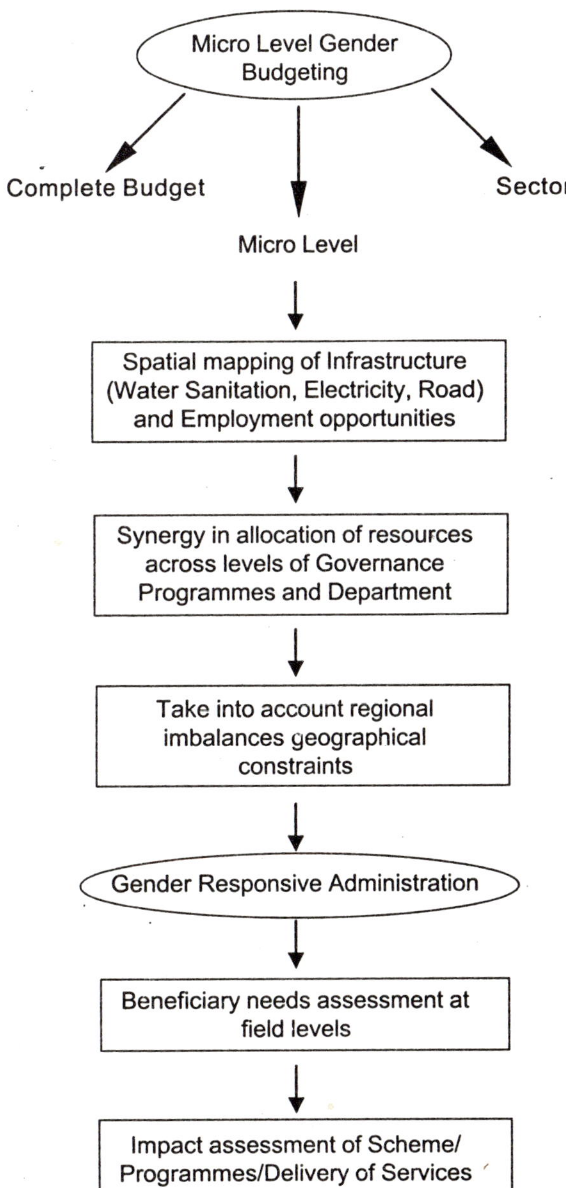

allocation and gender sensitive progamme formulation and implementation.

(b) Mainstreaming gender concerns in public expenditure. Fiscal and monetary matters etc.

1. Strategic Framework

While several countries across the globe have adopted gender budgeting initiatives, pioneering work was done in Australia and South Africa.

The Australian approach or the "Three-way Categorisation", distinguishes between:

I. Gender-specific expenditure;
II. Equal opportunity expenditure for civil servants; and
III. General expenditure (the rest) considered in terms of its gender impact.

In the South African "Five Step Approach" the five steps are:

I. Analyzing the situation of women, men, girls and boys;
II. Assessing the gender-responsiveness of policies;
III. Assessing budget allocations;
IV. Monitory spending and service delivery; and
V. Assessing outcomes.

In India the strategic framework for gender sensitivity in resource allocation has been earmarking a specified minimum quantum of funds/benefits for women in all women-related sectors, supplemented by targated interventions for women in various sectors like health, education, employment, training, micro-credit, etc.

Specific focus on gender-based resource allocation is seen from the Eighth Plan onwards.

The Eighth Plan (1992-97) highlighted for the first time a gender perspective and the need to ensure a definite flow of funds from the general developmental sectors to women.

The Ninth Plan (1997-2002) adopted 'Women Component Plan' as one of the major strategies and directed both the Central and State Governments to ensure "not less than 30 percent of the funds/benefits are earmarked in all the women's-related sectors.

Special vigil was advocated on the flow of the earmarked funds/ benefits through an effective mechanism to ensure that the proposed strategy brings forth a holistic approach towards empowering women.

The Tenth Plan reinforced commitment to gender budgeting to establish its gender-differential impact and to translate gender commitments into budgetary commitments.

The Department of Women Child Development as the nodal Department in GOI for gender budgeting took the initiative in 2004, of defining a broader strategic framework for gender budgeting covering a wide gamut of activities which collectively would contribute to strengthen the gender budgeting initiative.

2. Approaches to Gender Budgeting Initiatives in India

A wide variety of women empowering initiatives have been taken up over the last few decades in the government and civil society. A few milestones in the context of gender budgeting are briefly mentioned below to enable reflection on the different approaches to gender budgeting:

I. The Government of India adopted the Women's Component Plan approach for ensuring gender sensitive resource allocation. Reviewing the performance of the WCP during the Ninth Plan, the 10th Plan documents indicates that 39% of the GBS of 15 women-related Ministries/Departments flowed to women under the Women's Component Plan.

II. The first formal exercise in gender budgeting at the national level was undertaken by the National Institute of Public Finance and Policy (NIPFP) when they analyzed the Union Budget. The Report of NIPFP categories public expenditure under three main types:

(a) Women specific allocations which are specifically targeted to women and girls,

(b) Pro-women allocations which are the composite expenditure of schemes with women component, and

(c) Mainstream public expenditure that have gender differential impacts.

The study highlighted the low proportion of women-related allocation in the Union Budget and the tendency for revised allocations being less than budgeted projections. The report recommended the following priority actions for gender-sensitive budgeting:

- Mechanism to collate gender disaggregated data from relevant Department be developed to obtain the gender-wise relevant statistical database, targets and indicators.
- Gender audit of plans, policies and programmes of various ministries with pro-women allocations should be conducted.
- The provisions for women in the composite programmes under education, health and rural development, etc. should be segregated to protect the provisions by placing restrictions on their re-appropriation for other purpose.

III. Studies in selected states were commissioned by Department of Women and Child Development through the National Institute of Public Cooperation and Child Development using the same model.

IV. The Department of Women and Child Development also commissioned a study on gender analysis of budgets of all states for the period 1993-94 to 2006-07 so as to generate a time series data on budgeted expenditure for women by State Governments for the years 1993-94 to 2006-07.

In this report, the programmes for women have been classified under 5 sectors—

(a) **Education and Training:** General education of girls above senior secondary level, training of women in technical education, extension work, etc.

(b) **Women in Need:** Pension/financial assistance for destitute/handicapped women and widows and their children for purposes like marriage/education, etc., shelter homes, rehabilitation of prostitutes, etc.

(c) **Health:** Maternity and Child Care, hospitals for women, community health programme for women, etc.

(d) **Women Empowerment Programmes:** Working

women hostels, self-help group schemes, women cooperative banks, etc.

(e) **Miscellaneous** measures

Apart from highlighted that more than 50% of expenditure on women is from the state budgets, the study also brought out significant variations in interstate positions on trend of expenditure on women seen in correlation with female population.

V. At the state level, the State Government of Karnataka was a pioneer in gender budgeting of public expenditure. The state undertook earmarking resources for women in most sectors. State like Kerala and Tamil Nadu have achieved a high degree of progress in gender-related indicators on literacy, health, employment, etc. through introduction of several successful gender related programmes (especially through the self-help group movement).

VI. The initiatives taken in the last two years by Ministry of Finance have reinforced the commitment of the Government to adopt gender budgeting as a tool for women's empowerment.

- Recognizing the need to spread gender budgeting initiatives in the entire Government Machinery, the inter-Departmental committee recommended that all departments establish a 'Gender Budgeting Cell'. To begin with eighteen departments were asked to reflect scheme-wise physical targets and expenditure benefiting women in their performance Budgets for 2006-07.
- The Department of Women and Child Development has drawn up detailed guidelines on gender budgeting initiatives for these cells and workshops have been organized for dissemination of gender budgeting practices and initiatives.

VII. There are several studies on status of women and public expenditure for women in sectors like agriculture, industry, labour and so on and at micro-level covering gender analysis of budgeting practices and implementation at Panchayat levels. Considerable research also exists on gender impact of important government programmes like the Employment Guarantee Scheme, Swarajyanti Gram Swarozgar Yojana, etc. These studies have highlighted important areas of concern like:

- Overall inadequacy of allocation for women in budgets at national and state level.
- Multiplicity of schemes with small budgets which have limited impact and coverage.
- Too many layers of administration impede smooth flow of funds and lead to delay in implementation
- Shortfalls in implementation on account of gender insensitivity in implementing agencies or failures to address core gender-related issues. Scheme formulation not in line with field level requirement. Scheme design does not address barriers to access by women.
- Lack of availability of gender disaggregated data to isolate women expenditure in pro-women schemes.
- Physical targets and achievements not transparently indicated
- Lack of involvement of women in decision-making.

Summarizing the above:

- Gender budgeting activities in the government is mostly, *ex-ante:*

I. A conscious decision to earmark funds for women-related programmes and enhance allocation under women specific programmes and pro-women programmes.

II. Implement women specific schemes for training and skill up-gradation (STEP, Swawlamban, Training women in agriculture extension activities, etc.) and mobilize collective power of women through self-help group based schemes (Swayamsidha, Swashakti, Kutumbashree, SGRY), extend micro-credit (Rashtriya Mahila Kosh) and so on.

III. Address improvement in women-related macro-indicators like literacy, maternal mortality rate (MMR), etc. through focus on coverage of women in education and health services.

- Gender Audit has focused on :

I. Analysis of impact of the expenditure and review of effectiveness of public programmes targeted for welfare and development from the point of view of design and implementation and comments on status of access of women to select public services.

II. Adoption of a few macro-indices like MMR, work participation, literacy, etc. that dominate the measurement of gender status and highlighting gender differentials to focus attention on need for enhanced allocation for women in certain sectors like health, education and employment.

With this background, we may examine Gender Budgeting as a "tool" for women's empowerment. The starting point would logically be looking at the constituents of "women's Empowerment". These are defined in the 10th Plan document quoted below:

Social Empowerment—to create an enabling environment through various affirmative development policies and programmes for development of women besides providing them easy and equal access to all the basic minimum services so as to enable them to realize their full potentials.

- **Economic Empowerment**—to ensure provision of training, employment and income-generation activities with both 'forward' potential women economically independent and self-reliant
- **Gender Justice**—to eliminate all forms of gender discrimination and thus, allow women to enjoy not only the *de-jure* but also the *de-facto* rights and fundamental freedom on par with men in all spheres, viz. political, economic, social, civil, cultural, etc.

What is the Gender Budgeting Tool?

As mentioned earlier, gender budgeting initiative in India has been undertaken through several different approaches. Some of the prominent approaches are discussed below.

(A) Quantum and Trend Analysis of Gender-based Resource Allocation and Expenditure

The term gender budgeting by its very definition and nomenclature has underpinnings in financial resource allocations and thus most of the gender budgeting exercises focus on quantitative resource allocation for women, under gender specific and pro women categories of public expenditure.

It is no doubt necessary to get a macro-position on trend of allocation for women. However, this approach has several limitations as a means of empowering women. Some of these are listed below:

(a) The general concern expressed is—when women are under 50% of the population, why should public expenditure on women be less than 5% of the Budget? There is no apparent rationale behind a WCP of 30% and that too only in the social sector's budget? Why not 50% or 75%.

(b) Core issues like design of program and its effectiveness from the gender perspective, too many small interventions, barriers to access, etc. remain opaque in macro-level analysis of quantitative allocation for women.

(c) A rising trend in allocation of funds for women does not necessarily translate into enhanced benefits or wider coverage. The rise in allocation may just cover enhanced cost of delivery of services with no increase in quantity of services or even quality.

(d) The tendency is to analyze expenditure of each level of Government in isolation. For example, gender analysis of Union budgets is carried out without linking state expenditure. In the federal set-up this gives an incomplete picture. Any comment on say expenditure on health for women is incomplete if we look at the government of India Budget or State Budgets in isolation.

(e) Without availability of gender disaggregated data it is difficult to comment upon the position of incidence of public expenditure from a gender perspective.

(B) Gender Audit of Sectors like Education, Agriculture, Health, Industry, etc.

Many gender budgeting studies have presented gender profiles of sectors like health, education, agriculture, employment and so on at national or state level. This is certainly a more effective mechanism than the first approach based on quantification of resources. However, inmost of these studies the issues raised are deficiencies in design and/or implementation of program, based on field level surveys. Little attempt has been made to benchmark the scale of resources required to empower women meaningfully, based on adequate availability of resources and reliability of services.

Effective improvement in health for women requires not only access to a medical centre but also transport (Road), employment (food), water and sanitation and so on. A sectoral approach is thus uni-dimensional when rated as an empowerment tool.

(C) Gender Audit Based on Position Reflected by Gender-related Macro-Indicators

Status and trends of certain gender-related macro-indices—MMR, Women's access to health, literacy states, participation in PRI, employment statistics, etc. are quoted as proxy indicators for level of women's empowerment. Adverse gender indices are cited as justification for enhancement in quantum of allocation. However, this approach again is constrained in that there is no benchmarking of the quantum of allocation required to achieve the targeted improvement in these indices. Thus the effectiveness of this approach is questionable.

(D) Women's Participation in Gender Budgeting through Fiscal Decentralisation and Local Level Institutions

This could *prima facie* be an ideal solution that would take into account field level requirements of women and with participation of women in planning and implementation, outcome achievement is more likely. However, desirable as it is, we have to recognize the constraints in the current context.

(a) The biggest Constraint is Limited Financial Devolution

The structure of public finances and expenditure in India is a multi-tiered one and resources flow to the field through several layers of administrations and through a variety of modes—Centrally Sponsored, Central Sector, State Sector, Additional Central Assistance and so on. The net result is that very little devolution of financial powers rests with the local level administrations. Further schematic designs and conditionalities leave them with virtually no flexibility. Accountability too is diffused. These problems are faced even in some of the states that are upheld as best models.

In a study commissioned by World Bank "India-Fiscal Decentralisation to Rural Governments", some key findings based upon studies in Kerala and Karnataka, indicate:

(i) Inter-governmental relations are mostly hierarchical. The design and implementation of the decentralisation program are a state government responsibility. However, implementation of key aspects of the programme is lagging.

(ii) In the absence of reliable information on the revenues and expenditures of local bodies, neither the State nor the Centre can lead a reasonable fiscal decentralisation programme.

(b) Another Constraint is the Limited Effective Participation of Women in Field Level Planning and Implementation

Women's participation in local administration is constitutionally provided. However, the effective impact would require immense capacity building and overcoming socio-economic barriers. Field level studies conducted in Karnataka indicate a few problems like: Elected Women Representatives (EWR) in PRIs are not well endowed or trained women technicalities of budgeting even though they may be aware of their needs at the local level like water, sanitation, security, etc., they are not always given an equal opportunity to express themselves or impose the perceived requirement of women.

(E) Identification and Promotion of Gender Audit-based Best Practices

There are abundant instances of best practices in the realm

of gender empowerment. Projects have been taken up to successfully demonstrate the strength women draw in collectivity self-help group schemes and cooperatives, etc. There are also projects reflecting the potential for women in skill up-gradation, micro-credit-based entrepreneurship, etc.

(F) Reliance on Women Specific Schemes

We device women specific schemes for nutrition, education, vocation training and so on. These are no doubt critical in the empowerment process. However, these tend to be uni-dimensional in focus and do not serve as a tool for holistic empowerment.

(G) Reliance on Convergence of Interventions

Give the multitude of schemes and programmes for women, spread across various Departments and Ministries of the Government, one approach towards empowerment of women is seeking to converge these interventions, mostly through self-help group (SHGs) or women cooperatives. This could prove an effective empowerment approach and also finds support in the 10th Plan documents.

While the SHG group and collective power of women is critical in the empowerment process, in the absence of an institutional mechanism for convergence, it would prove difficult to have universal success, given the involvement of a multitude of departments and schemes, at the functional level. Success stories rest on individual efforts rather than institutionalized mechanisms. Central sector schemes and centrally sponsored schemes have limited flexibility and may require a re-look at the design and implementation of the schemes. Further the SHG movement is not uniform in its success and spread across the country.

Summing up it is submitted that while all the above approaches have merit and benefits, but perhaps in isolation, these approaches are not complete in themselves to achieve women's empowerment.

EXTANT APPROACH TO WOMEN'S DEVELOPMENT

(1) While planning for women's empowerment, the outlook has been one of looking at women as a beneficiary

segment rather than as equal participants in the development process. As a consequence, the gender budgeting exercise has mostly focused on provision of resources and programmes for women in the social sector. Sectors like Education, Health, Nutrition, Employment, etc. are no doubt critical in the empowering paradigm, but it is necessary that we look beyond. Women must be recognized as equal players in the economy whether they participate directly as workers or indirectly as members of the economy. It has to be accepted that every policy of the Government—fiscal, monetary or trade, has an impact on the well being of women and that in many cases there would be a gender differential in the impact. Thus it is not adequate to restrict the gender differential in the impact. Thus it is not adequate to restrict the gender budgeting exercise to a few sectors of the economy which are traditionally considered as women-related. The analysis has to cover every rupee of public expenditure. It has to cover the way schemes are conceptualized and how women-friendly they are in implementation and targeting of beneficiaries.

(2) At present, very limited gender perspective is kept while formulating fiscal and monetary policies and taking decisions on issues like withdrawal or introduction of subsidies, etc., this has to be initiated if we are to speak of meaningful women's empowerment and thus has to form an integral part of the gender budgeting exercise. Without this, the Gender budgeting exercise may be enhancing resources in social sector but the impact may be nullified by say inflation, costlier credit, withdrawal of subsidy, imposition of taxes, excise/custom duties on essential commodities, etc. if a policy of the government, unwittingly has a significant gender adverse, bias, arresting that may be more critical than enhancing resources for women specific programmes. Thus there is a strong case for gender-based review of fiscal and monetary policies as an integral part of the Gender Budgeting exercise.

(3) If certain planning and implementation issues are not

addressed, the gender budgeting initiatives may meet the fate of several other development initiatives and remain more of a paper exercise with limited outcomes. More so given the limited bargaining power of women. These issues would include :

- Synergy in resources for women in various budgets—national, state and local.
- Weeding out overlapping interventions.
- Schemes design and implementation from gender perspective to consciously address socio-economic barriers faced by women in accessing services.

The administrative set-up in our country has multiple layers of governance and budgeting. Each of these has a multitude of Department and Ministries with their own programmes and schemes. The end result is considerable overlap in interventions for services and may not be to the benefit of women. For example, vocational training and skill up-gradation programmes are run by several GOI Departments besides the state government themselves, each government agency bearing administrative cost of delivery. Despite so many agencies, the country-wide geographic balance/ imbalance cannot be ascertained. This also makes it difficult to ascertain the total allocation flowing to women and conduct gender audit in a meaningful fashion.

(4) Reliance on the voluntary sector for outreach has come to stay. But this has to be institutional and optimized so as to ensure more transparency and accountability. The time has perhaps come to look upon the NGOs as "social contractors". The order of events needs to be implementing agencies from voluntary organisation more transparent to promote accountability, especially at the field level.

(5) The gender budgeting tool based on resource allocations and concomitant follow-up activities and gender audit should not become an end in itself. We have to move away from looking at this exercise as an accounting

exercise with focus on "higher women-related allocations." The expected end outcome is women's empowerment thus this exercise has to be seen in the perspective of a process which entails looking at multi-dimensional activities, many of which do not necessarily have a specific allocation in public expenditure.

GENDER BUDGETING FOR WOMEN'S EMPOWERMENT—AN ALTERNATIVE STRATEGY WOMEN A STAKEHOLDER

Awareness about gender budgeting and policy level commitment to women's empowerment is at a peak today. Various enabling measures like setting up of gender budgeting cells in Ministries of Government of India, reflection of a gender budget statement in the Union Budget 2005-06 and adoption of the women's component plan by some states have been undertaken. The mid-term appraisal of the Tenth Plan has identified adverse child sex ratio, high MMR, wide gender gap in literacy and wage rates, violence against women and female foeticide and infanticide as burning issues for women besides vulnerability of women in low paid hazardous and insecure jobs in the unorganized sector and in export processing/special economic zones. These documents also state that there is a need to review the stagnation in implementation of the women's component plan.

It is thus perhaps an opportune time to explore an alternative strategy towards gender budgeting, with builds upon the vast experience gained in the past few decades.

The challenge is How do we make gender budgeting in as an effective tool for achieving women's empowerment?

There is no denying that participative budgeting with women being directly involved in the decisions related to planning, financing and programme implementation is the ideal situation. However in the extant Indian context, given the limited devolution of finances to local administrations and socio-economic and political barriers to women's effective participation, an alternative strategy is proposed.

AN ALTERNATIVE STRATEGY

The strategy proposal is Macro-level planning for micro

needs. The perspective on gender budgeting has to be turned upside down. It is not the allocation of resources in the budget at national and/or state levels that has to seen but the resource that flow to and are available to women at the field level, i.e. the women in the villages, cities and towns of the country that need to be monitored.

Two Inter-related Mechanisms are Suggested as a Part of the Proposed Strategy

(a) *Special Mapping of infrastructure and resources*: How do we translate financial commitments in to monitorable measures of empowerment? How do we overcome disparities in empowerment across various regions and across classes? Macro-level resource allocations and financial and physical indicators do not adequately address these questions. The solution offered is spatial mapping. The states have to be asked to do spatial mapping of social infrastructure and access to employment opportunities for women, clearly indicating resources available, overall gaps, and resource allocation required based on size of population and yardsticks for availability of facilities, etc. so that universalisation is achieved progressively, and allocation and interventions are more focused. These spatial maps would then form the basis for concomitant regional plans and projections on funds for gender requirements, with maximum local participation this would also enable taking in to account regional requirements and building in culture specific changes necessary in interventions for women. Such mapping initiatives have been undertaken over the past years but in a piecemeal manner, for relatively uni-dimensional issues but not for gender specific concerns. Thus the technology and methodology is in place.

(b) *Centralized coordination of Macro-level planning for micro-needs with the Planning Commission*: Till financial devolution improves and social changes take place and participative budgeting becomes a reality, the Planning Commission would have to coordinate Planning at Macro-level for Micro-level needs. Public expenditure flows to the end target group through a plethora of administrations, schemes, and agencies. So planning for and implementing and monitoring at the field level would require centralized coordination of all the interventions. The Planning Commission will have to takeover the role of coordinating gender budgeting initiatives in the realm of providing basic infrastructure for women, employment opportunities, economic empowerment, etc. deemed necessary for the well-being and development of women.

This suggestion being given in the gender budgeting context is not administratively impossible. It is to be found in the 10th Plan MTA document in the context of achieving balanced regional growth.

Through coordination, Planning Commission will have to essentially address all gender issues including issues like overlap in initiatives (across departments in Government of India and state governments), need for synergy in provision of funds at centre and state levels, etc., this would be facilitated by the information reflected by the spatial mapping exercise and benchmarking of financial resources required based on region specific requirements of women.

STRATEGIC MAP FOR WOMEN'S EMPOWERMENT

A strategic map is proposed to depict all the inter-related activities necessary for women's empowerment and to enable a better focus in resource allocation under gender budgeting. Taking a clue from Robert S. Kaplan and David P. Norton's paper (*Harvard Business Review*, Sep.-Oct. 2000) we may map our strategy under the following four components:

Client (women) Perspective	Internal processes Perspective	Financial Perspective	Learning Perspective

Stake Holders (Women) Perspective

- *Basic socio-economic infrastructure*: Health, Education, Water and sanitation
- *Economic Empowerment*: Economic identity, employment, Assets, Credit, Skills, markers, risk coverage, and

- *Social and political empowerment*: Political participation, gender equality in inheritance, marital laws, security.

The three concerns identified for the stakeholder are distinct in that they require a different strategy, funding pattern and implementation approach.

Basic Socio-economic Infrastructure

At the macro-level, provision of certain basic infrastructure on a universal access basis is necessary for survival and dignity of living. This would include—water, sanitation, electricity/power, roads, etc. It may be debatable whether expenditure on these utilities should be included in quantification of resources allocated for women and what percentage of this should be treated as a women's component. But it cannot be denied that these facilities are critical for the well-being of women. Particularly water and sanitation and fuel as the bulk of time for women go in water and firewood collection. Drudgery apart, this work is purely unpaid labour and leaves them with no time to pursue more remunerative options. Thus the economic identity of women gets downplayed despite the critical labour they put in for survival of the household. Connectivity by rail/roads again is often critical for survival in times of crisis on health grounds or to market produce or seek employment.

Another reason for ensuring universal availability of this critical infrastructure is the impact it has on effective delivery of other services particularly health and education and employment opportunities. Availability of medical services in crisis, manning of primary health centers and schools, etc. often suffers due to lack of availability of basic infrastructure like electricity and water/sanitation in rural areas. In a study carried out by World Bank (Anil B. Deolalikar, 2005) it has been concluded that universal road, electricity and sanitation coverage in the poor state would be associated with reductions of 40% in the child underweight rate and 60% in the infant mortality rate.

Thus provision of these facilities, i.e. water and sanitation and electricity/biogas may be deemed to be gender friendly and we may treat it as critical for women's empowerment. However, the focus has to be on universalizing these services with focus on adequacy, access and reliability. One drawback has been benchmarking. For this exercise to be successful it is necessary that we benchmarking. For this exercise to be successful it is necessary that we benchmark resource requirement of the physical infrastructure after establishing yardsticks for availability, translate these in to financial projections and then plan ahead. This has to go in tandem with spatial maps for progressive universal coverage and to facilitate monitoring.

Economic Empowerment

Despite the tremendous amount of effort devoted by women in the care economy and support in survival of the household, much of this is unaccounted for and unpaid. Creating an economic identity for women is critical for empowerment. This requires a more micro-level approach but coordination at planning commission level is still important because of the multitude of small budgeted interventions. Further resource allocation has to be seen in conjunction with reality reflected in spatial maps on access to productive livelihood in different areas of the country. Universal access to productive livelihood for women would serve as a stabilizing factor for the entire family. The strategy may entail tapping the economic potential of collective power of women besides training in the higher skills. This has to go hand in hand with gender mainstreaming. Induction of women in the workforce of the entire public machinery in greater numbers, opening up more training institutes, etc. and universalizing access to support services like accommodation. The approach has to be creative and gender sensitive.

Social and Political Empowerment

This entails relatively less of resource allocation and more focus on effective implementation of laws and legislation and change in societal attitudes on gender. Effective empowerment for women would rest on equity in political processes and participation. A successful strategy would entail more concentrated participation of women in this realm—through induction in law enforcing agencies and in legislating and administrative bodies.

INTERNAL PROCESS PERSPECTIVE

This would include:

(a) Exercise of preparation of spatial maps by each state up to say village/block/district level on gender friendly infrastructure and livelihoods/employment sources/asset ownership, etc. clearly indicating gaps in infrastructure and access to livelihoods.
(b) Developing yardsticks for access to socio-economic infrastructure.
(c) Coordination by Planning Commission for synergy in resource allocation center and state levels and facilitating convergence of multi-departmental interventions.
(d) Redesigning interventions from a gender perspective.
(e) Gender mainstreaming in all public expenditure.
(f) Developing monitoring mechanisms to ensure progressive universalisation of infrastructure and employment opportunities based on spatial mapping.
(g) Involving women self-help groups and women elected representatives in PRIs to take decisions and participate in programmes implementation and monitoring wit defined roles.
(h) Gender-based review of fiscal and monetary policies.
(i) Gender-based review of legislation and effective empowerment of gender-related legislations.

FINANCIAL PERSPECTIVE

Action areas would cover:
(i) Translation of physical projections in to financial projections based cn spatial maps of resource gaps, yardsticks for resources required to universalize availability of services for women's empowerment.
(ii) Enhancing allocation to universalize access to basic socio-economic infrastructure.
(iii) Re-prioritisation of resource allocation to cover infrastructure gaps and imbalances.
(iv) Synergy in state and national level resources.

(v) Monitoring utilisation of resources based on targets achieved.

(vi) Gender friendly review of revenue, tax and subsidy policies.

LEARNING AND INNOVATION PERSPECTIVE

This would require among other activities:

(i) Better fiscal management to stretch existing resources.

(ii) Employment generation for women in new areas.

(iii) Developing MIS to generate gender dis-aggregation in data harnessing technology for resource mapping.

(iv) Training of administrative cadres in gender mainstreaming.

(v) Social re-engineering through gender component in the education process gender issues compulsory in research, training and so on.

(vi) Capacity building for stakeholders (women) in budgeting, higher productivity skills and training, improve their bargaining power-collective strength through setting up self-help groups and cooperatives.

(vii) Bridging gap between research and administrative action, identifying impediments in effective implementation evaluation and micro-level reviews.

The above strategic map is only suggested as an example of the kind of activities holistic empowerment of women would entail. Approach requires considerable effort in areas like spatial mapping and benchmarking of resource. However, with the slow progress reflected in women's empowerment being a major concern, the effort is perhaps now required. Further the advances in Information Technology could be fruitfully harnessed to this end.

What Out to be Done?

The Mid-Term Appraisal of Tenth Plan rightly observed that all Ministries/Departments both in the Central Government and in the States should not be confined to the realm of some Ministries only which have historically been perceived as "women-related ". Moreover, ensuring that these funds sanctioned actually reach the women is also the responsibility of the Government. In this regard, a 'non-lapsable pool' of women's fund could be created in every State and also at the Centre. If there is under-utilisation of funds allocated for women specific programmes/schemes under any Ministry (Central or State), the balance amount of funds should be transferred to this pool however to ensure that funds actually reach the women rather than lying idle in the non-lapsable pool, checks and balances as well as incentives for quality of spending as well as monitoring outcomes will need to be put in place.

The watered-down language in the *Draft Approach Paper to the 11th Five Year Plan* ("towards Faster and More Inclusive Growth Approach to 11th Five Year Plan", Planning Commission, June 14, 2006), hereafter referred to as the draft Approach Paper, which talks about "appropriate provisions" for gender balancing (Gender Balancing, Section 5.6, page 64) is another area of concern. This could be a step backward from the 30% commitment under the WCP. The Government should reaffirm its commitment to at least 30% allocations for women as under WCP. One weakness of the WCP is that it treats women as one homogenous group but in reality, we know that there are layers and layers of discrimination even within women, thus adult women will be doubly discriminated and a differently-abled dalit women will be even more vulnerable. Thus WCP needs to factor in this intersectionality-framework while addressing issues of women, therefore, even in the WCP, there should be guidelines for designing programmes and schemes focused at the most vulnerable women, like dalit women, adivasi women HIV positive women, sex-workers, etc.

Bearing in mind the serious lacunae in the gender Budgeting statement prepared by the government, as highlighted in the previous section there is an urgent need to build the capacity of gender Budgeting cells that have been set-up in Central Government and the Planning Commission should take strong measures for getting the ministries/departments to implement WCP, and collect and report gender-disaggregated data on their programmes/schemes. Last but not the least, gender budgeting cannot be seen in isolation from the overall economic-political scenario. Identifying and listing resource allocations for women is only apart of the whole approach of gender Budgeting. The crux of the issue is the overall economic policy framework in which we operate.

CONCLUSION

Despite all legislations and policy commitments and planning, women remain a vulnerable group. If we are to translate the policy commitment of Women's Empowerment in to a reality we would have to beyond the current outlook on gender budgeting which excludes several dimensions of the problem. We have to go in for a more broad-based approach that addresses planning, adequate resource allocation, programmes design and formulation, targeted intervention and implementation based upon the requirement of women reading at the field level with their participation. This has to supplemented by relentless reality checks at the field level. Gender mainstreaming has to be a guiding force in all these activities to maximize out reach of public expenditure and benefits for women. Further universalizing accesses very important for meaningful outcomes. Inter-state and intra-state imbalances have persisted for a long time and need to be addressed more forcefully. Some overlap of gender and developmental issues will take place—this is inevitable given the wide gap in availability and requirement of socio-economic infrastructure in the country.

The strategy of macro-level planning for micro-needs and the Strategic Map for gender budgeting as a tool for women's empowerment has been proposed keeping in view the need for a holistic approach to empowerment of women. Any successful strategy for women's empowerment will have to account for the fact:

(a) Empowerment cannot be successfully achieved till all aspects—social, economic and political are addressed.
(b) Empowerment should cover women in all regions of the country.
(c) Gender concerns have to be mainstreamed in all aspects of public expenditure and policy as women are equal citizens in the country
(d) Participation of women in decision-making is necessary

given their specific needs and to recognize them as equal members of society.

(e) Societal attitudes have to be re-engineered.

Resource Allocation and public expenditure are important in the empowerment process and thus gender Budgeting has a very critical role to play. However, the tool of gender budgeting has to lend itself to this process based upon the requirements of women's empowerment. The allocation and expenditure process has to be focused and appropriately prioritized. The tool should not become an end in itself. The gender budgeting tool thus has to be honed through:

(a) Spatial mapping of status of women and resources to ensure progressive universal coverage.

(b) Coordination of the flow of public resources to facilitate and ensure convergence of resources with synergy across within various levels of government. No doubt the resource allocation involved would be of a high order. However, this investment itself could contribute to gender empowerment if utilized in an efficient outcome-oriented manner with more involvement of the stakeholder (women) in decision-making and implementation. Further this would lay the foundation for other women specific interventions to be effectively implemented. Lastly, meaningful empowerment of women in India would have to rest on a shift in societal attitudes.

REFERENCES

Anil B. Deolalikar: Attaining the Millennium Development Goals in India (World Bank, 2005).

Annual Report, 2004-05 of Department of Women and Child Development, Government of India.

Eighth Five Year Plan Document, Planning Commission, Government of India.

Gender Budgeting in India, UNIFEM and NIPFP ; 'Follow the Money Series', *South Asia*, Vol. 3; Gender Budgeting in India.

India—Fiscal Decentralisation to Rural Governments, (January 2004, World Bank).

Maitreyi Krishnaraj, Divya Pandey, Aruna Kanchi; Research Centre for Women's Studies, SNDT Women's University, Mumbai. 'Follow the Money Series—South Asia', Vol. 5; Gender Sensitive Analysis of Employment Guarantee Schemes.

Mid-Term Appraisal of Tenth Five Year Plan (2002-07), Planning Commission, Government of India.

Ninth Five Year Plan Document (1997-2002), Planning Commission, Government of India.

Nirmala Banerjee, Joyanti Sen, Sachetana, Kolkata—Swaranjayanti Gram Swarozgar Yojana—A Budgetary Policy in Working; 'Follow the Money Series—South Asia', Vol. 6.

Nirmala Banerjee, Poulomi Roy: 'What does the State Do for Indian Women?', *EPW*, October 30, 2004.

Robert S. Kaplan and David P. Norton: Having Trouble with Your Strategy? Then Map It (*Harvard Business Review*, Sept.-Oct. 2000).

Seventh Five Year Plan Document, Planning Commission, Government of India.

Sixth Five Year Plan Document (1980-85), Planning Commission, Government of India.

Tenth Five Year Plan Document (2002-07), Planning Commission, Government of India.

Issues of Gender Equality and Empowerment of Indian Women

Birendra Kumar Jha

"Where women are respected, there Gods delight, and where they are not, there all works and efforts come to naught"

(*Manu-Samhita iii, 56*)

From the time immemorial it has been realized that women may play a vital role in the social and economic transformation of a country. For Swami Vivekanand "A nation would not march forward if the women are left behind." Of course, the real development of society is neither possible nor desirable by leaving half of the population in dark and depression. Realizing this virtue Gandhi advocated for the empowerment of women and gender equality. He writes, of all the evils for which man has made himself responsible, none is so degrading, so, shocking or as brutal as his abuse of the better half. He was in favour of educating women and giving them all freedom which men enjoy. India's first Prime Minister, Pandit Jawaharlal Nehru, realizing the role of women, stated, 'In order to awaken the people it is the women who has to be awakened. Once she is on the move, the household moves, the village moves, the country moves and thus, we build the India of tomorrow.' Our former President A.P.J. Abdul Kalam said, that 'empowering women was pre-requisite for creating a good nation. According to him, when women are empowered, society with salability is assured. Empowerment of women is essential as their thoughts and their value systems lead the development of a good family, good society and ultimately a good nation'. But these progressive thinking are yet to be realized even after 60 years of Independence.

GLOBALLY IMPORTANT

The issue of gender equality and women's empowerment has gained globally importance and international agencies now focus on women centric gender-based politics initiatives. In 2001 the United Nations Population Fund (UNFPA) had promised gender equality and empowerment of women by 2005 as one of the eight—Millennium Development Goals (MDGs). World Bank, World Health Organisation and UNFPA accept women as disadvantaged gender globally, more so in developing countries like India. The high priority accorded to promotion of gender equality and empowerment of women at global level reflects a global affirmation of women's rights and gender equality as core value of development. For promotion of gender equality and empowering women the target is to eliminate gender disparity in primary and secondary education, preferably by 2005 and in all levels of education no later than 2015, and for monitoring progress of this target, indicators selected are:

- Ratio of girls to boys in primary, secondary and tertiary education.
- Ratio of literate women to men (15-24 years).
- Share of women in wage employment in the non-agricultural sector.
- Promotion of seats held by women in national parliament.

The first Human Development Report (1990) also touched gender issues. The Human Development Report (1995) analyzed the gender issues in detail. In this report Maqbub-Ul-Haq, the progenitor of the series of Human Development Reports emphasized the need of government international to promote gender equality and coined the slogan—'development if not engendered is endangered'.

The Earth Summit and in Rio, the Human Rights Conference in Vienna, the population conference in Cairo and the Beijing conference all were milestones in terms of advancing our understanding of the crucial role of the women in development and focusing the attention of the international community on issues concerning the role of women in the work place and in the society. The Hague Forum (1999) documented a widespread willingness to move ahead with the International Conference on Population and Development (ICPD) programme of action which has emphasized on empowering women and providing them choices through improved access to education and health services, skill development and employment. The ICPD has also stressed on involving women in policy and decision-making process at all levels.

The United Nations declared 1975-85 as the women's Decade. However, it is alarming to take down that even during this women's Decade, there has been global deterioration in the women's condition. A document in 1985, which reviewed the facts and studies concerning women from all over the world, states that the almost uniform conclusion of the Decade's research is that, with a few exceptions, women's relative access to economic resources, incomes and employment has worsened, their burdens of work have increased, and their relative and even absolute health, nutritional and educational status have declined.

GLOBALISATION

Promoting Gender Equality or Global Poverty

Does globalisation promote gender equality or global poverty. This is burning question a gender equality about, is more than a goal in itself. It is a pre-condition for meeting the challenging of reducing poverty, promoting sustainable economic growth and building good governance but globalisation has been seen to lead increasing feminisation of poverty. Globalisation has been categorized as free trade, unfettered markets and integration of economies of the nation states in the world economies. As per

World Commission on the Social Dimension of Globalisation (2004), "Our primary concerns are that globalisation should benefit all countries and should raise the welfare of all people throughout the world. This implies that it should raise the rate of economic growth in poor countries and reduces world poverty, and that it should not increase inequalities and undermines socio-economic security within countries."(WCSDG, 2004) India has entered into the global era since the commencement of economic reforms in 1991 (B.K. Jha, 2008) and it widely believed that globalisation which simply means the integration of the Indian economy with the world economy, has been deemed as the panacea for solving all problems (B.K. Jha, 2005) but its advocates overlook the fact that globalisation has raised both apprehensions and expectations, more often the former than the latter in respect of its impact on labour (T.S. Papola, 2004) particularly women labour. In response to a mounting burden of debt leading to balance of payment crisis, the government of India adopted a structural adjustment programme officially declared as New Economic Policy which have phased the economy towards liberalisation, privatisation, globalisation and marketisation, intending to achieve high growth rate and thereby solving the problems of unemployment and poverty. Globalisation has obviously had some positive impacts. India is now one of the fastest growing economies in the world and at the current GDP growth rate of 8% plus, India is poised to become an economic super of the 21st century, along with U.S.A., China, Russia and Brazil. But at the same time it is not less true that globalisation generally, while benefiting certain regions or groups, is marginalizing and distressing the vulnerable and disadvantaged regions and people and it is needless to say that the rural women are the main victim while labour markets are not yet truly global, labour has become a global resources, corporations go anywhere in the world to seek labour and import highly skilled labour from anywhere. In so far as women domination is already hurting them. Vibhuti Patel (2007) has rightly observed, the U.S.A. and Europe realized that best way to reduce the wage bill and enhance profit rates was to move industrial plants to poorer countries like India, Sri Lanka, Bangladesh, Indonesia, Philippines, Thailand, etc. The cheap labour of docile nimble fingered and flexible Asian women the last colony was found to be most attractive step enhances profit margins. This policy was given the appealing title of 'Integration of women in development'. Indian women are seen as the most flexible of the world's labour force and the lower supply price of these women provides a material basis of the induction of poor working-class women into export industries such as electronics, garments, sports goods, food processing, toys and agro-industries. Working class women are rigorously socialized to work uncomplainingly, under patriarchal control, at any allotted task however dull, laborious, physically harmful or badly paid it may be (Vibhuti Patel, 2007). The most worrisome fact is that the main strategy exacted by Indian manufacturers in collaboration with multi-nationals is switching of the production operations from organized sector to unorganized sector and the increased use of cheap and flexible labour force, i.e. women. (R. Akhoury, 2005) It is but strak truth that economic globalisation deep economic restructuring across countries and neo-liberal policies have led to trend of in formalisation for the female workforce resulting in 94% of the total women workers in the informal sector. A.M. Scolt realizing the intense concentration of women in the informal sector called it as the female sector (R. Akhouri, 2005) where women are employed in low-status-insecure-low paid jobs of casual nature in most cases. (B.K. Jha, 2006) Globalisation has pushed women workers to the informal sector thus depriving them of their trade union rights. By doing this, the women fall outside protective labour laws such as Maternity Benefits Act (1961), Employees State Insurance Scheme, Factories Act (1948), Equal Remuneration Act (1976), Bombay Shops and Establishment Act (1984), Plantation Labour Act and Child Labour (Prohibition and Regulation) Act (1976).

Increased openness to trade in the global era could cause important shift in the demand for skilled labour and hence cause the wage gap between skilled and unskilled workers to widen. This may increase gender inequality due to openness of international trade as women are generally represented in the pool of unskilled labour.

More shameful impact of globalisation lies in this fact that sex-tourism in India has reached massive proportions with globalisation. A new type of publicity material for foreign tourists shows scantily dressed women waiting for tourists at the beach or in the form of five star hotels. Worsening economic conditions force young, poor and lower middle class women to become prostitutes either for survival or by brute force. (Vibhuti Patel, 2007) It is needless to say that the burden of poverty falls more heavily on women than on men in the global era.

Will the globalisation help women to overcome social limitations ranging from lack of nutrition to limitations in participation in social, economic and political life? Unfortunately, the answer is unclear (Meenu Agrawal and Meenakshi Sharma, 2008) but what is more clear is the feminishahat of poverly in the global era.

A Conceptual Framework: Empowerment of women is an effective strategy to cope with gender-based discrimination and attain gender equality. Pursuit of equality aims at three levels namely polity, economy and society. Through facilitating and promoting equal participation of women by means of preferential treatment in education in employment and through other alternative measures and schemes generally designed to improve opportunities for them and protecting them from all forms of social injustice and exploitation.

Strictly speaking, empowerment is a dynamic agent of changes at the grassroots. It concerns gaining control and power over their own lives. It involves awareness raising building self-confidence enlarging capabilities, expansion of choices, increased access to and over human and physical resources. It makes people lives better, freer and more fulfilling. According to the World Bank (2004) empowerment is the process of enhancing an individual "or group" capacity to make choices and transform those into desired actions and outcomes, according to Sen and Batliwala (2000), or empowerment is the process by which the powerless gain greater control over resources and over ideology. The International women's conference at Nairobi in 1985 led to the opening of the concept of empowerment of women as a tool for redistribution of social power and control of resources in favour of underprivileged like women. The parameters of empowerment are multi-facets and multi-dimensional for the real upliftment of the down-trodden and weaker sections of the society, i.e. women. They include:

- To enhance self-esteem and self-confidence in women.
- Enabling women to gain equal access to and control over resources.
- To foster decision-making and action through collective process.
- To provide information, knowledge and skill for economic independence.
- Transforming the institution such as family education, religion, media, etc. and structure such as legal, political, economic and social, etc. through which ideology and practice of subordination is reinforced and reproduced.
- Indian's Global Position in Gender development: Over the past few years, gender equality and empowerment of women have been receiving special emphasis. The 8th March in every year has been celebrated as the International Women's Day. India celebrated the year of 2001 as the national women's empowerment year. However, in practice it is flattering due to various factors such as low literacy, restrictive social structure, predominance of patriarchal society, low exposure to growth opportunities, non-involvement in income generating activities as well as continuing socio-economic dependence over the years.

TABLE 1

India's Global Position

Country	*Gender Development Index*		*Gender Empowerment Measures*	
	1992	*2001*	*1992*	*2001*
Norway	0.911	0.937	0.752	0.836
Austria	0.901	0.935	0.568	0.738
China	0.578	0.715	0.474	0.321
India	0.401	0.523	0.226	0.240
Pakistan	0.360	0.466	0.153	0.173

Source: HDR 1995, 1999 and 2001, GoI, Economic Survey, 2001-02, p. 237.

The table shows that even our next door neighbour China is having much better position than India from both GDI and GEM point of view. As per Human Development Report (2005) India's GDI came to 0.586 and Human Development Index was found 0.602.

CRYING NEED FOR GENDER EQUALITY AND EMPOWERMENT OF WOMEN

Despite the constitutional provisions and other supportive measures to make the society gender just for effective empowerment, the facts and figures however, present an altogether different picture still women are fighting hard to get gender equality and empowerment. For instance, they are fighting hard to get their political justice with limited success in Panchayati Raj Institution where 33% seats are reserved for them. The women reservation bill is yet to be passed in our parliament which seeks to equalize the advantage of women participation in politics at the national level. Majumdar, Dipika has painted a very gloomy picture of women's status in these words, "Bride burning dowry death, wife beating rape, gangrape and prostitution show the subjugated and humiliated position of the Indian women. Few cases of bride burning or dowry death are brought to the notice of the police. Favour till eventually find their way to newspaper column, these show the horrifying and miserable conditions of Indian women. Wife beating by husband is also a mental torture leading to the suicide of the wife in many cases. Rape and gangrape are no longer personal problems, but social problems. Extreme poverty and economic necessity of women are sometimes associated with the problem of prostitution" (Majumdar, Dipika, 1998). A very dangerous increasing trend of crimes and violence in different forms against women tells the real tale of women's status in the Indian society.

Undoubtedly, violence against women is also an evil reflecting lower status of woman. One in every three women globally is subjected to violence during her life time. One in four women is exposed to domestic violence and this represents one of the main causes of injury and deaths among women worldwide (Forum for Women and Development, 2005). Thus, what to talk of India, gender discrimination is quite glaring in economically developed countries.

TABLE 2

National Level Crimes Against Women: All India

Crimes	*1991*	*1998*
Rape	9793	15031
Molestation	20611	31031
Kidnapping & Abduction	12300	16381
Eve teasing	10283	8122
Dowry Death	5077	6917
Cruelty by Relatives	15949	41317

Source: NHDR, 2001.

Indian women, regardless of their caste, religion or class, never enjoys equal status in the family or society. Gender discrimination in South Asia is situated with deeply ingrained system of patriarchy which limits and confines women to subordinates role (Human Development in South Asia, p. 3). Starting with discrimination against the girl child even before she is born, the life of the average. Indian woman is one of deprivation in every sphere. The logic behind such discrimination is such that girls appear as a liability for the family as they have to be married off, often with huge dowry, whereas boys are considered an asset as they carry on the family lineage and support the family in times of financial need and bring in dowry (Human Development in South Asia, 2000, pp. 122-23). Studies by Bumiller (2003), Kapoor (1993), Kartekar (1998), Mosses (1994) and UNFPA (1997) confirmed this view and reported a large number of cases of 'missing girls' in India. Indeed it may be Highly shameful to take down that 84% gynaecologists in Mumbai admitted to performing sex-determination tests as per report of Human Develop mint in South Asia, 2000. As a result there has been continuous decline in sex ratio of India since 1901 to 1971 from 972 to 930 women per 1000 men. In 1991 census it came down to 927 per 1000. However, there has been marginal increase in India's ratio in 2001, i.e. 930 male preference adversely affects females through inequitable allocation of food, education and healthcare, a disparity frequently reinforced throughout life and for this, they have also been adopting the methods of foeticide. A World Bank Report on women's health status in India, released in 1996, has grimly catalogued the variety of ways in which women are discriminated against. As girls, they get less vaccination, less education and less nutrition than their brothers and when they grow up they are less healthy than their male counterparts and succumb more easily to sickness and disease. An Indian woman is 100 times more likely to die of maternity-related causes than is a woman in the industrialized countries. It is needless to say that the intra-household distribution of labour and resources is loaded against women who work more and get a lesser share of food, health care, leisure and play. It is studied that in rural Punjab 21% of girls in poor families suffer severe malnutrition compared to 3% of boys in the same family. Indeed, poor boys are better fed than rich girls (UNDP, 1995). Is it not true that whatever food is available tend to be distributed disproportionately between males and females? No doubt, poverty accentuates gender gaps and when adversity strikes, it is women who often are most vulnerable (UNDDP, 1997, p. 64). India continues to have the highest concentration of poverty accounting for almost one-third of those with an income of less than one dollar a day, and it is estimated that women account for 73% of those below the poverty line. Even households that have enough women are disadvantaged in terms of food consumption because of traditional notions of what food women must not eat or that women must eat last. Income poverty explains only about 10% of the variation in child nutrition (Mahbub Ul Haq Development Centre, 2000).

Female education is the major awareness generating factor toward gender equality and empowerment of women. The impact of skill formation through education, though recognized from the very beginning as pre-condition of growth and modernisation, was not explicitly incorporated in the standard Harrod-Domar type growth model (B.B. Bhattacharya, 2007) but the success of the East Asian growth and the deferment of the law of diminishing return through upgradation. Of technology and skill formation prove to be eye-opener and the new theory of growth known as the endogenous growth model recognized explicitly the role of skill formation through education in continuous upgradation of technology and productivity of both male as well as female workers. The beneficial interactions between education and such socio-economic variables as fertility, health and gender discrimination, and a heightened level of human articulation, including the urge to 'question and improve oneself' improve one's immediate environment, develop self-propelling norms of progress and play better citizenry on the other, are now much better recognized (Knight, 1996; Birdsalletat, 1997). Gunner Myrdal was right enough in his observation when he said, "it (literacy) is a prerequisite for the acquisition other skills and the development of more rational attitudes" for him "persons who can read and understand drafts and written directives make better industrial workers than those who cannot. Farmers who can perform simply computations and can read pamphlets are more progressive cultivators than those not so equipped." To stimulate economic development it is an urgent need for a massive effort to make the whole population literate as rapidly as possible particularly in the precarious situation of the larger and poorer countries like India. But what to talk of India in almost all the South Asian countries the education system even at the primary level, is heavily biased against girls, and throughout the region the literacy rate is lower among women than among men." This is partly because governmental efforts in the educational field were so modest. Facilities for popular education were woefully inadequate and secondary schools were 'job-oriented' toward service in administration. But mainly the explanation lies in the popular attitudes dating back to pre-colonial times. The three Asian religions could little for the education of girls and generally placed women in an inferior position though Buddhism, was more egalitarian in this as in other respects (Gunner Myrdal, 1972). It is heartening to take down that our education network is the second largest and we have the third largest reservoir of scientific and technical manpower in the world. Undoubtedly, access to education has improved at all levels, and women, too have been a beneficiary of the same (Tilak, 1997) but then, the absolute improvement registered by all sections of the Indian society, can not hide the relative deprivation of women. The literacy rate of women has gone up from 39.29% in 1991 to 54.16% in 2001 recording the increase in female literacy by 14.8% outpacing that for male literacy, i.e. 11.7% resulting in reeducation in male-female literacy gap from 24.84%, in 1991 to 21.70% in 2001. Still there is wide disparity between the education status of women and that of men. Although the jump of female literacy rate 14.8% from 1991 to 2001 is a good sign, but fear is that under the new economic regime, with it presiding deities of privatisation and globalisation, their access to education would get further eroded, more so because the parents struggle for survival might leave no choice but rope in children as additional earning hands (G.K. Chadha, 2003).

TABLE 3

Literacy (1951-2001)

(*in %*)

Censes Year	*Person*	*Male*	*Female*	*Male-female gap in Literacy*
1951	18.38	27.16	8.86	18.30
1961	28.30	40.40	15.35	25.05
1971	34.45	45.96	21.97	23.98
1981	43.57	56.38	29.76	26.62
1991	52.21	64.13	39.29	24.84
2001	65.38	75.85	54.16	21.70

Source: Census of India, 2001.

It is nothing short of a national shame that nearly three-fourth of female workers against one-third of male workers were illiterate. As late as 1999-2000, only 7% of our female workers against 23% of male workers were educated. Still more painful is to notice that the proportion of illiterate female workers was as high as 78% in agriculture, 82% in mining-quarrying, 78% in construction, 58% in manufacturing, 48% in trade and 37% in community-social-personal services whereas the corresponding figures for male workers were 46%, 40%, 37%, 21%, 16% and 14% respectively (G.K. Chadha, 2004). Moreover, it is noteworthy that no gap in adult literacy rate is found in economically sound Norway, Japan and United Kingdom and even in Indonesia; a low gap in Thailand, China and Sri Lanka, but a very high gap in economically weaker Pakistan, India and Bangladesh is found. It is but true that after ten five year plans and sixty years of Independence we have 9.5 lakh primary and upper primary schools 75% of which are located in rural areas in 12.3 lakh habitations, 94% of the rural population has a school within one kilometer but a large number of female children are out of school. According to the Indian Planning Commission half the villages do not have a primary school till now. And a worrisome feature in this concern is that most children drop out of school for a variety of reasons ranging from poverty to parents unwillingness to get their children particularly girls educated due to socio-cultural inhibitions. Although one of the important recommendations of the national policy of Education is to promote empowerment of women through the agency of education, girls are particularly deprived of education.

Improvement in economic status is a more visible indicator of empowerment of women. Economic dependency makes women weaker and helpless which compels them to be dependent on their relatives. Sen (1990) claims that wage work increases the bargaining power of women in the household and the economy, and is therefore empowering. It is generally believed that an increase in employment of women would result in an improvement in their economic and social status. The Work Participation Rate (WPR) in India comes out as higher for males than females both in rural and urban areas. The data given by decennial census as well as by the national sample Survey Support this proposition and this can be explained in terms of socio-cultural norms and prejudices, traditional values, etc. which restrict the entry of women in the labour market. The table reveals that the female work participation rate has increased from 19.7% in 1981 to 25.7% in 2001 but still it is lower than the male work participation rate both in urban and rural areas, reflecting gender inequality in this concern.

TABLE 4

Work Participation Rate (WPR)

Year	*Female*			*Male*			*Persons*		
	Rural	*Urban*	*Total*	*Rural*	*Urban*	*Total*	*Rural*	*Urban*	*Total*
1981	23.1	8.3	19.7	53.8	49.1	52.6	38.8	30.0	36.7
1991	26.8	9.2	22.3	52.6	48.9	51.6	40.1	30.2	37.5
2001	31.0	11.6	25.7	52.4	50.9	51.9	42.0	32.2	39.3

Sources: Census Reports 1991, 2001, GOI.

As the agrarian economy has the capacity to carry a large number of disguised unemployed persons both male and female or absorb them at low levels of productivity, the urban rates of work participation are comparatively lower. Relatively a little role played by women in economic activities which increase their dependency, making them more vulnerable to men is one of the factors that lead to gender inequality. Collection of fuel, fodder and water, livestock-raising and kitchen gardening take away 4-5 hours of women's labour for unpaid care economy (Vibhuti Patal, 2007). As the 1998 UN Human Development Report there is no country in the world in which women's quality of life is equal to that of men, according to a compile measure that includes longevity, health status, educational opportunities and political rights and so today woman's right to employment seems however to have been widely accepted as a necessary condition for bettering women's welfare and empowering them. In comparison to other countries the engagement rate of Indian women above 15 years of age in economic activity is not very significant, which is only 42.5% whereas it is for Norway 60.3%, for the U.S.A. 60%, for Japan 50% in 2003. Thus, only 42.5% engagement in economic activities constituting 50% of male engagement is lower than even other SAARC Countries. For instance, in Sri Lanka only 43.5% of

TABLE 5

A Comparative Status of Women in India Female Economic Activity (Age 15 and above)

Countries	*Rate (%) 2003*	*Index 1990-100*	*as % of Male 2003*
Norway	60.3	111	26
United States	59.6	107	83
Japan	51.2	104	68
China	72.4	93	86
Maldives	65.4	101	80
Sri Lanka	43.5	108	56
India	42.5	105	50
Pakistan	36.7	129	44
Nepal	56.9	101	67
Bangladesh	66.5	101	76
Bhutan	57.1	100	65
Ethiopia	57.2	98	67
Burundi	81.7	98	89
Niger	69.3	99	75

Source: UNDP, Human Development Report, 2005.

women engaged in economic activities that constitute only 56% of their male counterpart whereas in Maldives 65.4% of women are engaged in economic activities constituting 80% male-engagement in economic activities. In Bangladesh, Nepal and Bhutan a little above 50% women are engaged in economic activities constituting about 76%, 67% and 65% respectively of their male counterparts.

Of course, employment gives income to employed and it can be a factor in self-esteem and indeed, in esteem by others (R.P. Sen and P.N. Maury, 2005). Their contribution to economy through self-employed and home-based work is gone unnoticed. While constituting a significant part of the emerging labour force, women are lowerer vulnerable due to low literacy rates and low levels of education. A major insecurity faced by the women workers is the lack of marketable skills due to their low level of education. They find it difficult to move to other alternative jobs because they lack requisite educational qualifications and skills. This basically highlights the need to focus on promotion strategies for increasing skills to improve the quality of employment, particularly among the vulnerable groups (Jeemal Unni and Uma Rani, 2005)

TABLE 6

Women's Representation in Parliament

Lok Sabha Members	*No. of Women Members*	*% of Women*
1st	22	4.3
2nd	27	5.4
3rd	34	6.7
4th	31	5.9
5th	22	4.3
6th	18	3.4
7th	28	5.1
8th	44	8.1
9th	28	5.2
10th	39	7.2
11th	39	7.2
12th	49	9.0
13th	44	8.0
14th	45	8.25

Source: Election Commission of India.

Representation of women at the decision-making levels is considered as the best way of empowering women and thus, achieving gender equality but the political participation of women reflecting women participation in decision making is very poor in comparison to other countries. Women's representation in Indian parliament could not touch 10% of the total members. The table given below clarifies the picture in this concern.

Undoubtedly, political participation of India women in comparison to other countries is poor.

TABLE 7

Women's Political Participation in Different Countries

Country	*Women's Govt. level % of total in 2005*	*Country*	*Women's Govt. level % of total in 2005*
Sweden	52.4	China	14.3
Spain	50.0	Sri Lanka	10.3
Finland	47.1	Bangladesh	8.3
Germany	46.2	Pakistan	5.6
U.K.	44.4	India	3.4
U.S.A	28.6		

Source: HDR, 2005.

The recent report of UNDP, 2007-08 of women at ministerial level percentage as well as country ranking on the basis of Human Development Index presents the real position of India.

TABLE 8

Country	*Women at Ministerial level (%)*	*HDI country ranking*
Spain	50.0	13
Norway	44.4	2
Australia	20.0	3
Chile	16.7	40
Bahrain	8.7	41
India	3.4	128
Yemen	2.9	153

Source: UNDP Report, 2007-08.

Various researchers in Indian context have shown that women representatives are not only less corrupt; they are also more responsive to community needs than men. A 2007 survey of OECD countries by the women's Forum for the Economy and society and various studies by the World Bank find that women are more difficult to corrupt than men and that there is less corruption when there are more women in positions of responsibility.

The Millennium Development Goal on gender equality lists the increase of women's political representation as a subgoal. Though women's political rights are formally recognized all over the world and codified into national constitution, the global average of women's share in Parliament stands at paltry 15.9% (IPU, 2005). In India the mid-term appraisal of the 9th Plan urged for empowerment of women socially, politically and economically. And by political empowerment its explanation is that "if women are to be politically empowered, the immediate need is to resort to different forms of affirmative discrimination so that women proportionate numbers reach critical places to ensure that their voices are heard."

GOVERNMENT POLICIES AND INTERVENTIONS

The constitution made necessary arrangements through appropriate legislation and supportive frameworks of rules and procedures for gender equality and empowerment of women. The constitution of India guarantees to all Indian women—

- Equality before the law—Article 14.
- Discrimination by the state on grounds of only region, race, caste, sex, place of birth of any of these—Article 15(1).
- Special provision to be made by the state in favour of women and children—Article 15(3).
- Equality of opportunity for all citizens in matter related to employment or appointment in any office under the state—Article 16.
- State policy to be directed to securing for men and women equally, the right to an adequate means of livelihood—Article 39(a).

- Equal pay for equal work for both men and women—Article 39(d).
- Provision to be made by the state for securing just and human conditions of work and for maternity relief—Article 42.
- To promote harmony and to renounce of practices derogatory to the dignity of women—Article 51(A).
- Articles 243D (3), 243D (4), 243T (3) and 243T (4) of the constitution makes provision for reserving not less than one-third of the total seats for women in the direct elections to local bodies, viz. Panchayati and Municipalities (NADR, 2001).

Besides these, the National Commission for Women (NCW) was set-up in 1992 in order to safeguard the rights and interests of women. It has been reviewing women-specific and women related legislations and advising the government to bring forth necessary amendments from time to time. There are about 42 central Acts concerning women of which 32 Acts have been reviewed by the NCW for their efficiency and removing gender discriminatory provisions. In addition, the Department of Women and Child Development (DWCD) is also in the process of initiating new legislation amending existing ones so that they become more potent in protecting women. This includes protection of women from domestic violence for which Domestic Violence Act, 2005 came into force on September 14, 2005. Of the 435 calls received by the West Bengal Women's Commission since April 2004, 285 cases related to family violence, women alleged that they were subjected to mental and physical harassment by their family members, especially mother-in-law and husbands, for dowry or divorce. The Act seeks to provide immediate and emergent relief to women who face situations of domestic violence.

As empowerment of women cannot be happen unless they are provided with adequate income generating activities, through wage and self-employment, a number of schemes such as Swyamsiddha, Swavlamban and support to Training-*cum*-Employment Programme (STEP) are in progress where women mobilized as viable SHG are utilizing micro-credit with the help of agencies like the Rashtriya Mahila Kosh for income generating activities or getting trained in various traditional trades and crafts such as poultry, bee keeping and weaving as well as newly emerging vocations such as the IT sector, or skill upgradation and capacity building.

Women as an independent target group accounting for 495.74 million, recording 48.3% of India total population have been receiving attention of the government right from the First Five Year Plan (1951-56). But from the Sixth Five Year Plan (1980-85) and onwards there has been marked shift in the approach to women's issues from welfare to development and the Ninth Five Year Plan (1977-2002) made two significant changes in the conceptual strategy of planning for women. Firstly, empowerment of women became one of the nine primary objectives of the plan, and secondly, the plan attempted convergence of existing services available in both women-specific and women-related sectors. The Tenth Plan (2002-07) reinforced the commitment to gender budgeting to establish its gender differential impact and to translate gender commitment. In Budget 2005-06, the Union government for the first time included a statement on gender budgeting, which presented the magnitude of allocation constituted about 2.8% of the total expenditure for various programmes/schemes under the 10 demands for grants that were expected to benefit women substantially whereas the total magnitude of gender budget showed a rise to 5.1% of the total in the budget estimates for 2006-07. Gender equality through empowering women is inculcated as a significant approach in the 10th Five Year Plan but in the process of gender equality, potency and exuberance of women, a lot more needs to be done, as most of women living in rural areas are illiterate and they are trapped in vicious circle of poverty and deprivations.

CONCLUDING REMARKS

Even after 60 years of Independence Indian women have been exposed to greater insecurity, poverty, illiteracy, unhealthy living conditions and backwardness and more than 75% of their work is in unpaid activities which are neither economically rewarded nor socially value or recognized. In the context of the overall importance of gender equality and empowerment of women, what is required now is to build up a scenario at the ground levels for appropriately effective action programmes.

Constitutional provisions and laws do not lead to social transformation unless followed by actions and social awareness of the discrimination that have been perpetuated on women from time to time. What is required is to break the barriers that hinder women's access to education, health and economic self-sufficiency. Lack of awareness and consciousness of women about their rights, interests and benefits provided in the constitution and different laws and inefficiency and lack of sincerity and seriousness of the authorities concerned who have been entrusted with the responsibilities for administration and enforcement of the said laws are the main hurdles which need to be removed on priority basis.

Women's empowerment and their due status in the society is the major responsibility for which specific programmes and measures in respect to issues where women are lagging behind men and losing human rights are highly desirable but the most desirable is to educate them properly because education is a prime factor for women's development and empowerment which opens opportunities for their participation in various fields of life. Plans, policies and legislations provide only the blue print for directing the upliftment of women's status in the society and these would not be successful without economic empowerment of women. Of course, empowerment in other spheres of life would more or less automatically follow economic empowerment. Micro-credit based income generating activities for economic empowerment is a good beginning opening the door of credit to the marginalized poor women who were denied access to traditional channels of credit. This is not enough. For empowerment of women it is desirable to facilitate and promote their equal participation by means of preferential treatment in education and employment.

Above all, the main obstacle in the way of gender equality and empowerment of women is our traditional social system and so there is need to change social outlook toward women. Till now it is found that even the educated women particularly in rural areas are not coming out of the social traditional trap, with regard to education, employment, healthcare, household work and public participation. Women are treated as respectable life partners but not work partners. Men are entitled to higher education, employment and better healthcare, women are not. Going by the relative performance of men and women, over the past few decades, no objective analyst would deny that women have outsmarked men in various fields. Why then the discrimination continues right from the cradle stage. For G.K. Chadha (2003) this question is addressed more to rural than urban areas, more to parents than the state and more to owns attitude of resignation than to male chuvinism. And the remedy too has to originate from these very quarters. But unfortunately, education and economic status are positively related to foeticides in India and so there is need to change in mindset of even Indian women. It has hardly ever been recognized that "failing to invest adequately in educating women reduces the potential benefits of educating men" (Giri, 1997). The failure to see through the man-woman complementarily has been a costly failure in terms of lost opportunity to raise productivity, to increase family income and to improve quality of life. The abolition of dowry system is a must for change in the outlook toward women. Till dowry system prevails in the society, such change seems to be difficult. Perhaps one of the major causes behind regarding female child as a liability is dowry system. For centuries women have been forced to enjoy an inferior status in the society and in the global era it is hoped that women remains no longer in that position but one should not forget that globalisation is a train which waits for nobody. Indian women are not on the driving seat of that train and they need to be seated on the driving seat because women leaders often end up prioritizing the needs of women, which are also the needs of the society. That can be possible through proper education which may prove instrumental in changes in their outlook toward their own female child. This is with reference to the editorial "Home Truths" (Oct. 15, 2007). It is ironic that in India where goddesses are worshipped by millions of men, over 40% women are subject to beating by their husbands.

References

Agrawal, Meenu and Sharma, Meenakshi (2008), Globalisation as a Challenge and Opportunities in Impact of Globalisation of Development (ed.), Meenu Agrawal, Deep & Deep Publications Pvt. Ltd., New Delhi.

Akhoury, R. (2005), Women in Unorganized Sector: Post-Reform Scenario Globalisation and Contemporary Economic Scenario, Abhijeet Publication, New Delhi.

Bhattacharya, B.B. (2007), Education, Skill Formation and India's Economic Development, Presidential Address, 90th IEA Conf. Volume.

Chadha, G.K. (2003), What is Dominating the Indian Labour Market, Presidential Address, ISLE 45th Conference.

Conference volume of Bihar Economic Association.

Different Governmental Reports.

Gunnar Myrdal (1972), Population Quality Asian Drama.

ILO's World Commission on Social Dimension of Globalisation (2004).

Indian Economic Association, 90th Conference Volume.

Indian Economic Association, 89th Conference Volume.

Jha, B.K. (2006), Wage and Employment Scenario in the Unorganized Sector in the Global Era.

Jha, B.K. (2008), Impact of Globalisation on Poverty and Unemployment: Evidence from Uttar Pradesh in Impact of Globalisation on Development (ed.) Meenu Agrawal.

Kurushetra.

Majumdar, Dipika: The Changing Status of Women in India in (ed.) Datta, Gupta, Politics and Society, Today and Tomorrow, K.P. Bagchi, Kolkata.

Mishra, S.K. and Singh R.P., Determinants of Female Empowerment and Reproductive Behaviour in India, *IEJ*, Vol. 50, Nos. 3&4.

Patel, Vibhuti (2007), Globalisation and Women in Bhartiya Samajik Ckintan, Vol. VI, No. 2.

T.S. Papola (2004), Globalisation, Employment and Social Protection, *ISLE*, Vol. 47, No. 3.

Gender Budgeting and Women Empowerment

Nayan Kumar, Subalal Yadav and Rana Pratap

INTRODUCTION

As per the 2001 Census, the total female population of India is estimated at 495.74 million. This is 48.3 per cent of the country's total population. The figure shows that women and children are vital human resource of the country. Thus, they are considered to be the most critical determinant for its overall socio-economic development. The economic reform measures initiated in the early 1990s and consequent fiscal policies were found to have widened gender differences in the country. Studies on gender budgeting in India indicate that India's impressive economic growth in the last two decades have not succeeded in addressing the issues like relative deprivation of women in India. Several macro-indicators on education, health, sex ratio, economic participation, etc. point towards the existing imbalance in the status of India's female population *vis-a-vis* men. The Gender Budgeting exercise has reflected government's recognition, acceptance and willingness to use fiscal policy in achieving its ends which are beneficial to women. This change of mindset indicates that this process is a powerful tool that can contribute to narrowing down gender gaps, especially in income, health, education, nutrition and living standards.

After 60 years of independence, a significant number of women face disparities in access and control over resources. These disparities get reflected in important social development indicators such as health, nutrition, literacy, educational attainments, skill levels, occupational status, etc. In addition, there are a number of gender specific barriers that prevent women from gaining access to their rightful share in the flow of public good and services. Unless these gender requirements and their felt needs are incorporated and mainstreamed in the planning and development process of the country, it is likely that the benefits of economic growth are likely to completely bypass a significant section of the country's population which does not augur well for the future growth of the economy.

Gender Budgeting is understood as a dissection of the government budget to establish its gender-differential impacts and to translate gender commitments into budgetary commitments. Thus gender Budgeting looks at Government budget from a gender perspective to assess how it addresses the needs of women in all sectors. It does not seek to create a separate budget but to provide affirmative action to address the specific needs of women. Gender responsive budgeting initiatives provide a way for assessing the impact of government revenue and expenditure on women.

Gender Budgeting lends itself to strengthening administrative processes and actions to achieve the targets for improvement in the position of women. It not only entails a look at allocation of resources for women but goes beyond to cover tracking the utilisation of allocated resources, impact analysis and beneficiary incidence analysis of public expenditure and policy from a gender perspective. Hence gender budgeting is not an accounting exercise as commonly perceived and understood. It encompasses incorporating a gender perspective and sensitiveness at all levels and stages of the developmental planning, programmes, schemes, processes and implementation. An important outcome of the application of Gender budgeting is that it paves the way for gender mainstreaming in the developmental process and in understanding how the needs of women can be addressed in not only "traditional" areas like agriculture, health, education but also in so called 'gender neutral' sectors like Power, Defense, Chemicals, Biotechnology, Commerce, Information Technology, etc. where, in the first instance, the gender implications do not seem apparent.

As the nodal Ministry for women, the Ministry of Women and Child Development has been undertaking several initiatives for empowerment of women. In this context the Ministry has honed Gender Budgeting as a tool for achieving the goals and targets enshrined for women in our constitution and Plans and Policies. In 2004-05 the Ministry adopted "Budgeting for Gender Equity" as a Mission Statement. A Strategic Framework of Activities to implement this mission was also framed and disseminated across all Ministries of Government of India.

BUDGETING FOR GENDER EQUITY

Broad Framework of Activities

Quantification of allocation of resources for women in the Union, States and Local Administration budgets and expenditure thereof:

- Refining and standardizing methodology and development of tools.
- Trend Analysis.
- Analysis of change in pattern, shift in priorities in allocation across clusters of services etc.
- Variations in allocation of resources and actual expenditure.
- Adherence to physical targets.

Gender Audit of Policies of the Government Monetary, Fiscal, Trade, etc. at Centre and State

- Research and micro-studies to guide micro-policies like credit policy, taxes, etc.
- Identification of gender impact of policies/interventions viewed as gender neutral.
- Micro-studies to identify need for affirmative action in favour of women towards gender imbalances.

Impact Assessment of Various Schemes in the Union and State Budgets

- Micro-studies on incidence of benefits.
- Analysis of cost of delivery of services.

Analyzing programmes, strategies, interventions and policy initiatives from the perspective of their impact on status of women as reflected in important macro-indicators like literacy MMR, participation in workforce.

- E.g. analysis of substance and content of various interventions at health of women and correlate the same with indicators like MMR to establish need for corrective action in formulation of scheme/approach.

Institutionalizing the Generation and Collection of Gender Disaggregated Data

- Developing MIS for feedback from implementing agencies.
- Inclusion of new parameters in data collection in Census and surveys by NSO, CSO, etc.

Consultations and Capacity Building

- Collation of research and exchange of best practices.
- Developing methodologies and tools for dissemination.
- Forums and Partnerships amongst experts and stakeholders.

Review of decision-making processes to establish gender equity in participation review of extent participation of women in decision-making processes and to establish processes and models aimed at gender equity in decision-making and greater participation of women.

Formulation and reflection of satellite accounts to capture the contribution of women to the economy by way of their activities in areas that go unreported like care economy unpaid work in rearing domestic animals, etc.

The year 2005-06 has been devoted to carrying forward this exercise and universalizing gender budgeting initiatives in the government at the Centre and states.

The term Gender Budgeting has been defined differently in

various documents on the subject. A simple definition is as under:

> 'Gender Budgeting is a dissection of the Government budget to establish its gender-differential impacts and to translate gender commitments into budgetary commitments.'

The Gender Budgeting looks at the Government budget from a gender perspective to assess how it addresses the needs for women in the areas like health, education, employment, etc.

Gender Budgeting does not seek to create a separate budget but seeks affirmative action to address specific needs of women.

Gender Responsive Budgeting initiatives provide a way of assessing the impact of Government revenue and expenditure on women. Critical activities constituting the gender budgeting exercise include:

(a) Addressing gap between policy commitment and allocation for women through adequate resource allocation and gender sensitive programme formulation and implementation.
(b) Mainstreaming gender concerns in public expenditure and policy.
(c) Gender audit of public expenditure, programme implementation and policies—relating to public expenditure, fiscal and monetary matters, etc.

The Challenge of Gender Budgeting lies in translating related policy commitments into budgetary allocations and outcomes. The commitments towards women are reflected in our Constitution, Policies, Legislations and plan documents.

Gender Commitments

The commitment to gender equity is well entrenched at the highest policy-making level—the Constitution of India. A few important provisions for women are:

- Article 14—Equal Rights and Opportunities in Political, Economic and Social Spheres.
- Article 15—Prohibits discrimination on grounds of sex.

- Article 15(3)—Enables affirmative discrimination in favour of women.
- Article 39—Equal means of livelihood and equal pay for equal work.
- Article 42—Just and Humane conditions of work and maternity relief.
- Article 51(A)(e)—Fundamental Duty to renounce practices, derogatory to dignity of women.

The National Policy for Empowerment of Women, 2001 envisaged introduction of a gender perspective in the budgeting process as an operational strategy.

These provisions are effected and supplemented by the legal framework. A few law and legislations that are in place—

Women Specific Legislations

- Immoral Traffic (Prevention) Act, 1956.
- The Maternity Benefit Act, 1961.
- The Dowry Prohibition Act, 1961.
- Indecent Representation of Women (Prohibition) Act, 1986,
- The Commission of Sati (Prevention) Act, 1987.
- Protection of Women from Domestic Violence Act, 2005.

Economic

Factories Act, 1948, Minimum Wages Act, 1948, Equal Remuneration Act, 1976. The Employees' State Insurance Act, 1948, The Plantation Labour Act, 1951, The Bonded Labour System (Abolition) Act, 1976.

Protection

Relevant provisions of Code of Criminal Procedure, 1973; Special Provisions Under IPC, The Legal Practitioners (Women) Act, 1923, The Pre-Natal Diagnostic Technique (Regulation and Prevention of Misuse) Act, 1994.

Social

Family Courts Act, 1984, The Indian Succession Act, 1925, The Medical Termination of Pregnancy Act, 1971, The Child Marriage Restraint Act, 1929, The Hindu Marriage Act, 1955, The

Hindu Succession Act, 1956 (and Amended in 2005), The Indian Divorce Act, 1969.

FIVE YEAR PLANS AND GENDER BUDGETING

The plan documents have over the years reflected the evolving trends in gender matters. Formal earmarking of funds for women began with the Women's Component Plan. However, gender sensitivity in allocation of resources starts with the Seventh Plan:

- The Seventh Plan introduced the concept of monitoring of 27 beneficiary-oriented schemes for women by DWCD. The exercise continues and the number of schemes covered is being expanded.
- The Eighth Plan (1992-97) highlighted for the first time a gender perspective and the need to ensure a definite flow of funds from the general developmental sectors to women. The Plan document made an express statement that "... the benefits to development from different sectors should not by pass women and special programmes on women should complement the general development programmes. The later, in turn, should reflect great gender sensitivity."
- The Ninth Plan (1997-2002) adopted the 'Women's Component Plan' as one of the major strategies and directed both the Central and State Governments to ensure "not less than 30 per cent of the funds/benefits are earmarked in all the women's related sectors. Special vigil advocated on the flow of the earmarked funds/ benefits through an effective mechanism to ensure that the proposed strategy brings forth a holistic approach towards empowering women."
- Tenth Plan reinforces commitment to gender budgeting to establish its gender-differential impact and to translate gender commitments into budgetary commitments.

EXTRACTS FROM TENTH PLAN

"The Tenth Plan will continue the process of dissecting the

Government budget to establish its gender-differential impact and to translate gender commitments into budgetary commitments—the Tenth Plan will initiate immediate action in tying up these two effective concepts of Women Component Plan and Gender Budgeting to play a complementary role to each other, and thus ensure both preventive and *post facto* action in enabling women to receive their rightful share from all the women-related general development sectors."

The Approach Paper to the 11th Five Year Plan talks of "Towards Faster and More Inclusive Growth". The stress is on including the excluded. The 11th Plan strategy for gender balancing takes care of the special needs of women such as clean cooking fuels, care for pregnant and nursing women, etc. This requires appropriate provision in government policies/schemes across Ministries/Departments.

The importance of Gender Budgeting has been stressed time and again in different forums. To provide further impetus to this objective, the Finance Minister in 2004-05 had mandated the setting up of Gender Budgeting Cells in all Ministries/ Departments and highlighted the perceived need for budget data to be presented in a manner that brought out the gender sensitiveness of the budgetary allocations. This was followed by a more emphatic commitment in the Budget speech of 2005-06, wherein the Gender budgetary allocations were reflected in a two-way classified Gender Budgeting Statement in the Union Budget-The first Statement indicated those Ministries/Departments which identified allocation of 100% for Schemes/Programmes flowing to women and second Statement reflecting allocation of 30% and above but below 100% for Schemes/Programmes for women. In the year 2005-06, Gender Budget Allocation from Ministries/ Departments and 10 demand for grants was estimated at about 4.77% of the total Public Sector outlay. The 2006-07 Budget revealed an estimated allocation of 3.8% for women from 18 Ministries/Departments and 33 Demand for grants. The reason why there was an apparent fall in the Gender budget allocation between 2005-06 and 2006-07 was on account of a more accurate reflection of the actual amounts flowing to women through Programmes and Schemes. During the year 2007-08, an estimated 4.6% of the Public Sector outlay was identified as Gender Budget from 27 Ministries/Departments and 33 Demand for grants. The

Ministry of Finance in consultation with the Ministry of Women and Child Development has issued a Gender Budget Charter on March 2007.

CHARTER OF GENDER BUDGET CELLS

Composition of Gender Budget Cells

The GBC may set for itself, specific quarterly/half yearly/ annual targets to be achieved in terms of the following suggested areas of work :

(1) Identification of a minimum of 3 and maximum of 6 largest programmes (in terms of budget allocation) implementation by the Ministry and the major Sub-Programmes thereunder, with a view to conducting an analysis of the gender issues addressed by them.

- This is to be facilitated by describing the current situation with respect to the Sub-Programme (using disaggregated data in terms of beneficiaries as much as possible) and describing the activities for achieving the given output.
- Output indicators may be identified for measurement against performance in the coming year.
- Activities targeted at improving the situation of women under these programmes may be highlighted. In this regard, an assessment may be made of the extent to which sectoral policies address the situation of women, whether budget allocation are adequate to implement the gender responsive policy; monitoring whether the money was actually spent as planned, what was delivered and to whom; and whether the policy as implemented changed the situation described in the direction of promoting/ achieving greater gender equality.
- Results of this analysis may be included as an annex titled "Gender Responsive Budgeting Initiative" in the Ministry's Outcome/Performance Budget for the year.

- GBCs of such Ministries/Departments which have identified programmes where 100% of the budgetary allocation for the scheme is earmarked to benefit women, may undertake a similar analysis as described above. Results of this analysis may also be included in the Ministry's Department's Outcome/Performance budget for the year.

(2) Conducting/Commissioning Performance audit (at the field level wherever possible) for reviewing the actual physical/financial targets of the programme, the constraints if any, in implementation, the need for strengthening delivery systems, infrastructure/capacity building, etc.

(3) Organizing meetings/discussions/consultations with GBCs of related departments within the Ministry, field level organisation/civil society groups/NGOs working in the sector for exchanging ideas and getting feedback on the efficacy of sectoral policies and programmes.

(4) Suggesting further policy interventions based on findings of the above.

(5) Participating in and organizing Training/Sensitisation/ Capacity Building workshops for officials, concerned with formulation of policy/programme implementation and budget and accounts at the Ministerial level and also in the implementing agencies/attached/ subordinate offices and organisations under the administrative control of the Ministry.

(6) Apparently "gender neutral" programmes are not necessarily gender neutral in the impact they have, when seen through gender lens. Hence, in sectors like Defence, Power, Telecom, Communications, Transport and Industry, etc. GBCs may undertake an exercise to identify the possibility of undertaking initiatives/special measures to facilitate/improve access to services for women and their active participation in the decision-making process at various levels.

(7) Disseminate best practices followed by those Divisions

of the Department/Ministry implementing schemes, which have done good work in analysing the schemes/ programmes from gender perspective which have brought about changes in policy/operational guidelines.

(8) Prepare a Chapter on Gender perspective related to the Sector/Service covered by the Ministry and the impact of the existing policies/programmes and resources employed in meeting the specific needs of women for reflection in the Ministry's Outcome/Performance Budget.

Women's empowerment is a holistic concept which entails adequate resource allocation in all areas including health, education, water sanitation and nutrition, sustained employment, access to credit and asset ownership, skills, research and design technology and political participation. Further, regional imbalances have to be corrected. For this, it is necessary to focus on specific needs of women residing in villages and towns. Spatial mapping of social infrastructure and access to employment opportunities for women, would clearly highlight resources available, overall gaps, resource allocation required based on size of population and yardsticks for availability of facilities, etc. so that universalisation of basic socio-economic infrastructure is achieved progressively, and allocations and interventions are more focused. These spatial maps would then form the basis for concomitant regional plans and projections on funds for gender requirements, with maximum local participation. This would also enable taking into account regional imbalances within states and districts.

An action plan for gender budgeting is explained on next page.

Constraints

- Non-availability of gender disaggregated data.
- Need to train administrative cadres in gender budgeting perspectives and practices.
- Need for concerted multi-departmental action for successful and holistic empowerment of women.
- Need to build capacity and women as decision-makers.

GENDER BUDGETING —AN ACTION PLAN

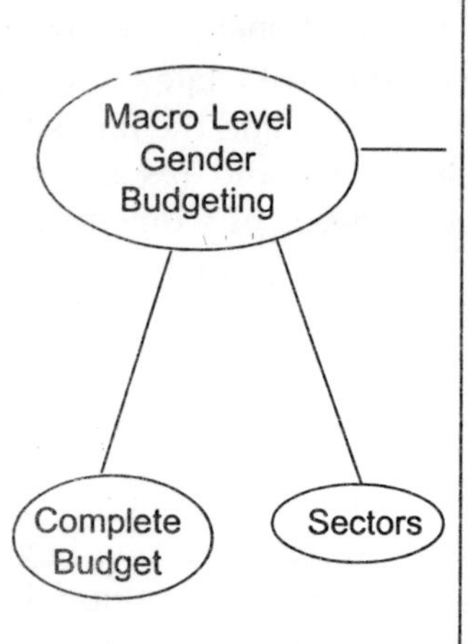

MACRO LEVEL INITIATIVES

- This entails preparation of a Gender-based Profile of Public Expenditure. This serves as a situational analysis/ Benchmark to identify gap areas in resource allocation for women.
- The exercise could be carried out for the entire Budget of a State or Ministry or for specific Sectors.
- Identification of gaps will enable enhancing/re-prioritizing allocation of resources towards women's empowerment.
- Monitoring flow of funds, gender friendly implementation and achievement of outcomes is an integral part of gender budgeting.

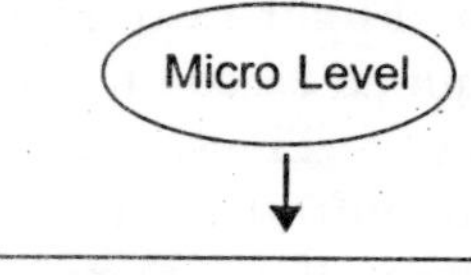

MICRO LEVEL INITIATIVES

↓

Spatial Mapping of Infrastructure (Water Sanitation, Electricity, Reads) and Employment Opportunities. →	• Spatial Mapping of resources available for women in the villages and towns and benchmarking public expenditure necessary to ensure adequate availability and access to essential services like health, education, water sanitation, fuel and employment gives a realistic picture of funds required for women.
↓ Synergy in allocation of resources across levels of governance, programmes and Departments. →	• The next step is to progressively translate gender-based spatial requirements in to resource allocations and create synergy in Resource allocation across levels of governance to ensure universal coverage.
↓ Take into account regional imbalances/geographical constraints. →	• Re-prioritize resource allocations to address—regional imbalances, infrastructure gaps.

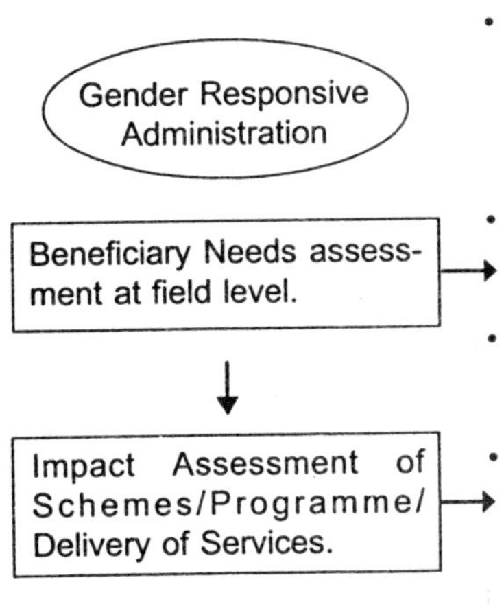

- The stage of Designing schemes and programmes should incorporate gender concerns identified through Beneficiary Needs Assessment at the field level.
- Programmes may be Redesigned from gender perspective-build in women's participation.
- Affirmative action may be taken to address gender barriers in access to public expenditure.
- Relentless monitoring and impact assessment of implementation and outcomes would enable suitable corrective action.

- Need for research into gender concerns in several mainstream sectors like Finance, Transport, Power, Wasteland Development, Roads.

CONCLUSION

To quote Dr. Amartya Sen in his keynote address on Transition to Sustainability in the 21st Century, at the Inter-Academy Panel called sustainability and freedom on International Issues, Tokyo, May 15, 2000, he said: "We need a vision of mankind not as patients whose interest have to be looked after, but as agents who can do effective things—both individually and jointly. We also have to go beyond the role of human beings specifically as 'consumers' or as 'people with needs', and consider, more broadly, their general role as agents of change who can given the opportunity—think, assess, evaluate, resolve, inspire, agitate, and through these means, reshape the world."

Thus Gender Budgeting Initiatives is an attempt to give women "agency", i.e. the power, the place in the structure of governance that enables them to direct the local and the macro-economy to serve their choices. This will enable women to direct the economy in a space where they can do so, especially for a start at the gram panchayat level where the bottom up approach and 'ought budget' will take over as shown in the successful Karnataka experience.

So, lastly, we can say that opportunities have to be enhanced for women so that they can generate income and be self-supportive. Women's empowerment must be accompanied by women's health. The patriarchal values need to change and public awareness that a nation cannot be healthy unless its women are healthy. Gender equality can bring efficiency in all economic sectors. But its a long way to go. The journey has just begun. This requires concerted efforts at all levels to make this endeavour a success.

REFERENCES

Annual Report (2005-06), Government of India, Ministry of Women and Child Development.

Annual Report (2007-08), Government of India, Ministry of Women and Child Development.

Kurukshetra (2007), March.

Kurukshetra (2008), January and March.

Singh, Dr. Gopal and Others, ed. (2003), Economic Empowerment of Rural Women in India.

Yojna (2006), October.

Theory of Gendered Approach to Development in the Third World Perspective

Shamim Akhtar and Shaishta Nagien

INTRODUCTION

Although the term 'gender' has been widely used over the past few decades, much of the academic interest in gender relations can be attributed to feminism (Waylon, 1996: 6). Feminists of all descriptions have characterized gender relations as relations of inequality and subordination, and feminist academics have been trying to make sure that gendered analysis is incorporated into the study of development. This paper attempts to examine such incorporation in the context of Third World Countries. It is organized under seven substantive sections. The opening section provides a brief historical background of the development policies and programmers determined by some international development agencies in The Third World countries. It also discusses how women get associated with these agencies and development programmers, and how the 'caucus' known as Women in Development (WID) came into being. Gender issues in modernisation theory, underdevelopment theory, and neo-liberalism are discussed in the next three sections follows an examination of gender analysis by a new set of feminist academics and of the implications of the efficiency approach of WID in the Third World Countries.

SOME INTERNATIONAL DEVELOPMENT AGENCIES IN THE THIRD WORLD COUNTRIES

A number of UN agencies and bilateral and multilateral agencies which have emerged after World War Second are dictating and the development policies and programmers in the Third World countries either directly or indirectly. As a specialized UN agency, the International Bank for Reconstruction and Development (IBRD), well known as World Bank, emerged in the aftermath of World War Second to advance loans for economic rehabilitation and development of countries which were particularly affected by the War. Although the chief sources of the World Bank's fund is capital subscription from member-nations and sales of its own bonds to private investors, one-fourth of the initial capital of the Bank was subscribed to by USA. To expand the Bank's lending policies and to invest in private enterprise, the International Finance Corporation (IFC) was created in 1956 and, in 1960; the International Development Association (IDA) was created as an affiliate of the Bank of offer long-term loans. By 1981, IBRD, IFC and IDA, collectively know as the World Bank Group, had advanced 3,383 loans, amounting to a total of approximately $ 85 billion, with IBRD's share alone amounting to about $ 60 billion. The World Bank Group progressively increased its lending activities during the 1980s, with confessional terms to the poorest nations. In a single year, during the mid-1980s, the World Bank Group lent more than $ 12 billion to developing member-countries, with $4 billion lent on confessional terms to the poorest nations (Plano and Greenberg, 1985). However, though almost all countries of the world are now members of the Bank, which has progressively increased the pace of its lending activities, the ability of the Bank to help developing countries meet their capital needs is limited.

International Monetary Fund (IMF) also emerged as a specialized agency of UN after the Britton Woods Monetary and Financial Conference of 1944 to promote international monetary cooperation. Its three main objectives were: (i) the promotion of exchange stability, (ii) the establishment of a worldwide multilateral of payments system, and (iii) the provision of monetary reserves to help the member-nations overcome short-run disequilibria in their balance of payments. Although most of the countries of the world are its members, voting power in the IMF is determined by the size of a member, contribution, with USA casting about one-fourth of the total. More important, the industrial nations function as a caucus to reach decisions in the IMF to defend currency values and to promote international liquidity. While the creation of IMF was aimed at preventing a return to the anarchic financial conditions of the 1930s, with its widely fluctuating exchange rates and competitive devaluation, exchange stability has been greatly weakened in recent years. The main problems facing the Fund have been persistent deficit in the balance of payment of most Third World countries. The situation is critical because many countries, especially the Third World countries, usually borrow money from IMF to make their annual payment to private and public banks and loan agencies on the principal and interest owed on outstanding loans.

In the broader context of development theory and the understanding of the basic concepts of WID, gender issues help place the evolution of thoughts and actions within the World Bank. 'Women in development' and 'gender and development' are not interchangeable. The former was applied to actions designed to ensure that women benefited or, at least, did not suffer from development efforts; on the other hand, the latter takes a broader view of the differences in behaviour expected of men and women, seeking their causes and their consequences for economic and human resource development. Through direct intervention in immediate situation, or through strategic changes in the legal and regulatory framework of the country, gender-related actions can prevent deleterious consequences and maximize the potential contributions specific to men or women. To this end, a shift from WID to gender approach has profound implications for the World Bank. Starting in the early 1970s, pressure from some staff and managers, as also some events outside the Bank, placed what came to be known as 'WID' on the Bank's agenda. In line with early sector papers on education and on population, some projects incorporated activities targeted for girls or women, but these did not represent more than 5 percent of investment lending until fiscal year 1978. A small number of staff and managers of the Bank began discussing informally the new topic of WID. The first working group of the Bank' Staff Association, formed in 1972, focused on the status of women in the Bank. Some members of the working group started a separate informal group to discuss emerging WID issues; soon, their efforts were reinforced by events outside the Bank.

GENDER ISSUES IN MODERNISATION THEORY

The first theoretical approach to development, namely, modernisation theory, discussed very little about women. In general, modernisation theory emphasized and approved the trend towards western capitalist modernity. It was argued that, if modernisation theory was followed in the Third World, Third World societies would catch up with the West.

Modernisation theory was subject to criticism from many quarters in the late 1960s. Women's issues of development theory also came to be criticized from different quarters. Since the early 1960s, UN has marked each official 'decade of development' with a declaration summarizing the lessons learnt from past experience and its priorities for the coming ten years. The declaration that announced the First Development Decade (1961-70) was devoid of any specific reference to women (Kabeer, 1996:1). Between the 1990s and 1970s, the feminist movement gained momentum, and the research done by women scholars pointed out that the so-called modernisation theory of development promoted by the development agencies had not benefited women and, in some cases, had adverse effect on women in the Third World. Women had not been given access to new productive opportunities, technology had not liberated them from domestic drudgery, gender neutral outcomes had not been led by market forces, and, in spite of the forces of modernisation, prejudice and preconceptions about women persisted in society (*Ibid.*, 19).

About the impact of modernisation on women in the Third World, more generally, there was a growing perception of the failure of development. This perception was combined with the unhappiness of the First World women, and was influenced by the second wave of feminism. These factors culminated in the emergence of the WID movement, which was inspired by liberal feminism (Waylen, 1996: 37). Remaining largely with the paradigm of liberal feminism, WID was, in part, a response to the inadequacies of the modernisation approach. It was argued that the process of economic modernisation marginalized women economically and socially, and increased their dependence on men (Boserup, 1970). Development project largely benefited men, often at the expense of women, displacing women from their traditional productive functions and diminishing the power, status and income they had previously enjoyed (Moser, 1993). Development planners ignored women's productive activities, partly because their national accounting systems ignored much of women's work within the household and subsistence economy, assuming women to be only housewives (Rogers, 1980).

The development projects where women were included was on sex-specific terms as housewives, mothers and 'at risk producers' (Kabeer, 1996: 5). M. Buvinic (1983) characterized development project as welfare approach to women and development, which identified women as a vulnerable group, needing help, particularly in their reproductive role. These projects concentrated on improving women's domestic skills such as childcare and nutrition (Rogers, 1980). Where the projects addressed women's need to generate income, it was through schemes which were in conformity with the dominant conception of women's role such as production of traditional handicrafts catering to insecure market, often for tourists or for export. Women's development projects were often ghettoized, leaving the majority to cater for men (Waylen, 1996:38).

Some policy proposals emerged from the WID critics. The solution to equality was observed as widening access to factors such as tools, technology and education. Women had to be integrated into development more effectively, and not allow it to pass them by. Starting from the assumption that economic development strategies had often had a negative effect on women, the equity approach acknowledged women's productive as well as reproductive roles (Buvinic, 1983). It argued that women had to be brought into the development process through access to employment and the market place. It placed great emphasis on the wider question of equity and on the need to reduce inequality between men and women. However, the WID group worked to influence United States Agency for International Development (USAID) policy and, as a result of its lobbying, a congressional amendment in 1973 mandated US assistance to 'move women into their national economies'. The WID approach was influential in determining the priorities for the UN Decade for Women (1975-85).

In spite of its essentially liberal feminist and reformist bent, the equity approach aroused hostility among development agencies and the Third World governments (Moser, 1993). This is mainly because 'The Decade' rhetoric of equity would have proved difficult to translate into policy, as it required a redistribution of resources throughout the development process. 'Focusing on all women, rather than poor women only, calls for equity at all levels, both among programmer beneficiaries and among programmer implementers' (Buvinic, 1983, cited in Kabeer, 1996:7). Defining women's problems in terms of the family's basic needs rather than unequal access to resources made the WID policy more acceptable within male dominated agencies. However, the new focus on women was adapted by the official agencies of development by linking it to the emerging concern with 'poverty alleviation and basic needs'. The poverty alleviation and basic needs strategy was important for women, particularly in the Third World countries, for two reasons: First, it focused on women's responsibility for family and child welfare by casting women in the role of managers of low-income households and providers of family basic needs; and second, it also incorporated the WID concern with women's productive roles with the recognition that these responsibilities had an economic component and, therefore, required income enhancing measures.

GENDER UNDERDEVELOPMENT AND DEPENDENCY THEORY

Dependency model, a key element of underdevelopment theory, arose from a growing disillusionment with economic strategies of development, especially as they had been applied in Latin America. Underdevelopment theory was developed, in part, as a direct challenge to modernisation theory. It arose as much as a reaction to classical Marxism as from deeply held objections to modernisation theory. Dependency theorists like A.G. Frank (1969), A. Emmanuel (1972) and D. Harrison (1988) argue that development and underdevelopment and underdevelopment are two aspects of the same system, namely, the world capitalist system. Indeed, both development and underdevelopment are regarded as part of the world process of accumulation, a process that commenced in the mercantile period, carried through into industrial capitalism and culminated in imperialism. The colonies, the semi-colonies and the neo-colonies existed primarily for the benefit of capitalist metropolis throughout this process and, as a direct result, became underdeveloped. It is only by breaking these links that genuine development can occur. They also concurred with the increasing disillusionment with the belief that the benefits of economic growth under modernisation would trickle down to the poor which provided the spur both to the International Development Organisation (IDO) to shift its emphasis to employment, focusing on the working poor and the potential of the informal sector, and to the agencies such as the World Bank to redirect their efforts towards the eradication of poverty and redistribution with growth (Waylen, 1996:39).

As a mark of this, towards the end of 1970s, an 'anti-poverty' emphasis emerged as the second WID approach. In part, it as a toning down of the equity approach, which had required agencies to interfere in the relations between men and women. An important part of this reorientation was the 'basic needs strategy'. The new focus on women could be accommodated within the development agencies by linking women to poverty alleviation and basic needs (Kabeer, 1996:7). Low income women could be identified, as a part of this new emphasis, as an important group to be singled out for particular attention. This was mainly because the existing projects had ignored their needs and women generally played the important role in fulfilling the basic needs within the household. This anti-poverty approach stressed income-generating projects for poor women often ignoring their reproductive roles and their interconnection with productive roles, and without the emphasis on increasing women's autonomy which was implied in the equity approach (Waylen, 1996).

Studies relating to the impact of the spread of capitalist social relations have been analyzed focusing on production and reproduction, and the links between them in both agricultural and industrial spheres in class and gender relations and the household in agricultural production (Deere, 1977; Beneria, 1982). The Green Revolution in India is cited as an example of the way in which the introduction of new techniques such as high yielding seeds and fertilizers altered the class position of different peasant households and the amount of productive labour undertaken by different groups of women both as unpaid labour within the household and as paid labour outside of it (Agarwal, 1986). The gendered nature of much industrial production in the Third World has also been highlighted in some studies. In the developing countries, women's participation in industrial labour force has risen faster than men's, increasing from 21 percent in 1960 to 26.5 percent in 1980, while the overall share of women in the labour force remained constant at around 32 percent (Jockes, 1987:80). In some developing countries—for example, Hong Kong (now part of China), South Korea, Taiwan and Thailand—women constitute more than 40 percent of the labour force. Women's participation was crucial to the success of manufacturing industry, the 'engine' of South Korea's economic development (Park, 1993:132); these female manufacturing industries accounted for 70 percent of total national export in 1975. Utilizing existing gender relations to their advantage, the multi-national corporations (MNCs) employ female labour, capitalizing on particular notions of skill with the payment of lower wages to women as well as transforming systems of outworking and household production (Elson and Pearson, 1981). However, the employment of female labour by the MNCs is often located in free-trade zones in developing countries and it is most marked in the electronics the textile industries (Mitter, 1986). Under the theoretical framework of GAD, the gendered nature of much industrial production in the Third World countries has been highlighted by these studies: women's labour has played a crucial role in the new international division of labour and the global accumulation of capital.

NEO-LIBERALISM IN THE THIRD WORLD COUNTRIES

The third theoretical framework of development, namely, neo-liberalism and the policy prescriptions accompanying it, while not strictly a corpus of development theory, has eclipsed both modernisation and underdevelopment theories and dominated development thinking since the early 1980s. Milton Friedman and Friedrich Hayek, who emphasis the unfettered working of the free market to promote economic growth provided the theoretical basis for many of its ideas. While appearing to be gender neutral, neo-liberalism carries with it the implicit assumption of certain gender relations and particular roles for women.

The widespread implementation of SAP by the Third World governments at the instance of international institutions has coincided with the predominance of the third variant of WID, the 'efficiency approach'. The efficiency argument has been clearly spelt out by B. Rogers (1980), who had stressed the advance impact of women's exclusion on development. In view of growing economic crisis in the Third World, she suggested that continued neglect of women's productivity was a costly mistake that planners could no longer afford to make. Gender-specific occupational segregation, with concentration of men in higher-level jobs and women in lower ones, is regarded as a stable and rigid phenomenon that exists in traditional as well as modern societies. Various studies underline the persistence of gender-segregated labour markets globally as being independent of level of industrial development or occupational diversification (Terrell, 1992; Anker, 1998). Even within the same occupation, women are paid lower wages relative to men and male-female earnings are not well explained by gender differences in human capital endowments (Coppin, 1995; Hotchkiss and Moore, 1996; Olsen and Coppin, 2001). Anker (1998) argues that human capital approach is becoming weak as more empirical evidence is taken into account. Many working women have a continuous working career in developing countries, as in industrialized countries, and yet the working experience has not improved women's occupational performance. Lower returns to education lead to inequalities in wages and job mobility.

However, the new policy equation has been constructed on an equality impoverished view of women's lives; it has defined women's economics agency as equivalent to that of men, ignoring their greater embeddedness in familial and domestic responsibilities. Here welfare is seen as complementary, rather than in opposition to efficiency. It suggests that the opposition posited in WID advocacy between welfare and efficiency needs to be rethought. Although WID advocacy shifted the grounds for investing development resources in women from welfare to efficiency, or from need to merit, Boserup (1970) spoke directly to a market conception of merit claims (Kabeer, 1996:25). However, market-led efficiency, with the WID emphasis on women as economic agents, served to underscore the 'gender grip' for women within the market solution. If the market is to be the primary mechanism for allocating resources, then, women, who generally have less purchasing power, will be unable to buy the support services they need to reduce their domestic labour overheads; if they are unable to buy these labour replacing services, they will also be unable to carry on the range of activities that would help them to increase their purchasing power. In its broader meaning, development can carry both negative and positive connotations—enriching a few, impoverishing the many.

The critique of development theory by feminist academics suggested that development plans and projects would not succeed unless women's potential and actual productive roles were recognized. However, part of the feminist agenda was incorporated into development thinking. Primarily, this agenda was executed in an instrumental manner—the improvement of women's life was seen as a mechanism to achieve other development goals, such as population control, rather than as a valuable end in itself. Subsequently, the feminist agenda has emerged as an independent action plan of IDO, World Bank, and the developed and the developing countries.

GENDERED ANALYSIS BY A NEW SET OF FEMINIST ACADEMICS

The 1980s saw the emergence of a new set of feminist critiques of much of the existing literature and policies and projects. While they are often overlapping and intersecting, three different lines of critique can be identified. The first derives from the work of Third World feminists, activists, researchers and policy-maker. There is now a growing feeling that there is a need to develop a Third World focus to understand the gender problem, focusing among others on gender subordination, value of women's work, empowerment, feminist ideology, and identity of women. Although considerable dependence is noticeable on western ideas, models and methodologies, there is not a discernible women's perspective on development in the Third World countries. Before the NGO's 85th Conference at Nairobi in July 1985, twenty-two activists, researchers and policy-makers prepared a document enunciating a Third World women's perspective on development, described as 'Development Alternatives with Women for a New Era' (DAWN) (see Sen and Grown, 1987). DAWN suggested that the problems of development were not unique to the Third World, even within the First World; there had always been those who had been marginalized in the process of market-led growth and whose dissonant voices had not been heard in the mainstream western feminist movement. The priorities for poor women from racially and nationally disadvantage groups were frequently food, housing, jobs, services and the struggle against racism rather than equality with men. DAWN was of the view that equality with men, who themselves suffered unemployment, poor work conditions, low wages and racism within the existing socioeconomic structures, did not seem an adequate or worthy goal (Kabeer, 1996:32).

The notion of global sisterhood was also challenged by the Association of African Women for Research and Development (AAWORD), a network of African researchers. AAWORD (1982) rejected the analysis and strategies of western women who insisted on prioritizing problems of equality between the sexes as the fundamental issue facing all women, and argued that the interest of men and women were opposed and mutually exclusive. Asian Women Research and Action Network (AWRAN) initiated a debate on the relevance of feminism in Asia and the special features of Asian feminism. The DAWN Report (1991, cited in Sharma, 2000:165) suggests going beyond the discussion of empowerment as good for women to the discussion of empowerment as critical for building accountability into the functioning of the public realm—both the state and the institutions of civil society.

The second line of critique has been labeled the 'post-modern feminist critique' of women and development theory and practice. This critique rejects universal constructs of truth, objectivity and neutrality. It replaces the unitary notions of 'women' and 'feminine' gender identity with plural and complexly constructed conceptions of social identity, treating gender as one of the relevant strands among others, attending also to class race, ethnicity, age and sexual orientation (Fraser and Nicholson, 1988:390-91). While some women share common interests and face some common enemies, such commonalities are by no means universal. They are interlaced with differences, even with conflict. This new feminism is more sensitive to local and diverse voices of feminism, and it rejects any universalistic feminist perspective. Whereas earlier feminism was concerned with understanding and recording commonly experienced oppression of women, the post-modernist feminist practice emphasis's diversity of women's interrelationships. However, post-modern feminism draws much of its inspiration from the work of DAWN (Parpart, 1993; Waylen, 1996). The third line of critique consists of mainly the First World feminist academies that worked to improve development analysis and policy of the Third World countries.

Of these three new lines of feminist critiques, the most important is that of DAWN, which has laid out the gender analysis in a wider process of development and social change in the Third World societies (Sen and Grown, 1987). All three critiques have criticized much of the WID and early GAD literature on several grounds (Waylen, 1996:43): first, they homogenize women. Second, the Third World women are seen as passive objects of policy, not agents of change in their own right; and third, as a corollary of the second, many of the policy prescriptions and projects are seen as primarily top-down ones, imposed from above.

Moreover, in the purely capitalist model of development and its doctrine of free-market economy and liberalisation, privatisation and globalisation, women have become victims of development and non-planners/policy-makers in the development process. Hence, most of these approaches have failed to achieve their objective of meeting the strategic gender needs. This is reflected in the increasing incidents of violence against women, dowry deaths, rape, sexual abuse, prostitution in the name of tourism promotion, and the declining sex ratio. The governmental policy of privatizing health and education sectors may have very adverse effects on meeting even the basic needs of women. Accordingly, DAWN emphasis's that development plans and projects would be more efficient and effective through women's economic contribution, but there must be a 'bottom-up' development approach through active participation and leadership of women.

IMPLICATIONS OF THE EFFICIENCY APPROACH OF WID IN THE THIRD WORLD COUNTRIES

That women's economic contribution brings about higher economic growth and productivity has been acknowledged in the progress reports of various countries. Improving women's education increases their efficiency as producers; it also increases women farmers' access to agricultural extension, credit services and other productive inputs (Quisumbing, 1994; Saito *et al.* 1994). The analysis of household panel data for Burkina Faso suggests that farm output could be increased by 6-20 percent through a more equitable allocation of productive resources between men and women farmers (Udry, 1996). A more equitable distribution of opportunities and resources between men and women leads more directly to higher economic growth and productivity (World Bank, 2000: 199).

A progress report on the World Bank's initiative for WID, which started during the 1980s, focuses on increasing women's productivity and income, because this is considered the best way to help women help themselves and contribute to economic performance, poverty reduction, slower population growth and environmental sustainability (World Bank, 1990:61). Progress in the Bank's lending has been most apparent in sectors (education, population, health and nutrition, and agriculture) that affect women's productivity the most. About two-fifths of the Bank's operations in the fiscal year 1989 included WID recommendations, as did almost all population, health and nutrition—PHN-projects (*Ibid.*, 61). About 40 percent of the Bank's operations approved in the fiscal year 1991 included specific recommendations for action to integrate women into the development process (World Bank, 1991:55). A review of some projects approved in the 1980s highlighted the need for more effective planning of WID action during project preparation and more effective supervision one project implementation had begun.

A primary component of then World Bank's WID initiative

had been the preparation of county-specific WID assessments and action plans. These assessments outlined specific programmers of action to assist women that could be implemented with the assistance of the Bank. About four-fifths of these action plans recommended raising the productivity and incomes of women farmers by improving access to extension and other agricultural support activities (*Ibid*.:62). A new operation policy directive issued in April 1994 states that it is the Bank's intention to reduce gender disparities and enhance women's participation in economic development by integrating gender issues into country-specific strategies (*World Bank*, 1994:37).

There have been success stories from several other Latin American countries: a study based on gender-disaggregated data for six countries (Chile, Colombia, Ecuador, Honduras, Mexico, and Peru) reveals that women account for the large share of beneficiaries under the current land-tilling programmers than under the past agrarian reforms (World Bank 2000:121).

A study on the effect of networking schemes, such as group-based micro-credit, suggests that these schemes have enormous potentials for reducing poverty and facilitating the empowerment of women. The interest reached a new peak with a micro-credit summit at Washington DC, in February 1997, which was considered the first step in a decade-long campaign seeking to ensure delivery of micro-credit for self-employment along with other financial and business services by 2005 to 100 million of the world's poorest families, especially the women of those families. In many developing countries of Africa, Asia and Latin America, a significant movement has been gathering momentum over the recent years, influenced mainly by the WID policy framework. Some of these micro-credit programmers—such as Bangladesh Rural Advancement Committee and Grameen Bank in Bangladesh—target women more than men, and the credit have greater productive potential for poor households in Bangladesh when women are the programmer participants (Pitt and Shahidur, 1998). In southern Africa, for the networking schemes of credit and saving facilities, women own an impressive share of small, informal sector business: 67 percent in Zimbabwe, 23 percent in Lesotho, and 84 percent in Swaziland, though training in entrepreneurial skills for women, who are typically cut-off from the normal paths of acquiring such skills, is critical. Group-based micro-credit schemes have helped women acquire non-land assets and have also had positive effect on girls' schooling (World Bank, 2000). Furthermore, the effect of micro-credit programmers on women's empowerment has largely been positive (see Rahman, 1986; Amin and Pebley, 1994; Pitt and Khandker, 1995).

Integrating WID initiative in the environmental area, Women, Environment and Development (WED) put forward two arguments: first, improving the status of women will assist the solution of environmental problem; and second, within environmental projects, women's sole participation will lead to an improvement in project efficiency (Sarker and Das, 2002:4407). The Rio Declaration (The UN Conference on Environment and Development at Rio, 1992) at the Earth Summit also acknowledges that women have a vital role to play in environment management and development from which they have been historically excluded (Sharma, 2000). Women's active participation and women's leadership have been stressed in the area of Natural Resource Management (NRM) Programmers in developing countries like India for protecting environmental degradation, sustainable development and efficient management of natural resources.

In Africa, community participation has helped restore forest resources in Gambia, and led to broader participation in rural development in Zimbabwe (World Bank, 2002:92). The progress report of Joint Forest Management (JFM) in India reveals some success stories relating to the involvement and active participation of women in the programmer. Chipko Movement in India, which hailed from women's activism, was independent of global environmental consciousness. Environmental campaigns in India have been successful in negotiating some changes in government policies. In the last two decades, conflicts over alternative uses of local resources have given rise to a variety of community initiatives. The National Forest Policy in India asserted that one of the basic objectives was 'creating a massive people's involvement with the involvement of women' (Ministry of Environment and Forest, 1988 cited in Sarker and Das, 2002:4408). Making a sharp departure from the part, JFM is a direct outcome of 1988 National Forest Policy, which acknowledges the dependence of the rural poor on forest resources for survival. Despite the ideological diversity of community initiatives and proliferation of non-governmental organisations working in the area of environmental action, poor peasant women are motivated for group action as they regard these organisations as the only protection against their vulnerabilities as individuals at home, at work and in society. Understanding that women are being deprived of their equal constitutional right to benefit accruing from the forest, the West Bengal Government's Forest Department has recently made efforts to establish a new management system of female Forest Protection Committee (Sarker and Das, 2002).

The WID approach has also broadened women's legal rights in many countries by increasing their political representation in local and national assemblies. Efforts are under way in at least thirty-two countries to increase women's political representation by reserving seats for them in local and national assemblies (World Bank, 2000: 119-20). In Panchayati Raj institutions in India, by law one-third of the seats are reserved for women. This has given rise to a new class of women (some 600,000 strong) with political influence. Similar reservation is under consideration for higher political bodies (*Ibid.*, 120).

CONCLUSION

Feminist academics have been trying to make sure that gendered analysis is incorporated into all areas and in all development plans and projects. However, new directions have emerged in both policy and analysis of development plans and projects, particularly in the Third World countries, with the predominance of the WID's efficiency approach through active involvement of women in development plans and projects. New areas and forms of analysis are being explored. The 'bottom-up' development schemes have entailed a vibrant civil society created through grassroots collective organisations. Acknowledging differences among women, these organisations have also necessitated greater consideration of the construction of identities and interests and have highlighted the need for alliances between different groups of women. Governments of the Third World countries have taken up legislative and reformative measures for smooth and successful functioning of gender-sensitive planning in various fields. A number of non-governmental organisations have become the torchbearers of this movement, even in remote areas in the Third World countries. Although parts of the feminists' agenda have been incorporated into development plans and projects of the Third World countries, the new direction has wider implications for gender equity and efficiency in all future development policy and planning in these countries.

REFERENCES

Agarwal, B. 1997, 'Environmental Action, Gender Equity and Women's Participation', *Development and Change*, 28(1):1-44.

Amin, S. and A. Pebley, 1994, 'Gender Inequality within Households: The Impact of a Women's Development Programmer in 36 Bangladeshi Villages', *Bangladesh Development Studies*, 22 (2&3): 121-54.

Association of African Women for Research Development (AAWORD), 1982, 'The Experience of the Association of African Women for Research and Development (AAWORD)', *Development Dialogue*, 1 (2): 101-13.

Buvinic, M., 1983, 'Women's Issues in Third World Poverty: A Policy Analysis', in M. Buvinic, M. Lycettle and W.P. McGreevey (eds.): Women and Poverty in the Third World (14-33), Baltimore: Johns Hopkins University Press.

Chen, M.A., 1991, 'Women and Wasteland Development' (Paper presented at the ILO Workshop on 'Women and Wasteland Development', New Delhi).

Coppin, A., 1995, 'Women, Men and Work in a Caribbean Economy: Barbados', *Social and Economic Studies*, 44 (2 & 3): 101-24.

Deere, C.D. and M. Leon, 1999, 'Institutional Reform of Agriculture under Neo-liberalism: The Impact of the Women's and Indigenous Movements' (Keynote Address at the Conference on 'Land in Latin America: New Context, New Claims, New Concepts', Centre for Latin American Research and Documentations, Centre for Resource Studies and Wageningen Agricultural University, Amsterdam, 26-27 May).

Debanarayan Sarker, Professor, Centre for Economic Studies, *Kolkata Sociological Bulletin*, Jan.-Apr. 2006 (45-66).

Emmanuel, A., 1972, Unequal Exchange, London: New Left Books.

Fernandes, W. and G. Menon, 1987, Tribal Women and Forest Economy: Deforestation, Exploitation and Status Change, New Delhi: Indian Social Institute.

Frank, A.G., 1969, Capitalism and Underdevelopment in Latin America, New York: Monthly Review Press.

Hotchkiss, J. and R. Moore, 1996, 'Gender Compensation Differentials in Jamaica', *Economic Development and Cultural Change*, 44 (3): 657-76.

Jaquette, J., 1982, 'Woman and Modernisation Theory: A Decade of Feminist Criticism', *World Politics*, 34 (2): 267-84.

Locke, C., 1999, 'Gender Policy in Joint Forest Management' in R. Jefferey and N. Sundar (eds.): A New Moral Economy for India's Forests? Discourses of Community and Participation (235-53), New Delhi: Sage Publications.

Mies, M., 1986, Patriarchy and Accumulation on a World Scale: Women in the International Division of Labour, London: Zed Press.

Mohanty, C., 1988, 'Under Women Eyes: Feminist Scholarship and Colonial Discourses', *Feminist Review*, 30 (1): 61-88.

Moser, C.O.N., 1993, and Gender Planning and Developing: Theory, Practice and Training, London: Routledge.

Olsen, R.N. and A. Coppin, 2001, 'The Determinates of Gender Differentials in Trinidad and Tobago', *The Journal of Development Studies*, 37 (5): 31-55.

Ortner, S., 1972, 'Is Female to Male as Nature is to Culture?' in Michelle Rosaldo (ed.): Women, Culture and Society (67-87). Stanford: Stanford University Press.

Parpart, J., 1993, 'Women and Development Feminist Critique of Women and Development Theory and Practice', *Development and Change*, 24 (4): 127-45.

Pitt, M. and S. Khandker, 1995, 'Household and Inter-household Impacts of the Grameen Bank and similar Targeted Credit Programmers in Bangladesh' (Paper presented at the workshop on 'Credit programmers for the poor: Household and intra-household impacts on programmer sustainability), Dhaka: World Bank and Bangladesh Institute of Development Studies.

Pitt, M. and Shahidur, K., 1998, 'The Impact of Group-based Credit Programmers on Poor Households in Bangladesh: Does the gender of participants matter?', *Journal of Political Economy*, 106 (5): 958-96.

Plano, J.C. and M. Greenberg, 1985, The American Political Dictionary (seventh edition), New York: Holt, Rinehart and Winston.

Quisumbing, A.R., 1994, 'Improving Women's Agricultural Productivity as Farmers and Workers, Education and Social Policy Department Discussion Paper 37, Washington, DC: World Bank.

Rahman, R.I., 1986, Impact of Grameen Bank on the Situation of Poor Rural Women (Working Paper 1), (Grameen Bank Evaluation Project), Dhaka, Bangladesh Institute of Development Studies.

Saito, K., M. Hailu and S. Daphune, 1994, Raising the Productivity of Women Farmers in sub-Saharan Africa (World Bank discussion paper 230), Washington, DC: World Bank.

Sarker, D. and N. Das, 2002, 'Women's Participation in Forestry: Some Theoretical Issues', *Economic and Political Weekly*, 37 (43): 4407-12.

Sen, G. and C. Grown, 1987, Development Crises and Alternative Visions: Third World Women's Perspective, London: Earth Scans Publications.

Sharma, K., 2000, 'Perspective for Gender, Poverty and Environmental Connections under Economic Reforms in India', in Centre for Women's

Development Studies (eds.): Shifting Sands: Women's Lives and Globalisation (140-72) Kolkata: Web Impressions (India).

Terrell, K., 1992, 'Female-male Earnings Differentials and Occupational Structure', *International Labour Review*, 131 (4 and 5): 387-405.

Udry, C., 1996, 'Gender, Agriculture Production, and the Theory of the Household, *Journal of Political Economy*, 104 (5): 1010-46.

Udry, C., H. John, A. Harold, and H. Lawrence, 1995, 'Gender Differentials in Farm Productivity: Implications for Household Efficiency and Agricultural Policy', Food Policy, 20 (5): 407-23.

Waylen, G., 1996, Gender in Third World Polities, Buckingham: Open University Press.

World Bank, 1990, 1991 and 1994, The World Bank Annual Report, Washington, DC: World Bank.

Gender Equity and Rights of Women: An Islamic Analysis

Shakeel Ahmad Khan

INTRODUCTION

Women constitute merely 50% of the total population of the world population while 1/2 earn 1/10 of worlds income and own less 1/10 of the worlds property. Some experts hold that if women's and unpaid work were factored into national accounting systems, GDP would increase by 30 to 40%. Gender discrimination begins with the very birth of a girl child and it continues life long. One-third of the women in the development world are subject daily to domestic violence. Now-a-days women empowerment is heatly debated but the statistic shows that nearly 3,50,00,000 women are missing in India alone. They have been either burnt, kidnapped, forced into trade or are facing other unmentioned atrocities. The ratio of female children compared to males goes on declining. Government has banned female infanticide and female foeticide but the onslaught is on its rise. Crimes against women are rampant. Dowry system, bride burning, female infanticide and foeticide, child marriages, forced abortions, sexual exploitation at home and work place, prostitution, drug abuse, risk of AIDS, gonorrihea, devadasi-system, sati, denial of education, low wages and discrimination at all levels are rampant. The review of women's rights (discussed at UN Fourth World Conference in 1995) showed that the progress has been actually dismal. Woman is considered inferior to men in every walk of life. Woman is a traditional maiden who is destined to live in distress, living under the fear of her frightening father, superior brother, suspicious husband and an ungrateful and careless son. She is tortured, humiliated, harassed and put to shame.

MATERIALISTIC, SELFISH AND IRRESPONSIBLE HUMAN ATTITUDE CAUSES DISCRIMINATION

The Holy Quran says, "O Mankind, we have created you from one man and one woman, and turned you into groups and communities for sake of introduction, and from the two spread many men and women on the earth". This verifies the fundamental truth that all human being are brothers and sisters irrespective of differences among them but since the very beginning man has suffered at the hands of man and non-else. Rousseau once said that man was born free but he find himself tethered shackled. Who has made these shackled and who change human beings? Definitely it is he who invents ever-new ways to oppress his brethren, to usurp their rights and shed their blood. For long time man is in search of peace and harmonious growth but it is nowhere visible. Man has become extremely self-centred and all the time he busy to raise his standard of living at the cost of humanity and encroachment of rights. All nations are involved too in the same pursuit as a whole. People want to control the limited material resources of this world for the benefit of fortunate few of developed societies. As a result, exploitation of the meager resources of the poor nations is going on unabated even in the so-called enlightened modern age. It has resulted only in chaos and uneasiness all around, culminating in regional wars and skirmishes, racial cleaning, economic slavery and global hegemony. People of poor countries are crying but there is none to come to their help except offering further loans by the world financial bodies and institutions. Thereby increasing their debt and economic dependence. It is going on in an unending chain. It is so because man had become selfish, greedy and very much materialistic in his approach. He wages every thing in terms of money and economic gains. Moral values have become commercial values and human values have little or no place in the process of market economy. The situation further worsens when man thinks that this is the only life and there is no life after death. So he must maximize his personal pleasure and comfort even at the cost of others. This materialistic attitude of life of human being only adds fuel to the fire. (*Radiance Views Weekly*, December, 2001)

Scientific and Industrial Development has made the human beings slaves of production, consumption and exploitation. Education at the moment is also meant only for material and economic gain. The existence selfish and irresponsible character of men and women and the nations is the greatest challenge before us.

Responsibility can exist only if a man ever conscious of the facts that he is accountable for all that he does on the earth. Islam elevates the human character to its highest points through the concept of and practice of monotheism, accountability in the hereafter, concept of trust and modern life of Prophet Mohammad(s) which the materialistic societies can never think about Islam means peace to prevent any kind of catastrophe in the society in order to prosperity and progress in the world. Don't create disturbances on the earth after it has been reformed and pray to God with fear and hope (Quran). Islam guides to utilise the instinct of human qualities which are inter-woven in the innate nature of human beings. The history of the Islamic society and state at Medina, during the period of the Prophet and his upright four caliphs, for about half a century, is an example of the Islamic model of life, to be followed by the whole world, even today. No better state or society, ensuring peace, justice, prosperity, and progress, was and has been established ever before and thereafter, in the whole history of mankind it provides the balance between man's material and spiritual requirement. Islam believes and claims also that the peace is not unattainable if we surrender to the one supreme God and act in full agreement with all rules and commandments of the supreme power. It denounces all the causes that can normally generate hatred. For example, caste, colour, sex are the basis of discrimination. Where people wish to subjugate other people they find it easy to take excuse on this find it easy to take the excuse on this premise. Islam recognises this basic cause and eliminates all sorts of inequality between man and man with one blow.

ISLAM CONDEMN AND OUTRIGHT REJECTS ALL KINDS OF OPPRESSION AND INEQUALITY

All people regardless of their colour, or race, or parentage are equal. An Arab is not better than a non-Arab and a non-Arab is not better than a black man and a black one is not better than a white one, except through righteousness and good deeds. All people are from Adam and Adam was created from dust. Operation of every kind is strictly abhorred in Islam. Islam establishes justice multi-dimensionally in the individual, collective as well as international sphere. It holds in condemnation all that is unjust and despotic. Acts of terrorism, coercion and aggression are strongly condemned in the Holy Quran. The common misconception about Islam is only due to international media.

GENDER EQUITY FREEDOM DIGNITY AND THE RIGHTS OF WOMEN IN ISLAM

Islam states that both the genders are equal before God. Islam establishes equality among men and women on spiritual, economic, social as well as intellectual front. The teaching of Islam sounded a death knell to the age-old anti-women traditions and saved woman from death, servitude, humiliation, and stigma of ignominy. Islam very clearly provides perfect equality of status and rights to women along with men. A woman has similar rights as a man in respect of her life, honour, dignity and freedom. She is free to create and control property as a man does. She is as respectable in the eyes of God as a man and equally shares the responsibility of being the vicegerent of God. Her position is not inferior or subservient to that of man. She has to discharge her duty as servant of God as well as member of human fraternity.

At the same time Islam recognises and provides for the biological, psychological and functional differences which exist between the two sexes. Men and women are complimentary to each other: two wheels on which the human life moves. Neither is complete unless it is complemented by the other. She has been given the additional duty of motherhood which is a hallowed position, all her own. She must be given perfect freedom to fulfil this duty of being the progenitor of new generations. She should not be overburdened with social and economic responsibilities outside house in such a way that interferes with the basic duty of hers.

Besides this, man has been given a certain degree, because of certain qualities bestowed upon him. It is neither in her interest nor in that of society to disturb this fine balance. That is why Islam stresses that men are the protectors of women and they have been given a degree above them.

Therefore, serious efforts must be initiated for re-Islamisation of our society for re-empowerment of women. "Give to man what is his and render to woman what belongs to her" should be our motto. It is not question of clash of sexes but reconciliation and balance between the sexes, as believing men and women have been declared by Allah to be the friends and supporters of each other. This reappraisal of gender relations in the Muslim society and corrective steps in the light of the Quran and Sunnah will certainly go a long way in developing an ideal society which will be a model for the strifetorn West which is facing an acute problem of disintegration of family and moral degeneration which eventually may lead to the "Death of the West" (*Readiance Views Weekly*, 2005)

RIGHT TO PROPERTY, BUSINESS, RULE AND WORK

Islam grants women vast economic rights. Muslim women have been given extensive rights of inheritance. She gets her share of legacy from her father, husband, children and other near relative. According to the Quran the woman is entitled to inherit half the share given to a man and she owns it entirely and her father, husband or any other relative has no right to it. Anything a wife earns is her own asset to dispose of, either to use it herself or to contribute it to the family budget. She has a full right to manage her possessions, as the desires. Islamic law makes no demand that women should confine themselves to household duties. In fact the early Muslim women were found in all walks of life. The first wife of the Prophet, mother of all his surviving children, was business-woman who hired him as an employee, and proposed marriage to him through a third party; women traded in the market place, and the Khalifah Umar, not normally noted for his liberal attitude to women, appointed a woman, Shaff a Bint Abdullah, to supervise the market. Against this backdrop the economic position of women was much stronger in Islamic History than in the modern environment. Other women, like Laila al-Ghifariah, took part in battle, carrying water and nursing the wounded. Women can be appointed to a judicial position to adjudicate in all matters. The Quran even speaks favourably of the Queen of Sheba and the way she consulted her advisors, who deferred to her good judgment on how to deal with the threat of invasion by the armies of Solomon. (Quran 27:32-35). Women have sometimes headed Islamic provinces, like Arwa Bint Ahmad, who served as governor of Yemen under the Fatimid Khalifahs in the late fifth and early sixth century. Women can do work like men, but they do not have to do it to earn a living. They are allowed and encouraged to take the duties of marriage and motherhood seriously and are provided with the means to stay at home and do it properly. (The Guidance) The Almighty has created men and women as equal, but with different capabilities and different responsibilities. Men and women are different, Psychologically are different. Men and women are equal in Islam, but not identical.

The Muslim woman has always had the right to own and manage her own property, a right that women in this country only attained in the last 100 years. Marriage in Islam does not mean that the man takes over the women's property nor does she automatically have the right to all his property if he dies intestate. Both are still regarded as individual people with responsibilities to other members of their family—parents, brothers, sister, etc. and inheritance rights illustrate this.

Women are thus well provided for: their husbands support them and they inherit from all their relations. They are allowed to engaged in business or work at home or outside the house, so long as the family does not suffer and the money they make is their own, with no calls on it from other people until their death.

In most of the cases, a woman inherits half of what her male counterpart inherits. However, this is not always the case. In case the deceased has left no ascendant or descendent but has left the uterine brother and sister, each of the two inherit one-sixth. If the deceased has left children, both the parents that is mother and father get an equal share and inherit one-sixth each. In certain cases, a woman can also inherit a share that is double that of the male. If the deceased is a woman who has left no children, brothers or sisters and is survived only by her husband, mother and father, the husband inherits half the property while the mother inherits on third and the father the remaining one-sixth. In this particular case, the mother inherits a share that is double that of the father. It is true that as a general rule, in most cases, the female inherits a share that it half that of the male.

JUSTIFICATION FOR NOT EQUAL SHARE IN PROPERTY

In Islam a woman has no financial obligation and the economical responsibility lies on the shoulders of the man. Before a woman is married it is the duty of the father or brother to look after the lodging, boarding, clothing and other financial requirements of the woman. After she is married it is the duty of the husband or the son. Islam holds the man financially responsible for fulfilling the needs of his family. In order to do be able to fulfil the responsibility the men get double the share of the inheritance. For example, if a man dies leaving about Rs. One Hundred and Fifty Thousand, for the children (i.e. one son and daughter) the son inherits One Hundred Thousand rupees and the daughter on Fifty Thousand rupees. Out of the one hundred thousand which the son inherits, as his duty towards his family, he may have to spend on them almost the entire amount or say about eighty thousand and thus he has a small percentage of inheritance, say about twenty thousand, left for himself. On the other hand, the daughter who inherits fifty thousand, is not bound to spend a single penny on anybody. She can keep the entire amount for herself. Would you prefer inheriting one hundred thousand rupees and spending eighty thousand from it, or inheriting fifty thousand rupees and having the entire amount to yourself? (Dr. Zakir Naik, 2005)

DOMESTIC WORK BY WOMEN IS OPTIONAL

In Islam Muslim women are not expected to do the

housework. If they have not been used to doing it, the husband is obliged to provide domestic help within his means and to make sure the food gets to his wife and children, already cooked. The Prophet(s) himself used to help with the domestic work and mended his own shoes. Women are not even obliged in all cases to suckle their own children. If a divorcing couple mutually agree, they can send the baby to a wet-nurse and the husband must pay for the suckling. If the mother decides to keep the baby and suckle it herself, he must pay her for her trouble! The womanly state in marriage is given full respect in Islam and so are the rights of children. No Muslim woman could feel ashamed to say she was only a housewife. She is the head of her household, although the husband has the final say in major decisions.

MAINTENANCE BY HUSBAND AND RIGHT TO DIVORCE

The Husband has the duty to support and maintain the wife, as stated in the Quran and this is held to be so even if she is rich in her own right. He has no right to expect her to support herself, let alone support his children or him. If she does contribute to the household income this is regarded as a charitable deed on her part. The wife must defer to her husband in respect for the fact that he maintains and protects her out of his means (Quran 4:34). If the husband wilfully fails to maintain his wife, she has the right to divorce him in court. In cases of divorce, the mother has first claim to custody of the young children, followed by other female members of her family, if she remarries or is unable to look after the children.

ISLAMIC MARRIAGE BASED ON EQUITY AND MUTUAL RESPECT

Although the Islamic marriage contract is a civil agreement between the two parties. It is not just a relationship of material convenience. "They are your garments and ye are their garments" (Quran 2:187). Love, mercy, intimacy and mutual protection and modesty are the qualities expected of an Islamic marriage. Husbands are expected to treat their wives kindly during marriage and even during and after divorce. Live with them on a footing of kindness and equity. "If ye take a dislike to them, it may be that ye dislike a thing and Allah brings about through it a great deal of good" (Quran 4:19). What you eat, drink and wear must be equally shared by you both. The Prophet(s) said: "The best among you are those who are kindest to their wives." Mahr is the gift the bridegroom gives to the bride in accordance to her family status at the time of marriage and it becomes exclusively her property. She also fully owns. Islam commands women to obey their husbands but in no way does it make him her Master. There are many prophetic injunctions in this content. Women as a mother has a very sacred position in Islam. Prophet(s) said: "Paradise lies at the feet of the mother."

ABOUT FAMILY WELFARE AND USE OF CONTRACEPTION

Contraception has never been forbidden in Islam, as the Prophet(s) gave permission for the withdrawal method, so long as the wife agrees. By analogy other methods of preventing conception are also allowed. The practical aspects of marriage are covered by the marriage contract, in which the wife can specify conditions and many Muslim women have taken advantage of this to take to themselves the right of divorce if, for example, the husband takes another wife (CARDS on Polygamy). It must include a marriage gift—sadaqah or mahr—to the wife from the husband of an amount and nature agreed between them.

NO FORCED OR CHILD MARRIAGE IN ISLAM

Parents have no right to force young women to marry against their will after they have reached marriageable age. There is much evidence in the hadith to show that forced marriages are not legal and the wife has the right to have them annualled. Islam being the great advocate of human dignity, it guarantees freedom in such vital and important social institutions. The Prophet(s) also advised that couple should see one another before getting married.

NO GENDER DISCRIMINATION IN GETTING EDUCATION

The first word of The Holy Quran begins with word 'Iqra' which means to read. Quran also means a book which is read again and again. All this reflects well the importance of education.

This is why to acquire education has been made compulsory for men and women both. The whole Islamic history if full of a complete and strong network of education and learning. During Caliph period of Islamic rule there was a well-managed centres of education without any gender discrimination. In 8th Century there was more than 100 teaching centres in Banghdad alone and such was the figure of centres in almost all Islamic capitals. Women figured prominently among the earliest scholars of Islam. The Prophet's wife Aishah was one of the foremost transmitters of Hadiths and like other wives and Companions of the Prophet was often surrounded by students wanting to learn from her. Women can be educated by men. The Prophet sent Umar Ibn al-Khattab to teach the Women of the Ansar. And women taught men too, not only the wives of the Prophet but many others later were teachers of men.

LOGIC BEHIND POLYGAMY IN ISLAM

The Quran is the only religious book, on the face of this earth, that contains the phrase 'marry only one'. There is no other religious book that instructs men to have only one wife. It was only later, that the Hindu priests and the Christian Church restricted the number of wives to one. It was only in 1954, when the Hindu Marriage Act was passed that it became illegal for a Hindu to have more than one wife. "Marry women of your choice, two, or three, or four; but if ye fear that ye shall not be able to deal justly (with them), then only one." Before the Quran was revealed, there was no upper limit for polygamy and many men had sectors of wives, some even hundreds. Islam put an upper limit of four wives. Islam gives a man permission to marry two, three or four women, only on the condition that he deals justly with them. "Ye are never able to be fair and just as between women. . ." Therefore, polygamy is not a rule but an exception. Polygamy awards women the dignity of a wife while saving her from the misery of prostitution. Males in other communities often maintain extramarital relationships are never able to obtain a legal or respectable status in the society. So it can be said that polygamy is in favour of women and not an anti-women act. And also it can be seen that polygamy is an exception, it is not a norm. Many people are under the misconception that it is compulsory for a muslim man to have more than one wife. By nature males and females are born in approximately the same ratio. A female child has more immunity than a male child. For this reason, during the pediatric age itself there are more deaths among males as compared to the females. During wards, there are more men killed as compared to women. More men die due to accidents and diseases than women. The average life span of females is more than that of males and at any given time on finds more widows in the world than widowers.

India is one of the few countries, along with the other neighbouring countries, in which the female population is less than the male population. The reason lies in the high rate of female infanticide in India and the fact that more than one million female foetuses are aborted every year in this country, after they are identified as females. If this evil practice is stopped, then India too will have more females as compared to males.

Even if every many got married to one woman, there would still be more than thirty million females in U.S.A. who would not be able to get husbands (considering that America has twenty-five million gays). There would be more than four million females in Great Britain, 5 million females in Germany and nine million females in Russia alone who would not be able to find husband. In Western Society, it is common for a man to have mistresses and/or multiple extra-marital affairs, in which case, the woman leads a disgraceful, unprotected life. The same society, however, cannot accept a man having more than one wife, in which women retain their honourable, dignified position in society and lead a protected life. Thus the only two options before a woman who cannot find a husband is to marry a married man or to become public property. Islam prefers giving women the honourable position by permitting the first option and disallowing the second. There are several other reasons, why Islam has permitted limited polygamy, but it is mainly to protect the modesty of women.

VEIL SYSTEM FOR WOMEN NOT AS A DISCRIMINATION

Islam wants a balanced and a just society sustain the women dignity and their rights. It decries all types of ills, evil and shamelessness in the society. To achieve peace at home and in the society, Islam prohibited women from dressing alluringly in public and cautioned against the free mixing of men and women commanding them to be modest and to resist temptation. Veil is a stepping stone for women to reach the apex of success while still maintaining her modesty and chastity fully intact. I is a natural inclination in women folk to observe it. Exposure of the female body is a source of sexual pleasure to women folk. Before we analysis the reasoning behind the veil system we must take look the status of women in pre-Islamic societies. In Babylonian Civilisation the women were degraded and were denied all rights under the Babylonian law. If a man murdered a woman, instead of him being punished, his wife was put to death. Greek Civilisation is considered the most glorious of all ancient civilisations. Under this very 'glorious' system, women were deprived of all rights and were looked down upon. In Greek mythology, an 'imaginary woman' called 'Pandora' is the root cause of misfortune of human beings. The Greeks considered women to be sub-human and inferior to men. Though chastity of women was precious and women were held in high esteem, the Greeks were later overwhelmed by ego and sexual perversions. Prostitution became a regular practice amongst all classes of Greek society. It is very painful to note here that when Roman Civilisation was at the zenith of its 'glory', a man even had the right to take the life of his wife. Prostitution and nudity were common amongst the Romans. Similarly the Egyptian considered women evil and as sign of a devil. In pre-Islamic Arabia before Islam spread in Arabia, the Arabs looked down upon women and very often when a female child was born, she was buried alive. History indicates that it was the darkest period in the history of mankind when Prophet Mohammad(s) was commanded to declare his mission. It was to be reclamation of the whole humanity. Islam uplifted the status of women and granted them their just rights 1400 years ago. Islam expects women to maintain their status. People usually only discuss 'hijab' in the context of women. However, in the Glorious Quran, Allah first mentions 'hajab' for men before 'hijab' for the women. "Say to the believing men that they should lower their gaze and guard their modesty: that will make for greater purity for them: and Allah is well make for greater purity for them; and Allah is well acquainted with all that they do."

The moment a man looks at a woman and if any brazen or

unashamed thought comes to his mind, he should lower his gaze. Hijab (Veil) also includes the moral conduct, behaviour attitude and intention of the individual. The Quran says that Hijab has been prescribed for the women so that they are recognized as modest women and this will also prevent them from being molested. It is but natural that nudity stirs the instinct of opposite sex. The fallout of such nudity is before us as the sexual and related offences have gripped the whole European society. Those who regard veil system as a form of exploitation now ask themselves which is more exploitative of women the mini skirt or veil?

Western talk of women's liberalisation is nothing but a disguised form of exploitation of her body, degradation of her soul and deprivation of her honour. It has actually degraded them to the status of concubines, mistresses and society butterflies who are mere tools in the hands of pleasure seekers and sex marketers, hidden behind the colourful screen of 'art' and 'culture'. United States of America is supposed to be one of the most advanced countries of the world. It also has one of the highest rates of rape in any country in the world. According to a FBI report, in the year 1990, every day on an average 1756 cases of rape were committed in USA alone. Later another report said that on an average every day 1900 cases of rapes are committed in USA.

RECENT SURVEY ON MUSLIM WOMEN: REVEAL SOME FACTS

This comprehensive survey was conducted in 40 districts, spread over 12 states, spanning all four regions—East, West, North and South of India. It is based on the answers of 9641 respondents, 80% Muslim and 20% Hindu and 60% urban and 40% rural. This survey has revealed certain heartening facts; lower incidents of divorce among Muslim Women at 0.41% (for Hindu 0.4%); lower rate of polygamy at 2.9%, which is around 4 to 5% among Hindus. (The media hype has made common Indians believe that polygamy is the distinguishing negative social trait of Muslim Community). It also reports that, in spite of being poorer, the Muslim women have a greater role in decision-making with regard to work, household matter and expenditure. There is greater consultation with Muslim women regarding family-size, expenditure, marriage, birth and death ceremonies and especially major purchases and investments. It is strongly so in spite of the known fact that in large part of the country Muslim women have been deprived of the share of inheritance ordained by Shariab—the divine Islamic law. According to MWS 26% Hindu women. It also confirms that Muslim women have greater level of political awareness.

National Muslim Women's status remains alarmingly lower in socio-economic aspects. Their educational level is above that of Dalits but lower than that of OBC's Poverty, not religion, is responsible for the lower literacy and educational standard. It is so in spite of the great stress Islam lays on education for men and women both. Their school enrollment is 40.7 per cent (Hindu upper castes 63.2%, Dalits 30.3%). All India figures for Muslim women indicates 17% junior school education, 10% higher secondary education and a meager 3.66% higher studies. Unfortunately, 60% Muslim women never attended any school and are almost illiterate. The need of the hour is a cool-headed examination of facts, stock-taking and heart-searching and paying greater attention to the prevailing conditions and problems of the half of Ummah: and sustained and concerted efforts to uplift our women—our mothers, sisters, daughters and wives—so that they may regain their elevated status conferred upon them by none other than our Creator Himself.

CONCLUSION

Poor governance, indifferent attitude of the government, lack of strong will power, lack of community support, lack of awareness even about the rights dignity and the status granted in Islam among Muslim women are the main huddles of their backwardness. It is only due to good governance and strong will power of the governments that Muslims of southern India are educationally and socially advanced compared to the Muslims of Northern India. We cannot ignore this established fact. It is actually painful that we always try to explore the escape route which is neither in the interest of the nation nor the community. Muslims being the largest minority and India having the largest Muslims population in the world, we can never realise the vision of a 'Developed India' by 2020 without developing this largest segment of population. Increase in literacy rate and reducing of poverty ratio among this community will naturally result in improved condition with control population as confirmed by several empirical studies. Illiteracy, poverty ratio, lack of entrepreneurship, poor awareness are purely socio-economic problems. It has nothing to do with the religion. If it is true then most of the Muslim countries of the world could not have achieved the high literacy rate among women. As per UNICEF report 2005 literacy rate among the women of some countries are like this—Bahrain 83%, Indonesia 87%, Lebanon 80%, Malaysia 83%, Iran 69%, Oman 62%, Qatar 94%, Saudi Arab 67%, Turkey 77%, Syria 60%, SAE 80%, Kuwait 80%-76%. Not only this work participation employment ratio entrepreneurship are also high compare to Indian Muslim women and it is also remarkable that all these strides are taking place in these countries within the preview of Islamic tenets. Even poor a country like Bangladesh has got success in sending 90% of its children to the schools. Tremendous changes can be brought in their conditions by liberal government attitude, community support and liberal banking policy. Moreover, SHGs formation, entrepreneurship development and training with financial assistance and marketing facilities for tiny enterprises like doll-making, candles, goatry, poultry, embroidery, carpet weaving, knitting centres can help to achieve gender parity in rural as well as urban areas. Attitudes of the so-called Muslims are customarily based on old cultural habits. In fact they have nothing to do with Islam. Adequate safety nets and social security systems that place women on an equal footing with men. Gender sensitive curricula and training for teachers using gender sensitive methods. There should be study for the causes and consequences of violence against women and the effectiveness of preventative measures. There should be integrated measures to prevent and eliminate violence against women.

References

Akhtar M. Siddiqui, Empowerment of Muslims through Education.

Danish, I., Empowerment of Muslim Youth in India.

Dr. Zakir Naik: Answers to Non-Muslims Common Questions About Islam.

Momin, A.R., Empowerment of Muslim in India: Perspective, Context and Prerequisites.

Mutahhani, Murtada (1981): The Rights of Women in Islam, Tehran World Organisation for Islamic Services.

Obaidullah, M., Islamic Financial Markets: Towards Greater Ethics and Efficiency.

Radiance Views Weekly, 2005.

Radiance Views Weekly, December 2001.

The Guidance, Vol. 1, No. 1, June 2006.

UNICEF, 2005.

Vahiduddin, S. (1996), The Place of Women in the Quran, Islamic Culture.

Women Labour in India, V.V. Giri National Level Institute, 1996.

PART IV

CRIME, VIOLENCE AGAINST WOMEN AND EMPOWERMENT

Violence Against Women: An Educated Woman can Eradicate Violence

Reeta Kumari

Violence against women occurs in every society rich or poor—having different forms of manifestations. One of the crudest forms of violence is the one, which takes place subtly and is sanctioned into the name of culture. Cultural beliefs and practices draw a very negative image of women who are to be suppressed and domesticated, which we all accept unconditionally, such deliberate subjugation of women is pure violence and negation of human,rights.

Violence violets human rights of life, liberty, equality, dignity, development and peace. Human beings are born male and female according to the biological sex given to them. These two are the wonderful creatures of nature whose mutual understanding and co-operation are essentially needed to guide the activities of the world. History is witness to the fact that women have been at the receiving end of psychological, social, economic, moral, ethical and even legal atrocities. Women face violence all through their lives, no matter what their socio-economic background, education, culture and religion. No place is safe for women, the home, the street, the educational institution, the office, the hospital and the police station. These are all places where they can be hit, raped, harassed and abused by men or other family members. Violence committed against women, in one form or the other, is a universal phenomenon prevalent in every region and society irrespective of the social or economic class to which the women belong. It is difficult to acquire accurate data on violence against women because of the social, cultural and legal barriers, lack of evidences and amount of secrecy and sensitivity involved.

In India, there has been a continuous rise in the total incidence of crimes committed against women over the years. During 2003, incidence of torture and molestation top the list contributing about 36% ad 23.4% respectively, of the total crimes committed against women, followed by the cases of rape and kidnapping/abduction. What is more disturbing is the fact that about 2.4% of the rape victims in 2003 were upto 10 years of age. Moreover, this is not the exact picture of the gravity of the situation as a large number of such cases simply go unreported because of the social stigma attached to it. Also, during 2002, about 74% of rape cases were investigated by the police out of total number of cases for investigation and in about 65% of cases a charge sheet was made. Further about 18.4% of the cases have been tried in court during 2002 out of the total number of cases for trial and only about 5% of cases a conviction was made. Situation in somewhat similar in respect of most of the other crimes committed against women. This can be shown by the Figure 1 given on next page.

The feminists have drawn attention to seven forms of violence which often go unnoticed. They are:

1. Domestic violence, murder, rape and battery by husbands or other male partners;
2. Genital mutilation, "female circumcision" or even more euphemistical "traditional practices";
3. Gender-based violence by police and security forces including torture of detained women;
4. Gender-based violence against women during armed conflicts;

FIGURE 1

Incidence of Crimes/Violence Committed Against Women

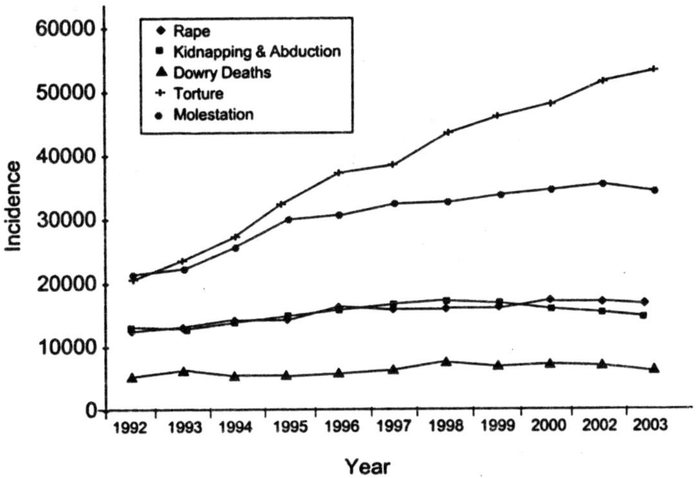

Source: *Women and Men India*, 2005.

5. Gender-based violence against women refugees and asylum seekers;
6. Violence associated with prostitution and pornography; and
7. Violence in the work place including sexual harassment.

Such types of violence occurs day-to-day life of women. Not only illiterate but educated women are also prey of it, in most cases they find themselves helpless. This situation is serious, we are in 21st century but our outlook concerned with female is too narrow. Several deep-rooted factors account for these types of violence with regard to women in the society. The factors are mainly cultural conditioning, perceptual discrepancy regarding the status of women, instructional structure of the society, traditional practices, preference for male child, dowry system, early marriage, poor education, economic dependence, limited political power, negative perception and some extent women themselves are responsible for increasing trend of violence against them.

HOW TO ERADICATE VIOLENCE?

Such violence can be controlled by the society only through the process of empowerment of women at every possible level. However, there has been an effort to make women conscious and awake of their position and importance, in the society and family. In this regard education plays important role. Education especially among women is cornerstone for social development to improve the prospects of general welfare of society. It would empower women to achieve many social, psychological, economic and political dreams which are denied to her customarily. It would actually accord women certain advantages in areas where they have traditionally lacked access or differential rights. Welfare schemes and policy measures are just not enough to promote education among women. Structural and attitudinal change across sections is desired in order to enhance educational and consequent socio-economic status of women in India. The importance of education for empowerment of women is undeniable. However, India still has one of the lowest female literacy rates in Asia. In 1991, less than 40 percent of the 330 million women aged 7 and over were literate, which means today there are over 200 million illiterate women in India. This low level of literacy not only has a negative impact on women's lives but also on their families and on society. If we want to empower women, the government must ensure education for her right from the childhood. The Indian government too has expressed strong commitment towards education for all. Sarva Siksha Abhiyan, the flagship programme for universalisation of elementary education has special focus on disadvantaged groups including the girl child. A sound foundation of educational environment through structures like Jawahar Navodaya Vidyalayas, Pratibha Vikashvidyalyas in every district of the country with fair representation for girl child would contribute enormously in national development through women education. In addition, the mid-day meal scheme has also improved girl's enrolment and retention in primary school. Ministry of social justice and empowerment is also implementing schemes of residential schools for scheduled caste girls in areas of very low literacy and award of scholarships to SC/ST Students with special emphasis on girls. "Mahila Samakhya," a women's education and empowerment programme being implemented in about 9000 villages in six states mobilizes and organizes women in groups called "sanghas" and through education makes them aware of their rights. The proposed scheme of Kasturba Gandhi Swatantrata Vidyalaya of residential schools for girls would also support universalisation of elementary education for girl child. As a result of number of initiatives and measures taken up by the Government, there is a rise in the percentage of enrolment of women. The rate of literacy among women too has gone up from 39.29% in 1991 to 54.16% in 2001. In fact, the increase in female literacy (by 14.8 percent) out paced that of male literacy (11.7 percent). The male female literacy gap has reduced from 24.8% in 1991 to 21.70% in 2001. Still, the rate of literacy among males is higher than females. For India as a whole, the gender gap in literacy has been decreasing since 1981. The data in Table 1 indicates that despite the improvement in rate of literacy, there continue to be a large gap between the literacy levels of men and women. Women as a whole are still disadvantaged in terms of education and its benefits.

TABLE 1

Literacy Rate in India

(in percent)

Census Year	*Persons*	*Males*	*Females*	*Male-female gap in literacy*
1951	18.33	27.16	8.86	18.30
1961	28.30	40.40	15.35	25.05
1971	34.45	45.96	21.97	23.98
1981	43.57	56.38	29.76	26.62
1991	52.21	64.13	39.29	24.84
2001	65.38	75.85	54.16	21.70

Source: Census of India, 2001.

It is obvious from the table that social and economic systems supported by patriarchal values continue to influence women's education right from the beginning. It is the great hurdles in the path of equal development of women in the society.

One of the major reason for lack of education among women in India is high dropout rate among girls at the early stages of schooling as compared to boys. As per data 45% of girls and 41% of boys drop-out of school attendance by age show the proportion of girls attending school decreases with age while for boys it remains somehow stable. In 1992-93 only 55% of girls aged 61% of the younger age group. The difference between the percentage of boys and girls becomes much more pronounced as we move up the level of education, this is mainly due to the higher school drop out rate among girls comparison to boys. The figures related to drop out percentages at different stage of schooling among boys and girls are presented in Table 2.

TABLE 2

Drop-out Rate of Different Stages of School Education

(in percent)

Year	*Primary*			*Elementary*			*Secondary*		
	Boys	*Girls*	*Total*	*Boys*	*Girls*	*Total*	*Boys*	*Girls*	*Total*
1960-61	61.7	70.9	64.9	75.0	85.0	78.3	NA	NA	NA
1970-71	64.5	70.9	67.0	74.6	83.4	77.9	NA	NA	NA
1980-81	56.2	62.5	58.7	68.0	79.4	72.7	79.8	86.6	82.5
1990-91	40.1	46.0	42.6	59.1	65.1	60.9	67.5	76.9	71.3
1992-93	43.8	46.7	45.0	58.2	65.2	61.1	70.0	77.3	72.9
1999-2000	38.7	42.3	40.3	52.0	58.0	54.5	66.6	70.6	68.3
2001-02	38.4	39.9	39.0	52.9	56.9	54.6	64.2	68.6	66.0

Source: Education in India (Various years), Department of Secondary and Higher Education, Ministry of Human Resource Development.

Generally speaking, the circumstances are difficult for girls, especially severe in states like, Bihar, Uttar Pradesh and Orissa.

After the above writings it is clear that among various reasons poverty is one of the prime cause of lack of education and higher drop-out rate among girls especially in developing states of India. Some of the offsited factors as reasons for dropping out as per girls are: reluctance of parents to send school, have to participate in domestic activities, helping in the fields, teacher's unfair behaviour, illness, death in the family and lack of interest in the studies spending on education, especially educating a girls child in rural areas is perceived as waste of money and resources as there is no immediate gain from education. Despite the clear advantages of female education, parents tend to prefer to educate their sons. Often a choice is made between sending either boy or girl to the school and parents would rather spend scarce family resources educating a boy as it is considered as a long-term and sure investment. Such type of mindset of girl's parents is encouraging factor in provoking violence against her. Generally, the root of violence germinated in the soil family in illiterate class mostly.

It seems true that women have some kind of inner power which in most of the cases lies in a latent form because majority of the Indian women have been socialized and conditioned in a manner that they do not question their powerless position and even they are not aware of their own potentials, status, individual identity and existence as a person.

It is high time that the sources through which women are likely to acquire the capacity to influence others, realize their potentials and experience power be studied. As an academician and researcher our main task is to disseminate the facts related to important issues and to contribute public awareness. It is hoped that with realisation of one's potentials, power and identify woman will be empowered to better her overall position within and outside the family, avoid all types of violence and exploitation and develop her personality.

It is suggested that by and large if a woman is:

- Able to realize her goals in life,
- Able to resist what she does not want to do,
- Can take decision on her own,
- Able to sustain herself without being emotionally dependent on others, and
- Competent in handling the affairs of their intellectual, domestic and social life, she is powerful (Pandey, 1994). She talks about some sources from where women are believed to derive their capacity to influence others. These sources are :

  (i) Socialisation process,
  (ii) Stress and crisis in life,
  (iii) Self-sufficiency, and
  (iv) Emotionally gratifying experiences in life.

SOCIALISATION PROCESS

A home which gives equal treatment and status to a female child, provides warmth love and security to her, encourages to her to be educated and self-independent. Bhasim (1972) suggested that one has to create better conditions for women, bring them up as "boys". Inculcate in them boldness, independence, freedom of thought and action and change the negative value of society. Under such condition a woman is expected to become as powerful, confident and self-sufficient.

STRESS IN LIFE

Stress in life weakens most of the women. It discouraged and compelled to give up the situation. On the other hand, some women take the adverse circumstances of life as a challenge for themselves.

EMOTIONALLY GRATIFYING EXPERIENCES AND SOCIAL EMOTIONAL SUPPORT

Love and support from the family members and relevant others provide emotionally gratifying experiences for a person. Such experiences could act as a source of psychological strength for a woman which may utilize for functioning efficiently and successfully in life. Such experience also help a woman stand strongly against adverse and difficult circumstances.

SELF-SUFFICIENCY

"Women Skill", competence, attribute, capabilities, achievements, guts, imagination and staying power has brought them up in the society." (*The illustrated Weekly of India*, January 7, 1996).

Preventive Measures—There are also few preventive measures which requires our attention. They are:

- Needful change in the attitude and mentality of people towards man raising awareness of the issue of violence against women and educating boys and men to views women as valuable performers in life, in the development of society and in the attainment of peace are just as important as taking legal steps to protect women's human rights.

- Re construction of the Socio-economic and cultural set-up.

The cause of violence against women's stemming from the socio-economic and cultural set up in Indian society should be changed. Although the Hindu succession Act (1955) provides equal share of property to daughters in parental property, but the reality is something reverse and the net result is subjugation of women. The act has remained a page of law book only. In many cases neither the parent care for rightful hiership to their daughters nor the daughter claim for it. Due to economic dependency on the husband and their in laws, they are tortured and learn to tolerate. In this regard the state government must regulate the reservation of economic opportunities for female according to their population.

Role of mass media in improving the status of women—In the 21st century we cannot forget the role of mass media in improving our condition. It is helpful in bringing social change in man dominated society. It highlights the fact in a very pathetic way which opens the eyes of the masses. Several incidence of violence against women were live telecast. It gives a sensational impact of on the mind of the male.

CONCLUSION

After the above analysis on violence related to women and their empowerment, one question arise here that can legislation protect women from culturally sanctioned discrimination and violence. The answer is simple no. in my view without giving a prime position and without their proper enforcement a civilized human society cannot be envisaged. In this regard one thing is important that they must be helped to help themselves. It means women must be aware about their own rights and their proper enforcement. Shoots of awareness are grown gradually among women. With the help of non-governmental organisations and mahila mandals, they work toward sensitizing other women by spreading awareness about their rights. They mobilize and organize women as a strong pressure group to participate vigorously in the development process and decision-making.

Circumstances have been changed very fastly. After the 60 years of India's independence, they are in condition to raise their voice against child marriage, torture and rape. It can be seen from the daily news that rapist is beaten to death by women victim herself or by mob of women.

It is fact that the Indian society has accorded differential status to women through out the history. But there has been a significant change in the status of women in modern India. They accept the power which is latent among women. In the words of ex-president A.P.J. Abdul Kalam, "Empowering women is a prerequisite for creating a good nation, when women are empowered, society with ability is assured. Empowerment of women is essential as their thoughts and their value systems lead the development of a good family, good society and ultimately a good nation". Women will gain power only when both men and women begin to respect and accept the contribution of women. The task is challenging for men dominated society yet not impossible because a woman is a wife, a mother, a daughter and so on.

References

Kurukshetra, January 2008.

L.N. Sharma, G.P. Ojha, M.M. Patnaik, Human Rights, Research Publication, Patna, 1999.

S.K. Ghose, Women in a Changing Society, New Delhi, Ashish Publishing House, 1984.

Shanti, K. (Ed.), Empowerment of Women, Anmol Publishing Private Limited, New Delhi, 1998.

Women and Men in India, 2005, Journal.

CRIME AGAINST WOMEN AND THE SCOPE OF WOMEN EMPOWERMENT

RAVINDRA K. CHOUDHARY AND MANOJ KUMAR MISHRA

1. INTRODUCTION

Crime against women is the most evocative, traumatism and political subject for discussion within India. Although it is not a direct issue of development yet it affects women's development; it restricts them from full participation in national development efforts and obtaining their due share in developmental efforts.

This subject has not been exhaustively studied but we know that throughout history, women in various continents of the world have been considered as the physically weaker sex. Crimes against women are assertion of dominance over them and come from the baser instincts of society. It not only represents the greater physical strength of men over women but also takes the form of the assertion of dominance of power and of riches over the women of the poorer classes. The powerful and the rich expect women of lower status to serve them in various ways one of which is sexual favours and in case they deny them by resistance, rape, kidnapping, molestation take place. Familial crime was rare in

Indian society. The phenomena which led to most crimes in Indian society were the frequent invasions throughout history. The conquering armies took vengeance over the women of the defeated by making themselves, raping them, selling them or even forcing them into marriages. The ancient Hindu scriptures have always taken a very dim view of crimes against women, Brahmins and cows. This is not however to say that crimes against women were not perpetrated during Hindu dominance or rule.

The Manusmriti to which one has to repeatedly refer in order to study social conditions during the first millennia and even subsequently, states that it is the duty of the king to protect the women of his realm. The wealth of women, whether they were married, unmarried or widowed had to be protected. Respect to the woman for her clastity and personal dignity, went so far as to prohibit talking to women in lonely or secret places even by their relatives. Sexual assault and rape were severely punished. A 'shudra' was to be awarded a death punishment if he raped a Brahmin woman. If a lower caste man cohabits with a higher caste woman, he could be killed but if he raped a Brahmin woman. If a lower caste man cohabits with a higher caste woman, he could be killed but if he did that with a woman of the same caste, he should give money on a demand being made to that effect by the girl's father. If an unmarried girl was raped by anyone the criminal could be punished by loosing his limbs. Women who were not chaste were also liable to punishment. A young woman cohabiting willingly with a higher caste man would not be punished but if she cohabited with a lower caste man, she would be punished by confining her to the house. If a woman proud of her beauty committed adultery to insult her husband, she was supposed to be thrown to the dogs to be bitten. Even in primitive Vedic time lesbianism was known and such girls were liable to be punished as criminals.

Some data of crimes against women during the medieval period of Rajasthan's history is known as a result of the studies being conducted by the Centre for Historical Studies, Jawaharlal Nehru University, Delhi. These studies reveal that the predominantly feudal and hierarchical environment of Rajasthan infuel crimes of sexual nature were considered the most heinous. Adultery, rape, forced marriages and elopement with a married woman were considered as great crimes. Before the onset of purdah which seems to have originated on a large scale after contact with Mughal Society, there was relatively free interaction between the sexes. This combined with polygamous marriage and the absence of husbands on frequent wars occasionally led to adulterous unions even among royal women. The wife of Lakha, the ruler of Kelakot in Rajasthan formed such a union with a Dome (a low caste man) employed by her husband, while he was absent in a war. The husband returned and on hearing of his wife's infidelity, punished her by presenting her to her paramour the Dome. A Jaisalmer prince's claim to the throne of Jaisalmer was once set aside because of his relations with an older woman.

Criminal molestation of women, whether it led to rape or not, was known by a rather flirtatious title of cham-chori or stealing the sex of a woman. Punishments for this crime varied according to the caste of the criminal. Fine was the usual remedy upon receiving a complain from a woman herself or her guardians. The 'Adsatta' records of Jaipur state show that these fines could be very heavy ranging between 5 to 65 rupees. These fines are a strong penalty, keeping in view the value of money those days. In the pargana of Chatsu in Jaipur state during the year 1744 and 1749 out of a total number of 150 criminal cases, fifty related to Cham-Chori. These included criminal assaults by men on daughters-in-law, sisters-in-law and lower caste women. Crimes against Rajput women were fewer as they belonged to the ruling class. Bringing home someone's wife illegally or remarrying her was also a crime.

Although crimes existed society looked down upon them and pushed the criminals severely. It is important to note that crimes of husband and their families against wives were very infrequent.

2. DOES SOCIAL SYSTEM INFUEL CRIME AGAINST WOMEN

It appears that the most powerful explanation for crimes against women is the existence of a patriarchical society where women are considered the weaker sex and the possessions of men. The low social and economic and political empowerment of women leads them to be considered as easy and soft targets. Moreover, the premium on female chastity is so high in society that crimes of a sexual nature against women are hushed up as they are likely to ruin a girl's life and bring the family dishonour. The attitude of the police in many cases is to treat the female victim as an accused and therefore she is afraid to approach them. In case women themselves and their relatives try to lodge FIRs in police stations, the atmosphere for their access is not congenial for women. In India, among all religions, marriage for women is considered as an obligatory experience in life. Arranged marriages being the order of the day the personal nature of the husband often remains hidden till well after the marriage. The social and economic standing of the future husband takes precedence over his personal nature and habits. The husband's parents further believe that the girl is in their possession and often load her with all domestic drudgery and social and economic harassment. The parents of the girl instead of building the confidence of their daughters to resist such treatment, give them the message that it is their duty to adjust in the marital home, thus barring her return back to the maternal home. The girl naturally becomes unresisting to the humiliating treatment meted out to her in her husband's home which in most cases happens to be a joint family in rural areas and in a majority of cases in urban areas also young couples cannot set-up homes of their own. Many crimes are due to disputes over women and domestic tension due to arranged marriages. It is also true that a substantial number of crimes in the lower middle class and the middle class occur due to the existence black money which has resulted in aggressive display of wealth during marriages and in the giving of dowries to daughters. This creates a vicious atmosphere where everyone from the richest in the land, to the poorest, thinks that display of wealth and giving of dowries is called for during marriage celebrations. When the expectations of the other side are not met, it results in domestic disharmony, domestic violence and dowry-related deaths.

3. CONSTITUTIONAL FRAMEWORKS FOR PROHIBITING CRIME AGAINST WOMEN

Sensitivity about controlling crimes against women exists in the political and administrative ethos of the country. The Indian Penal Code (IPC) introduced in 1862 and subsequently amended contains punishments for rape, kidnapping and abduction, homicide for dowry. Dowry deaths or their attempts, torture, both mental and physical, molestation, sexual harassment and importation of girls as offences were added on later. Four specific laws dealing with crimes were passed after independence besides several amendments carried out in the IPC. The first such act was a reflection of the mentality of our leadership on the social welfare of women and hence the Immoral Traffic (Prevention) Act was passed in 1956 banning the trafficking of women for prostitution. The Dowry Prohibition Act was passed in 1961 banning the giving and acceptance of dowry. The Representation of Women Act was passed in 1986 making such representation of the women in the media an offence. The recruitment of women to the police begun and some police stations meant exclusively for women have also been set-up.

In spite of enactment of above said IPCs the violence against women has been showing an alarming trend. During 1997 to 1998, the percentage rise in total crime against women has increased by 8.26, it has showed a declining rate of increase during 1998 to 1999 but again in 2002, the rate of increase was 8.08%. The five yearly trend of rise in crime against women has showed an accelerated rate say 21.49% (during 1997 to 2002). In this scenario, we have to inquire about the scope of women empowerment in India in general and that of Bihar in particular. For detail please see Table 1. The data of Tables 1 and 2 reflects that the crime against women has increase by 87% during the period of 10 years. Table 3 reflects the state-wise distribution of crime against women. This huge rise in crime against women highlights the failure of all measures undertaken by Government to control such crimes for safeguarding the women.

4. STATE-WISE DISTRIBUTION OF CRIME AGAINST WOMEN IN INDIA

The state-wise percentage contribution to total crimes may be seen from Table 3. It shows that Uttar Pradesh has contributed the highest percentage of total cognisable offences committed against women at 13.3 per cent of the total crimes committed against women occurring in the state. This is followed closely by Madhya Pradesh with a contribution of 12.1 per cent and Maharashtra at 10.9 per cent and Rajasthan at 9.3 and Andhra

Pradesh at 8.5 per cent. As far as rate per 1,00,000 persons is concerned Rajasthan (23.4) has contributed the highest percentage followed by Madhya Pradesh (20.5), Tamil Nadu (18.4), Jammu Kashmir (18), Haryana (15.5) and Andhra Pradesh (15.1). The Uttar Pradesh rate is 10.7. After viewing the state-wise picture it would be pertinent to have a sympotic view of various crimes in India as whole with the aid of Table 4.

TABLE 1

Trend of Total Crime Against Women During 1992 to 2002 National

Year	*Total Crime*	*Crime Rate %*	*% Increase During 1992 to 2002*
1992	79037	—	—
1993	83954	6.22	—
1994	98948	17.86	—
1995	105723	6.85	—
1996	115723	9.46	—
1997	121265	5.24	—
1998	131338	8.31	—
1999	136712	4.10	—
2000	141373	2.78	—
2001	143765	2.48	—
2002	147678	2.57	86.85

Source: Crime Report, 2005, Ministry of Human Affairs, Government of India (New Delhi).

5. CRIME AGAINST WOMEN AND THE CASE OF SUICIDAL DEATH

The crime situation is also reflected through the accidental deaths and suicides data published by the National Crime Records Bureau. Women constitute only 40.09 per cent of all suicides committed. Out of twenty different categories of accidental deaths during 1994, 72.2 per cent of all deaths by fire had women as their victims compared to 27.8 per cent men. Death due to poisoning constitutes another 40.09 per cent although here the male percentage is 59.1 per cent. it is obvious that accidental death due to fire may not be as accidental as it appears. Another interesting point is that the majority of accidental deaths by fire occur to

TABLE 2

Incidence of Crimes Against Women: National

Crime	*1990*	*1991*	*1992*	*1993*	*1994*	*1995*	*1996*	*1997*	*2002*	*Absolute increase per cent*	*Average annual growth rate per cent*
Rape	9581	9793	11112	11242	12351	13367	14846	15330	16373	33.0	4.8
Kidnapping and abduction	11699	12300	12077	11837	12998	13994	14877	15617	14506	11.1	1.7
Dowry deaths	4836	5157	4962	5817	4935	4927	5513	6006	6822	8.6	1.3
Torture	13450	15949	19750	22064	25946	32006	35246	36592	49237	126.9	14.6
Molestation	20194	20611	20385	20985	24117	27993	28796	30764	33943	31.7	4.7
Sexual harassment (eve-teasing)	8620	10283	10751	12009	10494	4527	5671	30796	10155	41.2	5.9
Crimes under special laws	-	-	-	-	8105	7888	11049	11081	—	—	—
Total	68317	74093	79037	83954	98948	105723	115723	121265	147675	56.2	7.7
Crime rate per cent	-	8.7	9.1	9.5	11.0	11.0	11.5	—	—	—	—

Source: Ministry of Human Resource Development, Department of Women and Child Development, Government of India, New Delhi, various years.

TABLE 3

Incidence and Rate of Crime Committed Against Women in State and Union Territories During 1993

State/Union Territory	*Incidence of Total Cog. Crime*	*Percentage contribution to all India total*	*Estimated mid-year population (In lakhs)*	*Rate of Total Cog. Crime*	*Rank**	*Rank***
India	131338	100.0	9709.3	13.5	—	—
Andhra Pradesh	11201	8.5	741.7	15.1	9	6
Assam	3388	2.6	256.5	13.2	12	13
Bihar	71.5	5.4	969.6	7.3	22	7
Gujarat	6658	5.1	471.0	14.1	11	9
Haryana	3002	2.3	193.4	15.5	8	14
HImachal Pradesh	778	0.6	64.2	12.1	14	14
Jammu and Kashmir	1715	1.3	95.4	18.0	5	16
Karnataka	5516	4.2	509.8	10.8	17	10
Kerala	4799	3.7	317.8	15.1	10	11
Madhya Pradesh	15865	12.1	774.0	20.5	2	2
Maharashtra	14266	10.9	894.1	16.0	6	3
Orissa	4450	3.4	353.0	12.6	13	12
Punjab	1238	0.9	231.0	5.4	27	17
Rajasthan	12159	9.3	520.1	23.4	1	4
Tamil Nadu	11201	8.5	608.8	18.4	4	6
Uttar Pradesh	17497	13.3	1640.4	10.7	18	1
West Bengal	6811	5.2	772.5	8.8	21	8
Delhi	2556	1.9	130.4	19.6	3	15

Note: *Rank on the basis of Rate of total consable crimes (Col. 6).
**Rank on the basis of Percentage share (Col. 4).

Source: Crime in India, 2004, Ministry of Home Affairs, Government of India, New Delhi, 2004.

TABLE 4

Disposal of Crimes Against Women Cases by Police During 1997 and 1998

Crime Head	*Total No. of Cases for Investigation including pending cases*		*Percentage of cases investigated*		*Percentage of cases charge sheeted*		*No. of cases pending investigation*		*Percentage of cases pending Investigation*	
	1997	*1998*	*1997*	*1998*	*1997*	*1998*	*1997*	*1998*	*1997*	*1998*
Rape	20736	20864	71.7	72.1	62.4	62.1	5828	5793	28.1	27.8
Kidnapping and abduction	23448	24966	62.8	61.3	36.1	35.9	8586	9565	36.6	38.3
Dowry deaths	7543	8938	72.3	72.7	63.5	63.8	2048	2393	21.2	26.8
Molestation	34937	35594	86.8	85.0	79.1	77.0	4528	5306	13.0	14.9
Sexual harassment	6131	8578	92.4	92.1	89.3	88.3	461	668	7.5	7.8
Cruelty by husband and relatives	43130	49532	80.5	79.1	67.9	65.9	8268	10248	19.2	20.7
Immoral Traffic (Prevention) Act	9076	9898	86.8	89.3	86.5	89.1	8268	10248	19.2	20.7
Dowry Prohibition Act	3853	4649	70.8	75.3	59.3	62.4	1100	1142	28.6	24.6
Indecent Rep. of Women (P) Act	96	206	85.4	80.1	81.3	62.1	14	41	14.6	19.9
Saṭi Prevention Act	1	0	100.0	—	100.0	—	0	0	0.0	—

Note: Similar details for important of girls (upto 21 years of age) are not available.
Source: Crime in India, 1998, Ministry of Home Affairs, Government of India, New Delhi, 2000.

women in the age group of 18-30 years, that is, those newly married or who have been married for only a few years.

The data regarding suicides again indicates that a high percentage of women commit suicide in areas where males are involved. Of all suicides committed in 1995, 53.3 per cent related to quarrels with parents-in-law, spouse, love affairs; 51.6 per cent were due to dowry dispute, 95.6 per cent, death of dear persons and 35.5 per cent, illegitimate births which again reveals women's unequal position in social relationships leading to suicides. The crime data 1990-95 shows that suicides among females has increased by more than 20 per cent.

It has been known for several years that women do not have easy access to police stations totally manned by men because of their own in built inhibitions about talking to strange men about their most intimate experiences. A better mechanism for dealing with crimes against women is the recruitment of women police and the setting up of special cells in the police for prevention of crime against women. These special cells have come into existence in most states and women police officials have been also recruited. The strength of women police in the highest rank of Inspector Generals and Deputy Inspector Generals is very inadequate as per data available till 1995. The Annual Crime Report of 1995 shows that in the ranks of Director General of Police and Inspector General of Police, six posts of women are sanctioned but eleven women had actually been posted. In the ranks of Assistant Superintendent of Police and Deputy Superintendent of Police while fifty posts had been sanctioned only thirty-four were in position. About 2,084 posts for women Inspectors, Sub-Inspectors and Assistant Sub-Inspectors existed but only 1,620 were posted against them. Vacancies also existed at the level of officials below Assistant Sub-Inspectors. This means that the grass root woman police force needs to be strengthened. The number sanctioned is most adequate and on top of that not filling them is even more appalling.

In the metropolitan city of Delhi, nine cells dealing with crimes against women have been set-up spread over the three different ranges and manned by officers of the rank of Assistant Commissioner of Police.

Shelter homes for women who are abused by their families are absolutely necessary as women bear many tortures since they cannot take shelter anywhere else. These shelters should impart legal literacy, skill training and above all counseling to the families for rehabilitation of their inmates.

6. CRIME AGAINST WOMEN AND THE ROLE OF SOCIETY AND NON-GOVERNMENTAL ORGANISATIONS (NGOs)

It is imperative that voluntary organisations are associated with the cells meant for prevention of crimes against women and also awareness generation programmes on women's rights are done at a much higher level than at present. These organisations can also play a prominent part in preventing crimes against women during civil disorders and caste and communal riots. The rise in the literacy status of women would lead to better awareness of their rights, as well as access to information relating to criminal administration.

The empowering of women economically would also help in building confidence. Awareness generation programmes for administrators, parliamentarians, police officials, and judiciary on gender sensitisation issues would lead gradually to the realisation of the society's responsibility for handling crime against women. Above all police officials of all ranks need to be recruited to women's cells.

7. CRIME AGAINST WOMEN: AN INTERNATIONAL COMPARISON

Any assessment of the crime situation must in order to be realistic have a comparative analysis of crimes against women in other countries.

Table 5 indicates the population and the number of cases relating to rape and sex offences obtained from the Interpol which give a comparative picture. Here it would be noticed that the United States of America tops the lots as far as rape cases are concerned. This phenomenon is also very high in Canada. The data of this table highlights that the crime against women is higher in highly developed nation, i.e. crime against women is not closely concerned with the socio-economic composition and condition of society but much more decided by the status of women in our society.

TABLE 5

Recorded Cases of Sex-Offences and Rape International Statistics (1991-93)

Country	*Population (In Million)*	*Rape*			*Sex Offences*		
	1993	*1991*	*1992*	*1993*	*1991*	*1992*	*1993*
Bangladesh	115	448	589	501	545	753	549
Canada	28.8	35570	NA	NA	39851	NA	38934
China	1300	NA	NA	47033	NA	NA	NA
France	57.5	5068	5356	5605	23732	25404	26569
Hong Kong	5.9	114	116	103	2178	2052	1962
Japan	124.8	1603	1504	1611	4779	5009	5191
Malayasia	19.7	706	716	266	1276	1353	509
Nepal	19.2	116	135	189	116	135	189
Singapore	2.9	74	80	79	857	914	984
Sri Lanka	17.5*	374	371	NA	426	424	984
USA	257.9	106590	109060	104810	NA	NA	NA
UK (England)	50.7**	4045	NA	NA	29423	NA	NA

Notes: *Population in 1992; **Population in 1991; NA—Data not available.
Source: Crime in United State of America—A Statistical Profile, Interpol Data.

TABLE 6

Law Enforcement, Courts and Prisons No. 308, Forcible Rape-Number and Rate; 1970 to 1992

Item	*1970*	*1980*	*1985*	*1986*	*1987*	*1988*	*1989*	*1990*	*1991*	*1992*
Number										
Total	37990	82990	88670	91460	91110	92490	94500	102560	106590	109060
By Force	26888	63599	71060	73453	75456	75441	78441	88541	91522	93825
Attempt	11102	19391	71610	18007	17654	17049	16089	16019	15068	15235
Rate										
Per 100000 Population	18.7	36.8	37.1	37.9	37.4	37.6	38.1	41.2	42.3	42.8
Per 100000 Females	30.4	71.6	72.3	73.9	73.0	73.4	74.3	80.5	82.5	83.5
Per 100000 females 12 years old and over										
Average Annual percent Change in Rate										
Per 100000 Population	NA	6.1	3.9	2.2	-1.3	0.5	1.3	8.7	2.7	1.2
Per 100000 Females 12 years old and over	NA	6.0	4.3	2.3	-1.2	0.7	1.4	8.2	4.5	-0.4

Notes: NA: Not Available represents annual average from prior year shown expect for 1980 from 1979; and for 1985, from 1984.

Source: U.S. Federal Bureau of Investigation. Population at Risk Rates and Selected Crime Indicators, Annual.

Table 6 gives the rape cases registered in the United States from 1970 to 1992—these have risen from 37,990 cases in 1970 to 1,09,060 in 1992. Considering the fact that this country has an approximately 20 crore population compared to India's over 100 crore figure, the figure is very high. The Human Development Report 2000 gives recorded rapes at the rate per 1,00,000 women aged 15 and above as 267 women for Canada, 96.8 for USA, 199.1 for Australia, Japan 3, France 27.1, Sweden 49.9, Sweden 49.9, Israel 28.4, Bahamas 220.5 and Jamaica 127.8 while India Stands at 4.6. The rate for India comes close to the figure of 15,031 rape cases recorded for 1998 given by the Crime Records Bureau of India. This is not to say that we in India can be complacement. What is surprising is that even in a traditional society like Japan, the rate is quite high compared to the population. In France and UK again the incidence of crime related to rape and sex offences is high. This is not to say that if the crime rates against women are higher in developed countries compared to India, the situation here can be ignored but considering the size of population, its diversity, differences in cultural situation and status of women, the incident of crime in India is within moderate limits. A strong media and awareness generation drive and tighter control over the functioning of the police could lead to further reduction of crime against women.

CONCLUSION

To conclude the whole discussion we can say that Indian women are at the cross roads of their destiny. There is a great upsurge in conciseness about their rights among all sections and classes of society in all regions of the country. No doubt, there has been a tremendous increase in developmental activity for women since eighties with a great leap forward in the nineties. There are ample examples are found in regard to women empowerment amongst various regions of the country and it is a matter of great pleasure for us but news concerned with crime against women published in daily newspaper not only neglected the whole efforts and achievements in the path of women empowerment but illucidates our dream to enter into the new millennium with the hope to achieve a great equity for women.

REFERENCES

Choudhary, Rabindra Kumar, Role of Women in Economic Development in Bihar, Ph.D. Thesis Awarded by Patna University, Patna.

Crime in India, 1998, National Crime Records Bureau, Ministry of Home Affairs, Government of India, Standardisation in Police, New Delhi, 1998, pp. 219-41.

Evaluation Report of Mahilla Samridhi Yojana, 1996, Programme Evaluation Organisation, Planning Commission, Government of India, New Delhi, 1996.

Hargovind Sastri, The Manusmiriti (Hindi), 5th Edition, ed., by Gopal Sastri Nene, Chaukhabha Sanskrit Sansthan, Varanasi, Chapter VIII, Shoka 4, 5, 6 and 7.

Human Development Report, 2000, UNDP, Oxford University Press, New York, 2000.

Nainsi Nainsiri Khyat, Rajasthan Oriented Research Institute, Jodhpur, Vol. II, pp. 232-34.

Ritu Tiwari, 'Elite Rajput Women in Medieval Rajasthan', Ph.D. Thesis, Centre for Historical Studies, School of Social Science, Jawaharlal Nehru University, New Delhi, 1995.

Women and Development, The Indian Experience by Mira Seth, Sage Publication, New Delhi.

INDEX

Access to:
Cooperative and Local Women's Organisations, 72
Activities of Rural Women, 76
Agricultural and Allied Activities:
Issues of Women, 16
Ahmad, Reyaz, 91
Akhtar, Shamim, 184, 247
Annan, Kofi, 17
Appropriate Training Programme, 73
Azad, Parveen, 56

Basic Socio-economic Infrastructure, 203
Bihar:
Status of Education, 177
Access to Education, 177
Budgeting for Gender Equality, 235

Capacity Building, 72
Chattopadhyay, Kamaladevi, 96
Child Care, 133
Child Sex Ratio, 108
Chaudhary, Ravindra K., 295
Composition of:
Gender Budget Cells, 241
Constitutional Provisions for Women:
Policy Commitments, 24
Crime Against Women and the Role of Society, 305
Crime Against Women in India:
State-wise Distribution, 299
Crisis in Agriculture, 35
CSWB (Central Social Welfare Board), 25, 69

Development in the Third World Perspective:
Theory of Gendered Approach, 247
Development Strategy and Employment, 31
Domestic Work by Women in Optional, 272

Economic Empowerment, 204
Access to Resourcers, 71
Economic Empowerment of Womens and Globalisation, 83
Economics of Women Education, 175
Education, Agriculture, Health, Industry:
Gender Audit, 195
Educational Empowerment, 70
Emotionally Gratifying Experiences, 292
Empowering Women:
National Policy, 127
Empowerment:
Approaches, 70
Empowerment of Women and Education, 170

Empowerment of Women and Globalisation, 3
Exposure to Mass Media, 73
Extant Approach to Women's Development, 197

Family Affects Work Negatively, 129
Family Imposing on Work Stress, 129
Farm Women in Agricultural Operations, 77
Fear of Sexual Harassment, 147
Female-Male Literacy Rate, 150
Financial Perspective, 205
Five Year Plans and Gender Budgeting, 239
Fixed Schooling Hours, 147
Foodgrains Production:
  Crisis, 39

Gandhian Philosophy and Women's Empowerment, 91
Gandhi, Mahatma, 91
Gender Audit of Policies, 235
Gender Bias, 71
Gender Budget Cells:
  Character, 241
Gender Budgeting:
  Action Plan, 187
  Tool, 193
  and Five Year Plans, 239
  and Women Empowerment, 233
  for Women's Empowerment, 200
Gender Commitments, 237
Gender Equality, 21, 131
  and Rights of Women, 266
  the Millennium Development Goals, 23
Gender Issues in Modernisation Theory, 250
Gender Parity in Education, 108
Gender under Development, 252
Getting Education:
  No Gender Discrimination, 274
Globalisation, 86
Global Poverty, 213
Global Child Sex Ratio, 109

Health and Nutrition, 71
Higher Education, 114

Importance of Women Education, 144
Indian Lok Sabha:
  Representation of Women, 20
India:
  Women and Education, 143
  Literacy Rate, 289
  Approaches to Gender Budgeting Initiatives, 189
  Perspective of Sex Ratio, 110
  Enrolment of Women in Higher Education, 115
  Labour Force Participation Rates, 48
  Globalisation, Empowerment Question and the Case of Women Workers, 42
Institutionalizing the Generation, 236
Internal Process Perspective, 205
International Development Agencies, 248
Inter-personal Relationship and in-laws, 36
Islamic Marriage Based on Equity, 273
Islam:
  No Forced or Child Marriage, 274
Issues of Gender Equality, 211

Jha, Birendra Kumar, 211

Kalam, A.P.J. Abdul, 3
Khan, Shakeel Ahmad, 266
Kumar, Bipin, 3
Kumar, Nayan, 233
Kumar, Reeta, 285

Lack of:
  Hostel Facilities for Girls, 47
  Qualities Female Teachers, 147
  Transport Facilities, 147
Learning and Innovation Perspective, 206

Lewis, W.A., 31
Local Women's Organisations, 72

Mental Health, 130
Micro-Credit Programmes, 72
Mishra, Manoj Kumar, 295
Muslim Women:
  Recent Survey, 270

Nagien, Shaishta, 247
National Economy:
  Women's Contribution, 68
National Level Crimes Against Women, 219
New Set of Faminist Academics, 256
Not Equal Share in Property:
  Justification, 272

Organised Sector Employment and Planning, 32
Organised Sector Employment:
  Dynamics, 33

Plans Period:
  Development of Women, 25
Polygamy in Islam:
  Logic, 275
Prasad, Anjali, 125
Prasad, Jyoti, 125
Prasad, Mahesh Chandra, 66
Pratap, Rama, 233
Prohibiting Crime Against Women, 298

Ranjan, Rajesh, 158
Rights of Women in Islam, 269
Rupam, Roma, 170
Rural Areas:
  Factors Responsible Illiteracy among Females, 146
Rural-Urban Literacy Rates, 113
Rural Women and New Millennium, 74
Rural Women:
  Time and Energy Distribution, 78

School Education:
  Drop-out Rate, 290
Self-Sufficiency, 292
Sharma, Indradeo, 30
Sharma, Praveen, 83
Shukla, Rajesh, 158
Shukla, Ranjana, 158
Suicidal Death, 300
Singh, Parmanand, 42
Singh, R.U., 175
Singh, Ranjeev Kumar, 170
Sinha, Mithilesh Kumar, 105
Social and Political Empowerment, 204
Social Empowerment, 70
Socialisation Process, 292
Stakeholders' (Women) Perspectives, 202
State-wise Female-Male Literacy, 153
Status of Women, 6, 70
Stress and Working Women, 130
Stress for Working Women:
  Role Ambiguity, 129
  Work Amount, 129
  Available Time, 129
  Invested, 129
  Work Conflict, 129
  Family, 129
  WIF Strain, 129
  FIW Strain, 129
  FIR Strain, 129
Stress in Life, 292

Technological Empowerment, 72
Tenth Five Year Plan:
  Extracts, 239
Theoretical Perspectives and the Globalisation, 44
Third World Countries:
  Neo-Liberalism, 254
Trade:
  Adverse Terms, 37

Unorganised Women Workers, 30
Upliftment of Women Education, 148

Veil System for Women, 176
Violence Against Women, 285
Violence:
How to Eradicate, 288
Women:
Appropriate Technology, 73
Specific Legislations, 24, 238
Maintenance by Husband, 273
International Status, 7
National Status, 10
Seats in Parliament, 14
Wage Employment Outside Agriculture, 15
Economic Growth, 21
Economic, 25
Protection, 25
Social, 25
Specific Legislations, 238
in the Public Sector, 140
in Organised Sector, 141
Domestic Duty, 145
Marital Status, 135
in the Eleventh Plan, 118
Employment Scenario, 118
Women Education in India:
Problems, 145
Women Education:
Perspective, 112
Women Enrolment:
Stage-wise Distribution, 115
Women's Political Participation, 226
Women's Empowerment:
Strategic Map, 202
Fund Allocation, 78
Policies, 80
New Roadmap Required, 105
Stress and Mental Health, 125
Historical Perspective, 4
and Development During Globalisation, 66
Indicators, 13
Need, 11
and Globalisation, 56
and Planning Process, 69
through Gender Budgeting, 184
Women's Representation in Parliament, 225
Women's Work, 84
Work Affects Husband Negatively, 129
Work Imposing on:
Relaxation, 129
Strain, 129
Family, 129

Yadav, Subalal, 233